The Body in Arabic Love Poetry

Edinburgh Studies in Classical Islamic History and Culture
Series Editor: Carole Hillenbrand

A particular feature of medieval Islamic civilisation was its wide horizons. The Muslims fell heir not only to the Graeco-Roman world of the Mediterranean, but also to that of the ancient Near East, to the empires of Assyria, Babylon and the Persians; and beyond that, they were in frequent contact with India and China to the east and with black Africa to the south. This intellectual openness can be sensed in many inter-related fields of Muslim thought, and it impacted powerfully on trade and on the networks that made it possible. Books in this series reflect this openness and cover a wide range of topics, periods and geographical areas.

Titles in the series include:

The Body in Arabic Love Poetry: The 'Udhri Tradition
Jokha Alharthi

Arabian Drugs in Early Medieval Mediterranean Medicine
Zohar Amar and Efraim Lev

Towards a History of Libraries in Yemen
Hassan Ansari and Sabine Schmidtke

The Abbasid Caliphate of Cairo, 1261–1517: Out of the Shadows
Mustafa Banister

The Medieval Western Maghrib: Cities, Patronage and Power
Amira K. Bennison

Christian Monastic Life in Early Islam
Bradley Bowman

Keeping the Peace in Premodern Islam: Diplomacy under the Mamluk Sultanate, 1250–1517
Malika Dekkiche

Queens, Concubines and Eunuchs in Medieval Islam
Taef El-Azhari

Islamic Political Thought in the Mamluk Period
Mohamad El-Merheb

The Kharijites in Early Islamic Historical Tradition: Heroes and Villains
Hannah-Lena Hagemann

Medieval Damascus: Plurality and Diversity in an Arabic Library – The Ashrafīya Library Catalogue
Konrad Hirschler

A Monument to Medieval Syrian Book Culture: The Library of Ibn 'Abd al-Hādī
Konrad Hirschler

The Popularisation of Sufism in Ayyubid and Mamluk Egypt: State and Society, 1173–1325
Nathan Hofer

Defining Anthropomorphism: The Challenge of Islamic Traditionalism
Livnat Holtzman

Making Mongol History: Rashid al-Din and the Jami' al-Tawarikh
Stefan Kamola

Lyrics of Life: Sa'di on Love, Cosmopolitanism and Care of the Self
Fatemeh Keshavarz

Art, Allegory and The Rise of Shiism In Iran, 1487–1565
Chad Kia

The Administration of Justice in Medieval Egypt: From the 7th to the 12th Century
Yaacov Lev

The Queen of Sheba's Gift: A History of the True Balsam of Matarea
Marcus Milwright

Ruling from a Red Canopy: Political Authority in the Medieval Islamic World, From Anatolia to South Asia
Colin P. Mitchell

Islam, Christianity and the Realms of the Miraculous: A Comparative Exploration
Ian Richard Netton

The Poetics of Spiritual Instruction: Farid al-Din 'Attar and Persian Sufi Didacticism
Austin O'Malley

Sacred Place and Sacred Time in the Medieval Islamic Middle East: An Historical Perspective
Daniella Talmon-Heller

Conquered Populations in Early Islam: Non-Arabs, Slaves and the Sons of Slave Mothers
Elizabeth Urban

edinburghuniversitypress.com/series/escihc

The Body in Arabic Love Poetry
The *'Udhri* Tradition

Jokha Alharthi

EDINBURGH
University Press

Edinburgh University Press is one of the leading university presses in the UK. We publish academic books and journals in our selected subject areas across the humanities and social sciences, combining cutting-edge scholarship with high editorial and production values to produce academic works of lasting importance. For more information visit our website: edinburghuniversitypress.com

© Jokha Alharthi, 2021, 2023

Edinburgh University Press Ltd
The Tun – Holyrood Road
12 (2f) Jackson's Entry
Edinburgh EH8 8PJ

First published in hardback by Edinburgh University Press 2021

Typeset in 11/15 Adobe Garamond by
Servis Filmsetting Ltd, Stockport, Cheshire

A CIP record for this book is available from the British Library

ISBN 978 1 4744 8633 0 (hardback)
ISBN 978 1 4744 8634 7 (paperback)
ISBN 978 1 4744 8636 1 (webready PDF)
ISBN 978 1 4744 8635 4 (epub)

The right of Jokha Alharthi to be identified as author of this work has been asserted in accord-ance with the Copyright, Designs and Patents Act 1988 and the Copyright and Related Rights Regulations 2003 (SI No. 2498).

Contents

List of Plates	vi
Acknowledgements	vii
Foreword by Sabry Hafez	viii
Preface	xvii

1	Introduction: A Critical Reappraisal of Scholarship of the *'Udhri* Tradition	1
2	Reconstructing the Past	32
3	*'Udhri* Tradition between Chastity and Sensuality	56
4	The Representation of the Beloved's Body	85
5	Present and Absent Bodies of the Beloved	127
6	Textuality versus Reality	164
7	The Representation of the Lover's Body in the *'Udhri* Tradition	189
	Conclusion	226

Appendix	233
Bibliography	249
Index	262

Plates

Located between pages 126 and 127

1 Layla and Majnun fainting. A lion attacking a person, *Khamsa* of Nizami, Herat. 1494–5
2 Majnun brought to Layla's tent, *Khamsa* of Nizami, Tabri. 1539–43
3 Majnun dies on the grave of Layla, *Khamsa* of Nizami, Iran. Timurid Dynasty. 1431
4 Majnun at the Ka' ba, *Khamsa* of Nizami, Iran. Timurid Dynasty. 1431
5 Layla in the palm grove, *Khamsa* of Nizami, Iran. Timurid Dynasty. 1431

Acknowledgements

I would like to express my grateful appreciation to Dr Kamran Rastegar for his kind encouragement and generous help throughout my study. The feedback he gave me has been very useful. I would also like to thank Professor Carole Hillenbrand for her fruitful discussion of my ideas and her valuable remarks on my work. The guidance that Dr Elisabeth Kendall provided me in the early stages of this thesis are very much appreciated. My deep gratitude goes to Professor Robert Hillenbrand, who expertly shared his insights on the subject of the portrayal of Majnun's story in Persian art. I am also indebted to his personal generosity in devoting time and effort to read through the entire typescript. I want to record also my thanks to Professor Marilyn Booth for reading my work and suggesting many corrections. I hugely benefited from her experienced guidance in matters of Arabic literature. In addition, I owe thanks to Dr Adam Budd, Professor Ahmad Darwish, Dr Christian Lange, Professor Gerard Van Gelder, Professor Khalil al-Shaikh, Professor Muhammad al-Tarabulsi, Professor Muhammad Lutfi al-Yusufi and Professor Walid Khalis for their suggestions during the early stages of my study regarding the sources I should consult. My gratitude goes to Ya'qub al-Harthi for his great help with searching for relevant sources and providing many of them for me. I would like also to record my warm thanks to Alasdair Watson, Ibtihaj al-Harthi, Khalsa al-Aghbari, Ula Zaaer and Zina al-Harthi for their great help in the translation of the Arabic poetry. I have indeed been fortunate in receiving so much support and encouragement from my husband Altayeb al-Harthi and from my family and friends, so my warmest gratitude goes to them.

Foreword
by Sabry Hafez

Benedetto Croce,[1] one of the major Italian philosophers of the twentieth century, divides theoretical mental activities into aesthetic and logic. Following in the tradition of Kant and Hegel, separating the critique of pure reason from the realm of taste and artistic judgement, Croce posits intuitive knowledge against conceptual knowledge. The former he associates with vision, contemplation, imagination, figuration and even representation, as the one pertaining to creative art and literature. For art is the work of imagination and is gained with the renunciation of concrete thought.[2] The latter, conceptual knowledge, is solidly anchored in reality and rational analytical thinking which produces the philosophical and the scholarly methodology. Hence it is always realistic, aiming at establishing reality against unreality, or at reducing unreality by including it in reality as a subordinate moment of reality itself, making a clear distinction between fantasy and thought.

In his major work on aesthetics Croce argues that art and creative literature are the work of imagination and lyrical intuition. Hence, artistic/literary talent is geared towards uniting the intelligible with the sensible and is endowed with the ability to construct and use imagination, contemplation, fantasy and configuration. Its conceptual counterpart is often connected to factual, logical, methodical and critical deconstruction of what the former has assembled and constructed. Such a formulation of intellectual activities posits one in a binary opposition to the other, suggesting that one can only excel in one or the other of these different types of intellectual endeavours.

Jokha Alharthi, the author of this book, defies such easy categorisations. She is as at home with the emotive and lyrical language of creative literature as with the measured, analytical and critical elaborations of a scholarly topic. In addition to her highly accomplished work in the field of the Arabic novel, which won her the prestigious International Booker Prize in 2019, she demonstrates in this book that she is also an accomplished critic and literary scholar. She first established herself in the field of Arabic narrative with two collections of short stories: *Maqati' min Sirat Lubna* (Extracts from Lubna's Life, 2001) and *Sabiyy 'ala Al-Sath* (A Boy on the Roof, 2007); three novels: *Manamat* (Dreams, 2004), *Sayidat al-Qamar* (Celestial Bodies, 2010), the first and only Arabic novel to win the Booker International Prize, and *Narinja* (A Bitter Orange Tree, 2016); and two children books: *'Ushsh Li-l-'Asafir* (A Nest for Birds, 2010) and *Al-Sahabah Tatamanna* (The Cloud Wishes, 2015).

Concurrently with her creative literary activities, she developed a career as an academic working for the leading university in her country: Sultan Qaboos University in Oman. Alongside her teaching she developed her research career, grounding it in one of the major biographical dictionaries of classical Arabic literature, *Kharidat al-Qasr wa Jaridat al-'Asr* by Al-Imad Al-Isfahani (519H/1125AD–597H/1201AD), publishing a book length study on his literary approach for selection and biographical compilation.[3] The *Kharida* (a twenty-one-volume dictionary) is a truly encyclopaedic work covering a large geographical area, extending from Iran to Morocco, and more than two centuries of Arabic literary production. Exploring such a rich resource in order to critically analyse its author's literary methodology and articulate the implicit criteria of his selection and compilation solidly grounded her in classical Arabic literature. It provided her with a deep understanding of those questions that are considered to be of great importance to the study of classical Arabic and prepared her to embark on her present work. Her work on the *Kharida* was significantly entitled *Mulahaqat al-Shumus* (Chasing Suns), a task that she has continued in both her creative and scholarly endeavours.

Her present book, *The Body in Arabic Love Poetry: The 'Udhri Tradition*, is an original endeavour to chase another set of suns, which emerged earlier than those covered by Isfahani. It is a distinctive and valuable contribution to the study of classical Arabic literature in general and Arabic poetry in particular. It traces patiently and methodically how the body is represented in the literary tradition of *'udhri* love poetry in the seventh and eighth centuries. No studies, either in Arabic or in English, have been undertaken on the depiction of the body in Arabic poetry of this period, or on the themes of sensuality and eroticism contained within it. This book, with its judicious analysis and composite orchestration of divergent material and conflicting interpretations, fills this gap through a persuasively argued thesis. It combines comprehensive close reading and insightful textual analysis of the tradition of *'udhri* poetry with a socio-cultural approach that situates it in the trajectory of its society and the common beliefs of its culture.

Her creative experience may account for her predilection for multiple interpretations rather than for a single truth behind the text; and this has enabled her to challenge the commonly accepted emphasis on chastity in *'udhri* poetry and, particularly, the absence of a clear concept of the body and sensuality. Faced with the ethereal nature of the beloved, it posits its new thesis that this tradition writes the body of the emaciated lover-poet and the corpulent and sumptuous beloved in the form, diction, imagery and content of its varied poetry. Contrary to the common perception of *'udhri* as chaste poetry of the imagined, it suggests that it is opulent with reality, sensuality and implicit sexuality. This makes it both new and relevant to the study of the perception and role of women in classical Arabic/Muslim culture, the literary and poetic representation of the body, women and feminist studies and multi-disciplinary cultural studies.

It begins with a thoroughly researched introductory chapter which constitutes a critical appraisal of the scholarship of the *'udhri* tradition in which it offers a brief history of the genre, the context and causes of its emergence, its development as a literary tradition and its authenticity as the natural product of its desert environment. Here the book situates its topic in the extensive narrative that surrounded this phenomenon, both by the seminal *Kitab al-Aghani* and the tradition of libertine Abbasid literature that followed.

From this very first chapter, the book demonstrates its command and comprehensive attention to the previous scholarship on the topic both in Arabic and Western languages. Most studies on classical Arabic literature are rooted in one of the two traditions. Those in English, for example, are grounded in Western/European scholarship and, in a truly 'Orientalist' stance, most of them pay little or no attention to the often vast works on their topic written in Arabic. Even those that may not be classified as Orientalist find it often tiresome to scrutinise a large body of work in a foreign language.

On the other hand, the ones written in Arabic pay little or no attention to the often insightful and highly valuable contribution of Western scholarship to their subject. Many of these works are written by academics with little or no access to Western languages, who are hence not aware of the importance of the literature on their topic in other languages. In this respect this book, written by a native speaker of Arabic with the ambition to contribute to Western scholarship on classical Arabic literature, by writing her contribution directly in English, is a welcome break with these practices. Unlike her creative work, which she writes in Arabic and is then translated by others into English,[4] this book is written directly in English. Hence it is firmly and competently rooted in both traditions of scholarship, which provides it with erudition, strength and importance.

The second chapter, 'Reconstructing the Past', locates the emergence of *ghazal* (love poetry) as a monothematic poem devoted entirely to the erotic theme in the Ummayad period. This is marked by the awareness that reconstructing the past is never free from its sedimentations in the present, for her primary interest in this early period is not to promote feminist revisionism of earlier literature but to offer new reflections on status, power, morality and desire. She distinguishes the *'udhri* poetry as a sub-genre of the *ghazal* that was created by the *mutayyamun* group of *ghazal* poets, and roots them and their work in earlier Arabic culture and its pre-Islamic perceptions. She persuasively refutes the division between *'udhri* and sensual love poetry, *al-ghazal al-sarih*, posited by some scholars, and places the book of al-Isfahani, *Al-Aghani* and its *akhbar* and narratives at the centre of her reconstruction of the past and the textual analysis of *'udhri* poetry. This brings in inter-textual interactions with Persian literatures and tenets of Sufism, which are intertwined with moral and ethical issues on the one hand and physicality and sensual concerns on the other.

The tension between *'iffa* (chastity) and sensuality is the main theme of the comprehensive and well-researched third chapter, '*'Udhri* Tradition between Chastity and Sensuality'. It grounds these concepts and the importance of the body first in the Qur'an and Islamic jurisprudence before dealing with their representation in literature. Maintaining the book's redeeming feature of critically engaging with the extensive research on the topic in Arabic and Western languages, the chapter focuses on the *'udhri* tradition and its textual elaborations on the body and sexuality and the Islamic discourse regulating the world of sexuality and love.

With Chapter Four, 'The Representation of the Beloved's Body', one arrives at the core thesis of the book and its distinctive contribution to the scholarship of Arabic *ghazal*. It painstakingly studies the way various *'udhri* poets wrote the body of their beloved, whether physically or allegorically, both in the anecdotes ascribed to *'udhri* poets in the culture and in the poetry itself. In doing so it carefully maintains a balance between contextual and textual aspects of their poetry. It demonstrates through close-reading and textual analysis of their diction and imagery how love as represented in their poetry and stories ascribed to *'udhri* poets is far removed from the Western concept of platonic love. Its clear grounding in reality, and literary representation of the body, is marked by detailed description of the beloved's desirable body and enticing curves, and demonstrates its physicality and sensuality in a manner that radiates eroticism. The comprehensive coverage of the major *'udhri* poets on the one hand, and Arabic and Western scholarship on them on the other, enables the book to persuasively write the body in this literary tradition and demonstrate how the conventional Arabic model of desirable female beauty permeates its diction and imagery.

This chapter posits a new understanding of this poetry as a highly revealing expression of the poet's creative engagement with his environment and society. The omnipresence of the beloved in nature and in the surrounding geography of the desert radiates with relevance and meaning, which the author draws out through sensitive textual analysis of selected poems. She demonstrates how the nature and geography of the Arab desert, with its fauna and flora, are entwined with the beloved's body as a major source of its imagery. In this respect the *'udhri* is not only a natural product of its socio-cultural environment, but extends its genealogy to pre-Islamic literature.

The author's study of the influence of the numinous Persian representation of the story of Layla and Qays, through poetry, painting and Sufism, on what might be termed the ethereal nature of the beloved, and how it led to a change of the perception of *ghazal* and elevated it to the realm of spirituality and mysticism complements rather that contradicts her findings. She shows how such ethereal beauty in the depiction of the beloved makes her radiate with sensuality and eroticism. Indeed it saves her from the mundane fate of becoming a mother. Although the Islamic attitude to marriage emphasises reproduction as the result of sexual enjoyment, the *'udhri* tradition makes no mention of children, for the beloved is usually depicted in an ethereal manner, eternally youthful, with no hint of potential motherhood.

The emphasis on the ethereal nature of the beloved at the end of this chapter leads naturally to the following chapter on the dynamics of the presence and absence of the body of the beloved. This chapter demonstrates that the writing of the body in *'udhri* poetry is not confined to its depiction as a concrete corporeal body and a model of ideal beauty but is caught up with the idea of her presence and absence. It can be observed in her gestures, speech, intimate body language such as glances, gazes, sighs and smells, as well as through her absence in the form of her phantom or her being in a location inaccessible to the lover. Her presence is often depicted as being part of the natural world in some metaphorical sense, but still physically absent. The phantom of the beloved (*tayf al-khayal*) is a frequently used convention of amatory poetry that has been utilised by the *'udhri* poets, as well as the longing for her place of residence where her omnipresence is to be found among the natural elements of stones, wind and water. The dialectics of the beloved's presence and absence generates a host of imagery and symbols associated with both, in a manner that enabled this poetry to take the pre-Islamic *wuquf ala atlal*, reminiscing on the old traces, to new realms of expression. Both the dwelling in which she resides out of the poet's reach and the home that she has vacated and the traces she has left behind generate rich images, metaphors and symbols.

The following chapter, 'Textuality Versus Reality', demonstrates the centrality of the textual in *'udhri* poetry; just to remember one's beloved while one is alone conjures her almost physically and inspires the lover to compose poetry. The paradox of the *'udhri* poet's complaint about love, and his embracing of it, engenders a complex perception of love and the persona of the poet at the same time. This led to the discourse of cultural value that developed around poetry, the perception of the poet as a hero and the representation of poetry as the ultimate goal. It is noteworthy that *'udhri* lovers were poets, and their poetry is in fact a confessional expression of their own sentiments and views of the world around them. This is essentially what earned them a place in most Arabic collections of poetry; their deep consciousness of the fact that they are poets itself shapes their romances. If the beloved is the feminine ideal, or is depicted as unattainable, her lover will suffer from his ardent love forever. Whether poetry is a sort of remedy, as several *'udhri* verses have suggested, or is an object in itself, its presence in this tradition is essential – the heroic gesture of the *'udhri* lover is that of being a poet. The lover is attached to his unique beloved, to whom he devotes his poetry. He reveres his beloved, the subject and object of his poetry, as much as his pre-Islamic predecessor celebrated his tribe. In the *'udhri* romances, the lover loses everything, including his beloved, except his ability to compose poetry. Being a poet seems to be his ultimate goal and heroic achievement.

The final chapter, 'The Representation of the Lover's Body in the *'Udhri* Tradition', begins by establishing the link between *'ishq* and sickness in classical times. It has been seen as a major cause of suffering, capable of subjugating, intoxicating and humiliating the lover. It often produces an enervated and depressed young man or woman suffering from lovesickness. In Arabic culture at the time, *'ishq* was seen as madness and submissiveness, as the malady of refined and sophisticated people. The book then demonstrates the effect of love on the lover's body in *'udhri* tradition and provides an exhaustive, highly detailed account of its corporeal manifestations. In *'udhri* poets' *diwans* there are numerous allusions to weeping, sickness, wasting away, paleness, malady, (*kabid maqruhah*) the damaged liver, even fainting and only the smell of the beloved's veil could wake him. Among the synonyms of love in the Arabic language, about twenty relate love, in varying degrees, to insanity, to a 'break with the commonly accepted norms of behaviour, whether on a personal or on a social level.' Yet, the changes that occur in the lover's body as he descends into lovesickness become signs of moral values related to the manners of love and to the literary values of its poetry.

In this final chapter the book provides a detailed close-reading and textual analysis of how the body of the poet/lover and his beloved are carefully written in *'udhri* poetry. It accomplishes its promise as a competent academic engagement with the original poetry under discussion and provides a persuasive new reading that challenges the traditionally accepted understanding of its nature and role. Its insightful textual analysis of *'udhri* poetry is matched by its rigorous appraisal of both Arabic and Western scholarship on the topic. The detailed manner in which this book demonstrates how the writing of the body permeates this poetry provides its readers with insights into the Arab community at the time, and into issues of status, power, morality and desire in Arabic culture.

This book is highly relevant to the study of Arabic classical literature and culture in general and poetry in particular. It fills a gap in the field and opens new venues for future investigation, for it adds a new dimension to the available studies on classical Arabic poetry. Its engagement with both Arabic and Western scholarship constitute an epistemological break with previous studies that will thrive and bear fruit. I expect it to become necessary reading in this field and that it may lead to new and fresh approaches to the study of the body and its significance in other classical texts. It will inspire students of literature to gain a fresh and more topical insight into classical Arabic culture and encourage them to venture into the realm of the unsaid. It is also relevant to a number of other academic disciplines, such as the study of the perception and role of women in classical Arabic/Muslim culture, the literary and poetic representation of the body, the role of the poet/ intellectual in his/her culture, women and feminist studies and multi-disciplinary cultural studies.

Notes

1. Benedetto Croce (1866–1952) was a major public intellectual whose complete works run into eighty volumes, but his main philosophy of the spirit is expounded in three major works: *Aesthetic* (1902), *Logic* (1908) and *Philosophy of the Practical* (1908). The ideas explicated in this paragraph are from *Aesthetic*.
2. See chapter one of Benedetto Croce (1921), *The Essence of Aesthetic*, trans. Douglas Ainslie, London: William Heinemann.
3. Jokha al-Harithi (2010), *Mulahaqat al-Shumus: Manhaj al-Ta'lif Al-Adabi fi Kitab Kharidat al-Qasr lil-Imad al-Isbahani*, Manama: Dar al-Suwaydi. In addition she compiled and edited the *Diwan* of a major Omani poet, *Diwan Abi-l-Hakam: Al-Shaikh Ahmad ibn Abdulla Al-Harithi*, Muscat: Centre for Omani Studies, Sultan Qaboos University, 2014.
4. Her second novel, *Sayyidat al-Qamar,* was translated into English as *Celestial Bodies*, trans: Marilyn Booth (Inverness: Sandstone Press, 2018).

Preface

The *'udhri ghazal* emerged as a remarkable literary genre in Arabic literature during the Umayyad period (seventh–eighth centuries CE). The leaders of this genre are famous poets who were also lovers (and whom I shall call "lover-poets"). They were known for their dramatic love stories and unique poetry, which presented such numinous figures as Majnun Layla, Qays Lubna and Jamil Buthaynah. Traditionally, scholars have assumed that there is no concept of the body in the *'udhri ghazal*. Most scholars to date have reproduced only commonly held ideas about the purity of *'udhri* love without doubting its supposed chastity. This book, however, argues that the body has a privileged position in the *'udhri ghazal*. It shows that the body's presence is represented, realistically or allegorically, in various ways, both in anecdotes about the *'udhri* poets and in their poetry. Although some critics have discussed the theme of the depiction of the beloved's body, it is the particular contribution of this study to illuminate what might be termed the ethereal nature of beauty in this depiction. Moreover, this book discusses the symbolic body in *'udhri* poetry. In many ways, then, it departs from the prevailing views on the *'udhri* phenomenon in studies of classical Arabic literature. In so doing, it opens the door to new discussions about the relationship between love poetry and Arab society in the classical age. It is also a contribution more generally to literary studies of representations of the body and is thus also relevant to scholars of comparative literature.

Please note that dates throughout the book are given first in the Islamic/Hijri (h) calendar, followed by the western/Gregorian (BC/AD) calendar.

*To my husband Altayeb,
my children Khuzama, Ibrahim, Yasmeen
and my sister Zina*

1

Introduction:
A Critical Reappraisal of Scholarship of the 'Udhri Tradition

> *'Udhri*, or chaste love poetry celebrates the lofty union of souls between a man and a woman that endures despite societal obstacles and legal limits, eternal beyond even death. *'Udhri* poetry turns the unattainability of physical union with the beloved into a spur to virtue, high devotion, and chivalry in the life of the lover, who ultimately dies as a martyr to love.[1]

This citation, from a popular website, exemplifies certain typical ideas about *'udhri* love and poetry that I intend to explore in this study. In both the popular and the academic view, *'udhri* love is nearly always considered as chaste love. In contemporary Arab society people still call chaste love '*'udhri* love'. This popular understanding assumes that the concept of the body is absent from the *'udhri* tradition, and likewise, most scholars who have addressed this tradition have simply reiterated these commonly held ideas about its virtues.

The significance of the present study lies in the fact that it will provide a comprehensive appraisal of the subject of the *'udhri* tradition. The term '*'udhri* tradition' encompasses not only *'udhri* poets and poetry but also the stories told about them. These poets lived in the seventh and eighth centuries and, about two centuries later, their poetry and love stories were collected and retold. This book aims to study and assess the various reconstructions of the *'udhri* tradition. In my reading, the human body is a vital feature of *'udhri* love and poetry. We can observe its presence, whether physically or allegorically, in a variety of ways, both in the anecdotes ascribed to *'udhri* poets and in the poetry itself. In fact, I would argue that some aspect of the body lies at the heart of even the most 'chaste' *'udhri* verses. Descriptions of the actual body of the beloved, or else its representation symbolically, in its presence or conversely in its absence, along with depictions of the emaciating and suffering body of the lover-poet, are all crucial aspects of the *'udhri* tradition, as my study intends to show.

Modern scholarly approaches to the subject tend to fall into several broad categories: some focus on the aesthetic side of *'udhri* love, whilst the majority address its historical and psychological dimensions, and yet other studies concentrate on one particular poet of this genre.[2] However, to the best of my knowledge, no studies have been undertaken on the depiction of the body in *'udhri* poetry or on the themes of sensuality contained within it.[3] This issue has been only partially investigated through a small number of general studies and even then mostly from a limited perspective. Hence, it is hoped that the present study will yield a more comprehensive appraisal of the subject. It will consider two specific points that have not previously been given the attention they deserve: firstly, how the attitude of the poet towards the body of the beloved is expressed, either literally or allegorically, in the *'udhri* tradition; and secondly, how the effect of ardent love on the lover's own body is depicted. Particularly careful consideration will be given to the attitude toward love and the body in Arab Islamic culture and its influence on the *'udhri* tradition. Another main concern of this study is to reconstruct the *'udhri* tradition itself. This book represents the first study devoted to the *'udhri* tradition to be written in English and the first to focus entirely on the presence of the body in the *'udhri* tradition in either Arabic or English. Previous thematic studies, as will be discussed, either overlook the subject or address only one particular poet of this genre.

'Udhri Poetry: a Brief Historical and Thematic Overview

Al-Ghazal[4] *al-'Udhri* is named after the *'Udhrah*[5] tribe that supplied this poetical tradition with many of its leading poets. Members of this tribe were generally said to have tender hearts and to seek a true love that usually led to death.[6] The *'udhri* poet Jamil b. 'Abdallah b. Ma'mar, better known as Jamil Buthaynah (d. 82/701), who is considered the leading light of this genre, was from the *'Udhrah* tribe. Nevertheless, there were *'udhri* poets from other tribes, such as Majnun Layla, who belonged to the Banu 'Amir. As one scholar has observed, 'the term *'udhri* was then used more broadly for a whole school of self-immolating poets of the central Arabian desert.'[7]

'Udhri love is a fatal love in that it leads to death. The *'udhri* loves only one woman, devoting his life and poetry to her and only rarely composing verses in another genre, such as praise (*madh*) or satire (*hija*). The beloved is portrayed in the *'udhri ghazal* as an ideal woman and her poet lover as a martyr of love. The recurring theme of suffering and torment in love is strong in the *'udhri* tradition. Another characteristic of the *'udhri ghazal* is the use of certain symbolic conventions and imagery.

The most important *'udhri* love poets are 'Urwah b. Hizam (d. 30/650), Majnun Layla (d. c. 68/688), Qays b. Dharih (d. 68\688), Jamil Buthaynah (d. 82/701), and Kuthayyir 'Azzah (d. 105/723). However, some scholars include other poets in the *'udhri* school such as Dhu al-Rummah (d. 117/735)[8] and 'Abbas b. al-Ahnaf (d. 188/804).[9] But the question of how to categorise these poets is still under debate: for example, not all scholars accept Kuthayyir 'Azzah as an *'udhri* poet.[10] In addition, one may argue that Dhu al-Rummah, in spite of his body of love poetry dedicated to his beloved Mayy, is concerned with different themes from the ones usually popular with *'udhri* poets and, moreover, his love story differs from *'udhri* love stories. Going further, while 'Abbas b. al-Ahnaf composes beautiful love poetry for his beloved Fawz[11], and while, in many respects, some of his themes are similar to *'udhri* themes[12], there is also a description of an orgy with singing girls in his poetry, which would be an unimaginable subject in *'udhri* poetry. Moreover, al-'Abbas's cultural environment was completely different from the *'udhri* environment and his poetry is closer to the manner of courtly love poetry. Given the controversies over whether some of these poets should be considered as part of this genre, I will focus only on those who are unambiguously and well-nigh universally considered to be *'udhri* poets.

Scholars do not differ sharply in historical detail about the *'udhri* poets, but they are at variance in their interpretations of these details, a matter which I intend to deal with later. I am not concerned here with citing anecdotes about the *'udhri* romances, as these can very easily be found in classical Arabic books such as *al-Aghani* and *Masari' al-'ushshaq*. Rather, I intend to comment briefly on the common tropes present in these love stories.

A considerable number of scholars have observed the striking similarities between the romances of various *'udhri* poets. To explain this, Jayyusi suggests that:

> The pattern of the *'udhri* love poetry and love tale was set early in pre-Islamic times. The earliest *'udhri* love poet in the Umayyad age was 'Urwah b. Hizam, and his tragic love story sets the pattern for the numerous love stories of the Umayyad period.[13]

'Urwah b. Hizam, in fact, lived before the Umayyad period and died during the caliphate of 'Uthman b. 'Affan. However, Jayyusi is correct about 'the pattern of the *'udhri* love poetry and love tale', which was set in pre-Islamic times. In pre-Islamic poetry we have the stories of 'Abdallah b. 'Ajlan, Hind's lover, and al-Muraqqish al-Akbar, Asma's lover, both of whom suffered love unto death. Nevertheless, al-Batal points out that in the *'udhri ghazal* new elements were introduced into the pre-Islamic stories to express the greater complexity of the new Islamic society, such as people's rejection of the new social roles set by the Umayyad authorities.[14] This may explain why *'udhri* love stories revolve around the same themes. The typical components of the *'udhri* poets' sentimental tales are[15]: the lover meets his beloved either during their childhood when they used to tend their families' flocks of sheep in the desert or they meet as adults in a sudden encounter. They fall deeply in love, a love that continues until death, and the lover consequently composes poetry describing his fatal love for his beloved. However, his beloved's parents turn down his marriage proposal, due to the disgrace that his verses have brought upon both their daughter and themselves – this in spite of the fact that they are from the same tribe and sometimes from the same family. In some cases, the demand for an exorbitant dowry prevents the marriage, so the lover goes to seek wealth while the parents force their daughter to marry another man, who generally has fewer good qualities than her lover. Then the beloved goes away with her husband. Her marriage intensifies her lover's passion, so the brokenhearted poet pursues his beloved and recites beautiful poetry that circulates far and wide, describing her beauty and his suffering. He continues in his endeavours to visit her after her marriage and they remain faithful in heart to each other until death. As a result of the poet's insistence on seeing his beloved and composing poetry about her, her parents complain to the ruler, who decrees that killing him is permissible. The ruler exiles him and the exiled poet wanders in the desert. In some accounts, his passion leads him into madness, but whenever he remembers his beloved, poetic inspiration comes. Eventually, the lovers die soon after one another and – in some accounts – are buried next to each other.

These episodes are motifs that are found in a number of *'udhri* romances. It is irrelevant for this study to review the minor differences between these stories. Instead, it is important to bear in mind the wider lines that constitute the essential framework of the love story, at the same time noting the way the structure is dependent upon symbolism. The legendary tropes in these stories can be observed through certain common features, namely, as al-Batal notes, the ambiguity surrounding the identity of the composers of these romances, and the repeated motifs within every single story which make all the *'udhri* stories concentrate on one theme, regardless of the minor differences in details.[16]

As one can see, the main characteristic of the plot is the poet's total devotion to love; this sentiment infuses all *'udhri* stories and poetry. The lovers are depicted purely as ideals of love, so that the reader knows nothing of their lives beyond this passion. The sentiments of love and the accompanying agony are told in *'udhri* poetry in a myriad ways. The lovers 'did not want to get rid of their pain, because pain is the only genuine criterion of true love.'[17] The beloved becomes the ideal of a timeless woman and seems to be almost immortal: 'Time cannot touch her, nor can her beauty and perception change.'[18] Her depiction in *'udhri* poetry reminds us of the *houri* who never ages, as described in the Qur'an[19]. Although *houris* are not described as passionate or even as lovers in the Qur'an, their eternal youth and beauty inspire the *'udhri* poet. who insists on drawing an out-of-time image for his beloved. The desert, being spacious and still, provides an appropriate setting for the unfolding of *'udhri* love stories. This vast tranquil space implies stability, which is compatible with the concept of unchanging time in *'udhri* poetry. So the desert is an ideal backdrop symbolising immutability and timelessness. The reader of *'udhri* stories and poetry loses all sense of time within the events of the love stories. Time seems to stop for the lovers as their passion tends to be detached and unaffected by temporality. Jacobi notes: 'Whereas the poet of the Djahiliyya abandons a futile love affair of the past, the *'udhri* poet perseveres in the face of hopelessness and despair. His love is preordained by fate and transcends death.'[20]

As their poetry shows, the *'udhri* poets, Kinany notes, 'were so possessed by their delirious passion that they came to believe that life without the beloved was meaningless.'[21] Majnun, upon the loss of his beloved, felt:

> As if the mountain-roads were the circle of rings
> Around me, never increasing in length or breadth[22]   [1]

The intimate relationship between love and death is a crucial element of the *'udhri* experience. Most of the lovers die because of their fatal love and so their poetry is full of references to death.[23] As Bürgel states: 'Such love is almost of necessity tragic. And its tragedy is a symbol of the incompatibility of the absolute and the concrete, of the ideal and the [sic] real life.'[24] As seen from the components of these tales, any love adventure needs the involvement of secondary characters to be foils for the main characters. A passionate love adventure could not be narrated without obstacles being created by others. These obstacles enliven the story and also help to make it eternal. The existence of others is the best guarantee for an everlasting and infinite love.[25] In *'udhri* stories the central theme is that the obstacles cannot be overcome and neither can the love itself be given up. Jacobi suggests that 'the conflict is obviously situated between generations: the parents represent the tribal community, against which the implicit polemics of the *'udhri* model are directed.'[26] It is noteworthy that in *'udhri* stories the lovers are rejected in one way or another by society, thus they are expelled out of society to the world of the desert, which symbolises their exclusion. Therefore, the figure of the blamer *'athil'* is a familiar figure in the *'udhri ghazal*.[28] The function of the blamer is to persuade the lover-poet to be more moderate or, in other words, 'to prevent the protagonist from making the heroic gesture'.[29] But for these poets, love was their chief object, it was a way of life that, moreover, gave it purpose.[30]

The *'udhri* poet does not want any woman other than his beloved, as she is preferable to any other creature; and, just as the lover's passion surpasses that of all other lovers, so too his beloved surpasses all other women. He would be pleased with very little from her[31] and she is both the cause of and the only cure for the poet's misery.[32] Intensity, despair and faithfulness are central to the love stories of the *'udhri* poets.[33] Their poetry concerns itself with the description of the lovers' suffering and yearning, and it also portrays their unattainable love as well as expressing their wishes and hopes for the future.[34] Although it is true that the beloved in *'udhri* poetry is typically portrayed as an aloof and inaccessible woman, nevertheless, I disagree with Kinany and Jayyusi who claim that *'udhri* love is an unreciprocated love.[35] I would argue that the portrayal of the beloved as an aloof woman (*bakhilah*) is, rather, a convention of classical Arabic poetry. Further chapters in this study will discuss this point in detail, and meanwhile, I will provide one example from Jamil's poetry on Buthaynah that shows the two lovers involved in passion:

> We were both on the point of crying for each other,
> And her tears were quicker than mine[36] [2]

Sources of *'Udhri* Poetry

These stories were collected and retold about 150 years after the *'udhri* poets' deaths. The stories and poetry of *'udhri* lovers were circulated from the end of the seventh century onwards, appearing in collections by numerous authors. The earliest extant version of the genre is to be found in an anthology of Ibn Qutaybah (d. 276/889), who collected the works of major Arab poets in his book *al-Shi'r wa al-shu'ara*.[37] Shortly after Ibn Qutaybah, Ibn Daud (d. 297/910) included in his *Kitab al-zahrah* some fragments ascribed to *'udhri* poets. Then al-Isfahani (d. 356/976) presented, in his famous work *Kitab al-Aghani* ('The Book of Songs'), a collection of numerous anecdotes and poetic fragments, which were either ascribed to *'udhri* poets like Jamil and Majnun, or referred to them.[38] His work is like a 'mosaic put together out of shards of prose and fragments of poetry'.[39] Al-Nuwayri (d. 733/1332), who relates various *'udhri* love stories in his encyclopaedia *Nihayat al-arab*, states that the *'udhri* martyrs of love were too many to count.[40] In any case, *'udhri* love stories, in more or less detail, appear in many classical literary works such as *Masari' al-'ushshaq* by Abu Ja'far al-Sarraj (d. 500/1106), *Rawdat al-muhibbin* by Ibn Qayyim al-Jawziyyah (d. 769/1349) and *Tazyin al-aswaq* by Daud al-Antaki (d. 1008/1599) where *'udhri* poets are transformed into the heroes of romantic stories. During the early 'Abbasid period, *'udhri* romances were very popular, numerous verses having been set to music.[41]

The Factors Contributing to the Rise of 'Udhri Poetry

The *'udhri ghazal*, like any other literary phenomenon, is complex and does not exist in a vacuum, being a result of many interrelated factors: religious, political, psychological, literary and historical. In Taha Husayn's view, this phenomenon is best explained by the sudden rise of languorous opulence in Mecca and Medina, cities that had lost their political weight in spite of having grown rich. Hence, wealthy poets in urban areas pursued profane love poetry while hopelessly poor poets in Bedouin tribes pursued *'udhri* poetry.[42] Clearly, Husayn relies on a vaguely formulated sociology of rising expectations and another scholar, Labib al-Tahir, has further developed Husayn's argument by linking the socio-economic factors of the *'Udhrah* tribe with the emergence of *'udhri* love.[43] However, the examples al-Tahir uses of poets who do not belong to this tribe, like Majnun, who is from the Banu 'Amir, make the link between this poetry and the specific economic situation of the Banu *'Udhrah* rather weak. Moreover, while social factors may have played a part in the emergence of these tales, we should be careful not to try to explain everything simply by the social environment.

To explain its emergence, Kinany associates the *'udhri ghazal* with Islamic monotheism, eschatology and ethics.[44] He says, for example: 'the Muslim religion had a bearing on all the aspects of *'udhri* love which we have studied so far, namely chastity, faithfulness, despair, resignation, the personification of love and the conception of an eternal passion.'[45] Shukri Faysal also emphasises the religious factor in the emergence of the *'udhri* phenomenon, as Islam purified people's souls.[46] Faysal says:

> From the chastity that was driven by religion and the love that was driven by desire emerged *'udhri* love. It was necessary for devout Muslims who were not so successful in their love to express this failure in one way or another. Subsequently, they found solace in poetry, a verbal art, with leeway to express their emotions; because *'udhri* love mirrored chaste and desirous love at the same time. So, this compensatory type of poetry was there to suppress the heat of emotions and elevate desires.[47]

Dayf, likewise, argues that following the ethical basis of Islam, *'udhri* poetry is characterised by chastity and perfection[48]. However, in spite of the popularity of Faysal's argument among contemporary scholars,⁴⁹ his limitation of the circumstances that led to the emergence of *'udhri* love to Islamic and societal factors opens the door to further discussion. There is no evidence that the Bedouin poets were more influenced by the moral teaching of Islam than other poets. In fact, to say that the Islamic influence was stronger on the Bedouin tribes than on the urban tribes is misleading for two reasons. Firstly, the Bedouin tribes are described in the Qur'an as hypocritical and unrighteous.⁵⁰ Secondly, during the Umayyad era there were unquestionably more devout men in Mecca and Medina than among the Bedouin tribes (*al-fuqaha' al-shu'ara'*); religious poets such as 'Urwah b. Udhaynah and 'Abd al-Rahman al-Quss lived in Medina, not in the Bedouin desert. Moreover, many anecdotes ascribed to *'udhri* poets present elements contradictory to what are predominantly considered the ethical principles of Islam.⁵¹ In any case, I would argue that the influence of Islam on the *'udhri ghazal* did go beyond poetic images and structures, but that this influence did not include the Islamic model of the relationship between man and woman. Thus, it may be wrong to assume that the influence of Islam helped distinguish the *'udhri* experience from other forms of Arabic poetry. Furthermore, the *'udhri* poets' use of religious language is meant to express the extent of their devotion. Thus, for Jamil, those who die of love are martyrs, no less than those who fall in *jihad*. At prayer, moreover, Majnun, instead of orienting himself towards Mecca, faces the place where Layla lives.⁵²

Several scholars emphasise the poor and sad quality of life in the desert along with a feeling of helplessness and also strict Bedouin manners as factors in the emergence of the *'udhri ghazal*.⁵³ Both Yusuf al-Yusuf and 'Ali al-Batal use a stratified social explanation to account for *'udhri* poetry. Al-Yusuf's analysis combines social and psychological readings of the *'udhri* phenomenon. On the other hand, al-Batal views the *'udhri* stories as legends and analyses them symbolically. Al-Yusuf's interpretation considers the political subjugation practised by the Umayyads and the social oppression that resulted from the increasing dominance of particular social values as the basis for his interpretation of the *'udhri* tradition. The experience of intense oppression leads to a loss of identity that is compensated for through the writing of poetry.⁵⁴ Al-Batal expresses a similar idea; arguing that the *'udhri* phenomenon, which circulated in the Hijaz desert, reflects the experiences of desert dwellers in the particular period when the poems were written. It also expresses the Bedouins' views on the political injustice practised by their leaders. Since freedom of expression was restricted, they referred to this injustice allegorically.[55]

However, the anecdotes told about *'udhri* poets and even their poetry indicate that they were not poor at all; the main reason that Qays was forced to divorce his beloved wife Lubna was to ensure that the wealth of his family remained within the family. Jamil, in addition, is depicted as a handsome man who wears expensive clothes. In one of his verses he says:

> I go amongst beggars and ask her family for hospitality,
> While my own wealthy and generous relatives are within reach[56]　　[3]

Furthermore, we should take many other considerations into account: the poets were not contemporaries of each other and they were not without their own social and political ambitions; Kuthayyir 'Azzah, for example, although conforming to the policy of dissimulation, eulogised the Umayyads. Therefore, the explanation that the rapid development of love poetry in the Hijaz was simply because the people of this region were not involved in politics is a fallacy.[57] In the Umayyad period not only the Hijaz but the whole Arab world was interested in the theme of love. It was a major theme in the work of many famous poets such as Dhu al-Rummah and Walid b. Yazid.[58] To provide an explanation for the phenomenon of love poetry in the Hijaz Jayyusi suggests that the poets in the Hijaz had more leisure time than those in the new provinces and could more happily turn their attention to that genre. In addition, the Hijaz's loss of its former status as the centre of Arabia must have caused a reaction which might have been expressed by amatory romanticism. Also, the long urbanised society of the Hijaz spread its style of living to all regions. Finally, Jayyusi suggests the possibility of the emergence of a poetic vogue that simply caught on, arguing that it has an element of excellence that transcends environmental and historical conditions.[59]

The Development of the *'Udhri* Phenomenon as a Literary Tradition

During the early Abbasid period in the late ninth century *'udhri* poets were transformed into the heroes of romantic stories that became very popular. Majnun, in particular, attracted the attention of writers on the theory of love, and his verses were eventually included in anthologies of poems by lover-poets and martyrs of love. The figure of Majnun also attracted mystics because Majnun's rapture was analogous to their own ecstatic states.[60] Hence, in the words of Jayyusi: 'It is appropriate to think that the appearance of such stories as Majnun's, though based on an existing tradition, started a fashion for a genre of love literature that proved to be enormously popular.'[61] The *'udhri* concept of love 'was imbued with a courtly flavour and projected back into an idealised Bedouin past. As a consequence, the biographies of poets reckoned among the *'udhri*s are embellished with legendary details.'[62] In modern Arabic literature Majnun's character has been a source of inspiration for many poets and authors, including Ahmad Shawqi and his poetic play *Majnun Layla*, which was first published in 1933. Except for a few scenes, the *Aghani* version of the story is replicated in Shawqi's play. In 1996 the Arab poet Qasim Haddad published a collection of poetry entitled *Akhbar Majnun Layla* in which he renders a new reading of the old legend. It is remarkable that, in Haddad's interpretation, the lovers are explicitly described as having a physical relationship.[63]

In Persian literature, Majnun's love for Layla is treated as a kind of adoration similar to the one reserved for God, and the legend was adopted by Sufis. The first adaptation of the Arabic fragments of the legend into Persian can be found in Nizami's *Layli and Majnun* (composed 584/118–19). Dols notes that Nizami's adaptation has the advantage of being consistent with the earlier accounts as well as being a fuller and more detailed narrative. Indeed, Nizami's style is characterised by an intense use of imagery[64]. In addition, the symbolic potential in the Arabic version of Majnun's story reaches its zenith with the Persian Sufi poet Jami (d. 1492/898). Jami's *Layli and Majnun* is a representation of the Sufi quest with a creative use of convention that is remarkable.[65] Inspired by Nizami, the Majnun legend has remained very popular with Turkish poets until modern times. The most famous adaptation of the story was by Fuzuli in 942/1535–6.[66] Further east, the romance was embraced in Urdu literature.[67] In the West, the Banu 'Udhrah, who die from love, appear in European literature in Stendhal's treatise *De l'amour* (1822) and Romantics such as Heinrich Heine with his poem *Der Asra*, which was set to music by Carl Loewe.[68]

The Authenticity of the *'Udhri* Tradition

The authenticity of the *'udhri* tradition, including its poetry and stories, has always been considered suspect by certain scholars and has been the subject of much debate. These scholars start with the influential classical source, the *Kitab al-Aghani*, casting doubts not just on the poetry ascribed to Majnun, but also on his actual existence. Al-Isfahani (d. 967/356), who devoted around sixty pages of *al-Aghani* to Majnun Layla, discusses the contradictory anecdotes that either confirm Majnun's existence and poetry or indicate that he is an imaginary persona. According to the *Aghani*, some reciters (*al-rawah*) claimed that when they had asked members of Majnun's tribe, the Banu 'Amir, about him, they denied that he had ever existed, some of them saying: 'Absolutely not, Banu 'Amir are much more serious [than Majnun]!'.[69] Al-Isfahani also quotes al-Jahiz as saying: 'People claim that every anonymous poem about Layla should be attributed to Majnun'.[70] However, many others confirmed that they had met Majnun and heard the poems being recited from his own tongue.[71]

The debate about the authenticity of *'udhri* poetry in general (and Majnun's very existence and the authorship of his poetry in particular) continues among modern scholars. I have no intention of reviewing all their points of view. Instead, I would like to briefly mention the major contributions relevant to the subject under discussion. Taha Husayn in *Hadith al-arbi'a* casts doubts on Majnun's poetry and his existence, which, in conclusion, he denies completely.[72] On the other hand, the Russian scholar Kratchkovsky has argued for the real historical existence of Majnun by relying on historical methodology.[73] However, Ghunaymi Hilal in his book *Al-hayah al-'atifiyyah bayn al-'udhriyyah wa al-sufiyyah* examines the different opinions and surmises that if we postulate that some of Majnun's fragments are fake, that does not mean that he did not exist at all.[74] 'Abd al-Qadir al-Qitt, likewise, has traced various examples of the same verses sometimes ascribed to Majnun, and at other times ascribed to Tawbah, Nasib or Qays.[75] However, as al-Jawari has observed, seeking credibility in *'udhri* stories is a difficult task, due to the fact that they were mainly circulated orally. Moreover, the comic and adventurous nature of these anecdotes made them more likely to be embellished with imaginary details. However, al-Jawari also demonstrates that modern scholars who have criticised this literary phenomenon may have failed to view it within its own historical context.

They have criticised the *'udhri* tradition according to contemporary norms in which such anecdotes would hardly feature.[76] Hamori also alludes to the oral tradition, arguing that:

> It has been suggested that *'udhri* poetry is the product not of Bedouin Arabia, but of Empire sophistication; that it is the romantic creation of the early 'Abbasid age, projected backwards in history at a time when biographies of Bedouin poets-lovers were a popular form of entertainment literature in Baghdad. But already the earliest 'Abbasid poets knew of these *'udhri* poets, and it is hardly likely that their romance-biographies (for which the *kitab al-Aghani* is now our principal source) did not from the first contain a core of poetry.[77]

In any case, these kinds of discussions are numerous and protracted. I would like to make it clear from the outset that the issue of authenticity of any particular *'udhri* anecdote or verse is not something that I will be concerned with in this study. How much of these stories and poetry is genuine and how much is the work of reciters is largely irrelevant here. The phenomenon is generally authentic in its being a product of a particular time and place, and it does not really matter if some *'udhri* verses are wrongly attributed or fabricated, or if some poets' stories are exaggerated. In fact, some degree of fabrication is inevitable when such romances grow into legends. As Khairallah has noted:

> Should a legend be realistic? Or is it rather the task of the critic to attempt an interpretation of a literary work that fascinated people's imagination? Is it sufficient to dismiss the love story of Majnun, because when compared with the love stories of Jamil and Kuthayyir, it appears to Husain to be 'the most insane and exaggerated among them, and the least meaningful'? Thus, by insisting on the necessity of realism, Husain denies the legend the benefit of the doubt, thereby missing the symbolism it may contain.[78]

Thus, I would agree with the scholars who focus on the questions of composition and structure, rather than the question of authenticity. Moreover, as has been stated in the text quoted earlier, the *'udhri* romances incline towards legend, hence it is quite natural for exaggeration to take place. The

Kitab al-aghani is the main source of such romances and I would agree with Suzanne Stetkevych that the poems and the anecdotes in this book

> ... have generally been either misused – that is, taken to be factual history in the modern sense – or else discarded because of their questionable historicity or obvious folkloric nature. But however unreliable they may be as a basis for factual literary biography, they nevertheless offer a rich vein of largely un-mined mythic /folkloric gold. For however far back the association of the *akhbar* with the poetry goes and whatever its nature, this association, I would argue, is not arbitrary but semantic. That is, the anecdotes somehow reflect, reinforce, or complement the meaning of the poems or the archetypal image of the poet. Furthermore, the explication of the structure and the symbolism of the many variant stories and anecdotes juxtaposed in the *Kitab al-aghani* narrative reveals that even apparently divergent or contradictory versions often yield what might be called the same mythic message.[79]

Moreover, al-Isfahani in *al-Aghani* presents many different and confused anecdotes, giving the responsibility for them to the storytellers (*al-rawah*) themselves. Contemporary scholars may then decide, according to their own criteria, which of these anecdotes are valid and which are not. Therefore, one *'udhri* story may appear in one scholar's opinion as an authentic story that fits with Jamil's character, while other scholars declare it to be a ridiculous fake. For example, the story that Ibn Qutaybah cites of Jamil and Kuthayyir's meeting, which resulted in the sending of Kuthayyir as a messenger to Buthaynah to make an appointment for Jamil,[80] is described by Hatum as 'the most honest story ever told about Jamil and his love for Buthaynah'.[81] Hence, he concludes from this story that their love is chaste and virtuous. On the other hand, Taha Husayn mentions the same story so as to refer to the silliness of the anecdotes told about Jamil. He even goes beyond that and ends up saying: 'This story is among the jokes that people used to mock the Bedouins with'.[82] This kind of contradiction supports my point of view regarding the matter of authenticity in the *'udhri ghazal*. Questioning the authenticity of these works should not concern us much here since there is no way to prove whether every single anecdote is valid or not.

A Critical Examination of Scholarship on *'Udhri* Poetry

Over the last century a considerable literature has been produced concerning the *'udhri* tradition, with several attempts to analyse this tradition from a variety of perspectives. Some of the studies focus on the tradition in general while others concentrate on one *'udhri* poet, most often Jamil or Majnun. However, since the heightened interest in the *'udhri ghazal* from the early twentieth century onwards, there have been very few studies on the literary aspects of this form, namely, its origin, its characteristics and related scholarship. It should be noted first that there are no English-language books devoted entirely to the *'udhri* tradition, though there are some studies of Majnun Layla, which will be discussed later. However, many studies have been written in Arabic, which include in their titles the phrase *al-ghazal al-'udhri, al-hubb al-'udhri* or *al-shi'r al-'udhri*. Nevertheless, few of these studies add anything new to the current level of knowledge. There are an even larger number of books that simply reproduce what is already common knowledge by expansion, stereotyping or going into verbose detail. Many of these works are based on a historical narrative approach, devoting much attention to relating stories about *'udhri* poets and including examples of their poetry without making any real effort to analyse this information.[83] Despite their increasing number, these studies make little attempt to address the subject of how the body is presented in the *'udhri* tradition, if they admit to its presence at all, and so they bear little immediate relevance to my study. Therefore, in the following pages, I will focus on the themes of desire, *'iffah* (chastity) and sexuality in the *'udhri* tradition from a scholarly perspective. It should be noted, however, that the issues addressed here are to be reiterated and discussed at greater length in the following chapters.

In the *Encyclopedia of Arabic Literature* Jacobi considers chastity among the main elements of *'udhri* love, a notion that, as mentioned earlier, I intend to question. Jacobi sees *'udhri* love as an 'elegiac counterpart to the frivolous eroticism of the Hijazi *ghazal*, represented by 'Umar b. Abi Rabi'ah'.[84] Gibb, likewise, in his early study *Arabic Literature: An Introduction*, views the *'udhri ghazal* as distinct from 'Umar and the other Makkan poets. He observes that 'from the moment of its creation, it achieved a great and growing popularity'.[85] Hamori, in a chapter on love poetry in the Abbasid period in *Abbasid*

Belles-Lettres, notes – as several scholars do[86] – that in the Umayyad period, the love-poem became independent and the *ghazal* emerged as a distinct genre. He states that whether the Hijazi love-poems are chaste or licentious has less to do perhaps with the poet's experiences than with the audience's expectations[87]. However, his chapter shows very little interest in the *'udhri* tradition.

In *Hadith al-arbi'a'*, first published 1924, Taha Husayn distinguishes between urban erotic poetry in the Hijaz and chaste Bedouin love poetry in the desert. He also notes the exaggeration found in the *'udhri* stories and ridicules the extreme behaviour of the lovers.[88] Clearly Husayn judges the phenomenon divorced from its legendary dimension and overlooks the aesthetics of its literary side. Making the same distinction between erotic and chaste *ghazals* in the Hijaz during the Umayyad period, Ihsan al-Nass, in his study *al-Ghazal fi 'asr bani Umayyah* [The *Ghazal* in the Era of the Umayyad Dynasty], published in 1976, suggests that the difference between the closed society of the Bedouin and the open society of the cities resulted in two types of *ghazal*: *'udhri* and sensual. Therefore, the *'udhri* poet's chastity is not the result of his inability to fulfill his heart's desire but a genuine chastity firmly rooted in the strict Bedouin code of behaviour.[89] However, one should bear in mind that al-Jahiz has another view of the issue, for he points out that men and women in Arabia would see and talk to one another freely.[90]

In terms of the themes of physicality and sexuality (or its absence) in the *'udhri ghazal* there are two main studies that have had a decisive impact on the others. These are Musa Sulayman's *al-Hubb al-'udhri* ['Udhri Love], first published in 1947, and Ahmad al-Jawari's *al-Hubb al-'udhri nash'atuhu wa tatawwurhu* ['Udhri Love: Its Origin and Progression], first published in 1948. First, it should be observed that both studies are entitled *al-Hubb al-'udhri*, not *al-Ghazal al-'udhri* or *al-Shi'r al-'udhri*. Does this mean, therefore, that the early studies regarded *'udhri* love as a separate phenomenon? For they give less attention to *'udhri* poetry and more to the essence of love itself. It is clear that this concern led both scholars to define 'love' in general and *'udhri* love in particular. However, Sulayman and al-Jawari differ over the matter that is paramount in this study: the physical presence in *'udhri* love. Al-Jawari defines *'udhri* love as an elevated aspect of love, which rises above sensual desire and physical lust.[91] Sulayman, on the other hand, casts doubt on the 'purified' nature of *'udhri* love. It is interesting to note that both of these early studies – concerning the presence or absence of the physical element in *'udhri* love – have had a strong influence on later studies. Many scholars on both sides of the argument have copied their ideas, even quoting their exact words.[92] However, it is difficult to give wholehearted support to al-Jawari's argument in favour of the sublimation of *'udhri* love,[93] since the ideas that he presents on the subject are extremely confused.

Sulayman's allusions to physicality in *'udhri* love can be considered as very early hints of a detailed discussion of this topic in the corpus of the *'udhri ghazal*. According to Sulayman, '*'udhri* poets were not angels . . . The sorrow resulting from the lack of sexual relations with their beloveds and their sensual beauty is not entirely absent from *'udhri* poetry.'[94] In his view, what we should understand about *'udhri* poets is their struggle for love and their making every effort for its sake rather than their rising above or disapproval of physical desires. He argues that there are many verses describing the beloved's body and the poet's lust for it. Although Sulayman's contribution is useful as an early source raising the question of the body in *'udhri* love, he gives readers only a few hints without providing any serious analysis of this issue, especially concerning *'udhri* poetry. Does literary creativity spring from desire? Sadiq Jalal al-'Azm's book *Fi al-hubb wa al-hubb al-'udhri* (1968) contains an important discussion of this idea. He puts forward many genuine and daring perspectives, maintaining that *'udhri* love is in fact a sensual love of which physical attraction is a part.[95] However, he argues, no physical contact actually takes place because the lover chooses to keep both his love and poetic inspiration alive by creating more obstacles between him and the object of his desire. Yet al-'Azm's discussion is limited to the prose material and, remarkably enough, does not address the poetry accompanying these prose fragments. He is not concerned with the interpretation of *'udhri* verses, which could be considered as essential for understanding the *'udhri* tradition. Moreover, his view of the *'udhri* poets as being masochistic is open to criticism.

On the other hand, both Mustafa al-Shak'ah in *Rihlat alshi'r min al-umawiyyah ila al 'Abbasiyyah* [Poetry from the Umayyad Era to the Abbasid Era] and 'Afif Hatum in *al-Ghazal fi al-'asr al-umawi* [The *Ghazal* in the Umayyad Period] proclaim that Jamil celebrates the chaste love which spread across the Bedouin desert after promiscuity was forbidden by Islam. They argue that no one can question the chastity and virtue of Jamil, Majnun and the other *'udhri* poets.⁹⁶ Hatum tends to generalise and make judgemental comments though, rather than presenting a critical analysis.⁹⁷ However, when Hatum addresses the question of 'physical innuendo in Jamil's poetry' he explains that this type of verse is merely an effort to imitate other famous poets like 'Umar b. Abi Rabi'ah. Therefore, he emphasises that we should not doubt Jamil's chastity and pure saintly love for Buthaynah merely from a reading of these incidental verses.⁹⁸ Yusuf Bakkar, likewise, observes that although *'udhri* poetry includes many physical innuendoes he stresses that we should not question the *'udhri ghazal* and the implied chastity of its poets.⁹⁹ Close analysis, however, indicates that Jamil and the other *'udhri* poets indicate more than these scholars wish to see.

The subject of *'iffah* (chastity) is also approached by al-Tahir Labib Jadidi in his study *Susyulujiya al-ghazal al-'Arabi: al-shi'r al-'udhri namudhajan*.¹⁰⁰ He presents a new view of *'udhri* poetry by relying on structuralist theories in discussing topics such as the relationship between the Arabic language and sexual life, Islamic monotheism and the adoration of a single beloved in *'udhri* poetry. The scholars discussed above have emphasised the social and political factors in the *'udhri* phenomenon, whereas Labib brings to light economic factors as well, drawing on Marxist theory. He attempts to engage with the question of the chastity of these poets: is it an aspect of poetic imagination or does it reflect reality? In Labib's opinion, the attitude of the *'udhri* poets towards sexual life differs sharply from that of Islamic tradition. Nevertheless, in my view, the signs of physical presence in *'udhri* poetry and anecdotes should not be ignored. Idealising the beloved does not mean that desire is absent. On the contrary, it is always there, depicted by the *'udhri* poets in several ways. Is it worth distinguishing between the presence of the desire and the impossibility of satisfying it? Moreover, as Labib himself notes, there are many erotic descriptions of the beloved's body within *'udhri* poetry. The subject of *'udhri* love is also briefly addressed by J. C. Bürgel in his article 'Love, Lust, and Longing:

Eroticism in Early Islam as Reflected in Literary Sources'. He classifies *'udhri* love as one of the major types of erotic love. Although he sees Jamil as active and cunning in terms of sensuality, he then says that he intends not to question the value of *'udhri* love.¹⁰¹

Are *'udhri* love stories ultimately about literary creativity? Al-'Aqqad [102] studies Jamil from the psychological angle by examining the narratives about the poet and trying to examine the balance between his love and his literary creativity. He concludes that Jamil and the other *'udhri* poets are the natural products of their era. That era itself is analysed in several chapters. Al-'Aqqad tackles the inconsistency between the *'udhri* ideal of immortality and chastity on the one hand and the *'udhri* verses mentioning physical contact on the other. Here, the author sees a link between what people wish to be and what they are in reality as human beings. Likewise, in *Love, Madness and Poetry: An Interpretation of the Majnun Legend*, As'ad E. Khairallah suggests that Majnun is torn between writing poetry and keeping his love secret, and therefore, by breaking the covenant of secrecy, Majnun has lost his blessed union with Layla. Khairallah emphasises the three dimensions of Majnun's character: love, madness and poetry. He is concerned with the link between the legend of Majnun and its mystical dimension, highlighting the significance of insanity as both a stigma and, in contrast, a sign of rebellion. This purity of vision and the courage to express it make the madman almost a poetic ideal. Khairallah discusses this significant question: are love and madness prerequisites for poetry? He concludes that Majnun seeks to satisfy his passion in a dream world – through poetry and insanity. Nevertheless, the author offers no explanation of the distinction between the omnipresence of Layla in nature and in the mind of Majnun and her physical presence in his poetry. He just mentions in passing that his insanity is another necessary means of communication with his beloved. Hence, the erotic dimension is absent from Khairallah's study and one might question his mystical interpretations of the manifestations of insanity. However, what is particularly interesting in his analysis of Majnun's insanity is his hint of the physical condition of Majnun, which becomes his distinguishing mark as the incarnation of the lovesick poet, in contrast with other heroes from this type of romance. A similar idea is expounded well in Michael Dols' book *Majnun: The Madman in the Medieval Islamic World*, which is a thorough examination of the subject of insanity in medieval Islamic society.[103] This study is useful particularly for its interest in the physical description of Majnun's madness and the causes of love.

André Miquel's comparison of Majnun and Tristan is concerned with the themes of society's norms, the tragic ends of the lovers and eternal love.[104]

The comparison between tragedy in Arabic love stories and Western literature is also the main concern of Manzalaouni's articles entitled: 'Tragic Ends of Lovers: Medieval Islam and the Latin West' and 'Swooning Lovers: a Theme in Arab and European Romance'. In spite of his important comments on the role of tragedy in love stories, the role of sexuality within the tragedy in these stories is not discussed.

Ruqayya Yasmine Khan's *Sexuality and Secrecy in the Medieval Arabic Romance of Majnun Layla*[105] is another valuable contribution to the subject of Majnun's romance. Khan argues that Majnun's romance is scarcely chaste and that it is about the competing models of courtship and marriage. She also maintains that a crucial component of the romance is the semiotics of secrecy. So it is the inability of desire to remain hidden, and its proclivity to express itself in and through language, that cause the tragedy. Thus there is a conflict between individual expression and social mandates. Khan also addresses the question of Islamic influence on this romance, yet, unlike other scholars, she emphasises the social conflict between the old Bedouin order and the new Islamic order. She sees Majnun as an anti-type of the Prophet and the Bedouin Wild Man as the embodiment of the Bedouin social order that opposes the Islamic one. In her analysis of 'secrecy' in this romance Khan concentrates on the fact that the revelation of desire is followed by the concealment of the desired object. Furthermore, by mentioning that the beloved is the subject of gossip the poet belies the image of the chaste maiden. The language itself engenders his desire. However, one should question Khan's view of Layla in particular. Is Layla really victimised by both her love and society and, moreover, does Majnun really make her a public disgrace? Despite the extensive range of this study, it focuses only on Majnun, whereas I intend to study the entire *'udhri* tradition, concentrating especially on its elements of physical presence.

Bouhdiba's work *Sexuality in Islam*[106] offers a significant contribution to the subject of sexuality in medieval Islamic communities.[107] Bouhdiba asserts that in the practice of love the Qur'an prescribes a balanced approach, but argues that this has not been translated into social practice. What was unified in revelation fell apart at the historical level. Themes such as sexual practice and prohibitions in Islam, the frontier of the sexes, the sexual and the sacral are discussed in detail in his study. Bouhdiba also addresses the subject of variations on eroticism: misogyny, mysticism and *mujun* (unrestricted pleasure), maintaining that they are three ways of dealing with a single problem. Misogyny encloses Muslims in their own empire, *mujun* releases their inhibitions, and mysticism sublimates them.[108] The sensuality of Paradise is also discussed in his chapter 'The Infinite Orgasm', where Bouhdiba argues that the sensual nature of Paradisiacal pleasures in the Qur'an indicates the wholesomeness of physical desire. The author quotes from Islamic texts that describe infinite pleasure with *houris*.[109]

Joseph Massad, in his study *Desiring Arabs*, traces the history of the unfolding of the concepts of culture and civilisation in the contemporary Arab world. It is an intellectual history of the representation of sexual desire in and about the Arab world. He argues that it was within the context of 'ethnopornography' that Arab readers began to read Orientalist accounts that emphasised Arab sexual life, often in a moralising manner. Influenced by this reading, they were overcome by a sense of crisis.[110] The *'udhri ghazal* is one of the elements that have been subjected to this kind of reconsideration by scholars in the Arab world – under the influence of colonial discourses on sexuality, Massad would argue. My study will partially make use of certain Western theories about the body and sexuality. For example, Freud's oft-cited article 'Creative Writers and Day Dreaming'[111] is particularly useful in understanding the relation between the wishes of the poets and their poetry. Georges Bataille, in *Erotism: Death and Sensuality*, demonstrates that eroticism assents to life to the point of death. He asks: 'what does physical eroticism signify if not a violation of the very being of its practitioners – a violation bordering on death, bordering on murder?'.[112] Bataille argues that only the beloved in this world can bring immortality to two mortal creatures. Hence, love spells suffering insofar as it is a quest for the impossible. We suffer from isolation in our individual separateness. He also demonstrates that the possession of the beloved object does not imply death, but rather that the idea of death is linked to the urge to possess.[113] This work highlights the connection between individuality, sensuality and death, themes of some importance to my study.

A significant effort has already been made to analyse and understand the concept of love in the classical Arabic sources. In his study *al-hubb fi al-turath al-'Arabi*, Muhammad Hasan 'Abdallah criticises the widely held view of separating Arab love into the *'udhri* and sensual categories. He believes that the phenomenon of love is more complex, being related to rituals, feelings, ideas and sectarian distinctions, all of which are expressed in poetry. He analyses many of the concepts that deal with love.[114] Raja' Salamah is concerned with the complex relationship between passionate love (*'ishq*) and its expression through the written word. In her voluminous and informative book *al-'Ishq wa'l-kitabah: qira'h fi al-mawruth*, the author makes a special effort to analyse the words for love in Arabic, of which there are, interestingly, more than a hundred, although some scholars do not consider them synonymous. Salamah draws a parallel between the image of the afflicted camel (*al-ba'ir al-sadim*) and the fate of the lover (*al-'ashiq*). She argues that longing is a form of energy, though a problematic one, as it cannot be easily satisfied. In that respect, it resembles fire. Indeed, many of the Arabic words used for love and longing are derived from the root word for 'fire'.[115] Khan's study is not confined to the *'udhri* tradition, providing as it does a significant contribution to the understanding of love in Arab culture and in the Arabic language. It also contains many references to the body and to death.

In her study *Theory of Profane Love Among the Arabs: The Development of the Genre* Lois Anita Giffen provides summaries of many classical Arabic works on love, thus identifying the reasoning behind the Arab theory of profane love. The information from Arabic lexicographers and philologists alongside the opinions of philosophers and physicians are another element in these works on the theory of love. Giffen also discusses the evolution of form and content in these works, concluding that they reveal certain common features, examining terms such as *'ishq* and *mahabbah* and their use. The concept of the martyrs of love is also analysed here: the author traces its development alongside the concept of martyrdom in Islam.[116]

The Structure and Trajectory of the Present Study

The *Kitab al-aghani* will be my main source for the stories told about *'udhri* poets such as Majnun, Jamil and Qays.[117] I will also refer to other classical sources such as *Al-shi'r wa al-shu'ara'* by Ibn Qutaybah. For the poetry, I will refer to the various poetic anthologies (*diwans*). The main sources of my study are the *diwans* of 'Urwah b. Hizam, Majnun Layla, Qays Lubna, Jamil Buthaynah and Kuthayyir 'Azzah. All of these works and their commentaries have been published during the last century. For the Qur'anic verses, Yusuf Ali's translation is used. Moreover, to achieve the objectives of this book, it has been necessary to consult the most relevant classical Arabic literature on love, particularly for the focus on the depiction of the lover's body and how it is affected by love.[118] The *Kitab al-zahrah (The Book of the Flower)* by Ibn Da'ud (d. 297/909), and *Tawq al-hamamah (The Ring of the Dove)* by Ibn Hazm (d. 456/1063) are two of the most important sources for my study and are closely related to each other. The *Kitab al-zahrah* is an anthology of Arabic love poetry, but is not just a collection of poetry as it also discusses the theory of love, being the first extant Arabic work on the topic. Some of the key topics in *al-zahrah* are: union with the loved one – being together (*wasl*), separation from the loved one – being apart *(bayn, nawa)*. The main reason for writing the poem in the first place is usually the pain of separation. There are other references to 'spurning or abandonment of the lover' (*hajr, jafa'*) and 'secret'/concealment (*kitman*).[119] In *Tawq al-hamamah*,[120] which is widely regarded as a masterpiece, the author proceeds in a rational manner to describe the essence and nature of love, its possible causes and symptoms as well as the frustration and perils surrounding it. This book is a prose work in which the passages of poetry, some composed by the author himself, are subservient to the prose text. Ibn Hazm portrays the tragedies of love, including examples from his own life, while keeping within the Arabic tradition of literature on love.[121]

Outline of the Present Study

The following will pursue a textual analysis of the classical sources using classical literary texts of '*udhri* narratives and poetry. The book consists of seven chapters, including this introduction. Chapter Two focuses on the ways in which stories and narratives about the poets and events throughout the ninth and tenth centuries gave rise to certain compositions that in effect established a tradition and reconstructed a past. The chapter will raise issues such as *al-ghazal al-sarih* vs. *al-ghazal al-'udhri*, and moral and ethical issues and their effect in reconstructing the past, with special consideration of the *Kitab al-Aghani*. In Chapter Three I discuss the concepts of sexuality, marriage and chastity in Islamic discourse; this touches on Islamic jurisprudence as well as Islamic culture in general. The implications of chastity as understood in the stories about *'udhri* poets and theories of love will also be discussed, taking into consideration the context of the ninth and tenth centuries. The problematic relationship that exists between the *'udhri* tradition and Islamic discourse around sexuality and love will be the main focus of this chapter.

In Chapter Four the theme of how the beloved's body is represented is set within the generic convention of classical Arabic poetry. Attention is drawn to the image of a corpulent woman and the depiction of a woman as a gazelle. Moreover, the chapter examines the ethereal aspect of female beauty in the *'udhri ghazal*. The presence and absence of the beloved's physical form is the primary subject of discussion in Chapter Five. I will argue that the bodily presence in the *'udhri ghazal* does not always take the form of a physical body – sometimes it appears through symbolic channels, where the symbolising of the body appears alongside its physical depiction. The themes of gestures, speech, phantoms, the beloved's house and her presence through nature will be examined in this chapter. This discussion leads to the central question of the subsequent chapter: does the beloved's absence enhance the poetry about her? Therefore, Chapter Six examines the friction between poetry and possession. By tracing the tropes of unfulfilled love and the idealised woman, the chapter offers an argument about the discourse of cultural value developed around poetry, the reception of the poet as a hero and the representation of poetry as the ultimate goal. In Chapter Seven I provide a discussion of the depiction of the lover's body in the *'udhri* tradition by analysing the vocabulary of sickness, healing, the physician and the use of magic, all of which affect the body. The discussion will embrace frequently repeated motifs and terms in the *'udhri ghazal*. The themes of madness and death will also be explored in this, the final chapter.

I have selected verses of poetry on the criteria of both internal evidence in the poetry itself and external evidence from the *akhbar* (historical anecdotes) that accompany the poems in the classical *'udhri* corpus. The goal here is not to offer a comprehensive account of the ways in which the *'udhri ghazal* refers to the body, but rather to examine in some detail a selection of texts in which the body is manifestly represented. It should be clear that the concern here is not the real historical figure of Layla or Lubna, but their literary representation. By analysing specific texts throughout all of the chapters and discussing the issues raised, I hope that the study will offer an original contribution to the subject.

Notes

1. http://muslimwakeup.com/sex, 5 April 2006.
2. These studies will be discussed in detail later in this chapter.
3. Except for one study which deals with secrecy and sexuality in the romance of Majnun Layla, a poet in the *'udhri* school. The author of this study is Ruqayya Khan and we shall discuss her work later in the introduction.
4. *Ghazal*: song, elegy of love, often also the erotic-elegiac genre. The term is Arabic, but passed into Persian, Turkish and Urdu and acquired a special sense in these languages. See Bausani, '*Ghazal*', p. 1,028.
5. 'A nomadic Arabian tribe of the Quda'a federation. Its pedigree is: 'Udhra b. Sa'd Hudhaym b. Zayd b. Layth. The 'Udhra were the central group among the descendants of Sa'd Hudhaym, and they incorporated several brother-clans such as the Harith b. Sa'd Hudhaym and Salman b. Sa'd Hudhaym. These 'Udhra are not to be confused with the 'Udhra of Kalb b. Wabara, i.e. 'Udhra b. Zayd Allat b. Rufayda b. Thawr b. Kalb. One of the latter 'Udhra was the genealogist Ibn al-Kalbi, who described the 'Udhra b. Zayd Allat at length. The 'Udhra lived in the area of Ashraf/Masharif al-Sham, which in this context refers to the northern Hijaz. They were particularly linked with Wadi Al-Qura.' See Lecker, *People, Tribes, and Society in Arabia around the Time of Muhammad*, p. 91.
6. See the references on the subject in al-Antaki, *Tazyin al-aswaq fi akhbar al-'ushshaq*, p. 19, and al-Sarraj: *Masari' al-'ushshaq*, vol. 1, p. 37.
7. Stetkevych, *The Zephyrs of Najd: the Poetics of Nostalgia in the Classical Arabic Nasib*, p. 115.
8. Dhu al-Rummah is perceived as an *'udhri* poet by Yusuf al-Yusuf: see *al-Ghazal al-'udhri dirasah fi al-hubb al-maqmu'*.
9. Zaki Mubarak studies him with Jamil and Kuthayyir: see *al-'Ushshaq al-thalathah*. Shawqi Dayf, likewise, perceives him as an *'udhri* poet: see *al-Hubb al-'udhri 'ind al-'Arab*.
10. This pretence can be traced back to a key source, namely the *Aghani*, where Abu al-Faraj al-Isfahani (d. 356/967) quotes anecdotes that show that Kuthayyir was not an honest lover like the other *'udhri* lovers but that he tried to imitate them. However, in my view, Kuthayyir's love story and his poetry would indicate that he is a true *'udhri* poet.

11. This name is a pseudonym to conceal her true identity and protect her reputation.
12. Among these themes are the suffering lover, the longing for an aloof beloved and the death wish.
13. Jayyusi, 'Umayyad poetry', in Beeston, *Arabic Literature to the End of the Umayyad period*, p. 424.
14. For more details see al-Batal, *al-Ghazal al-'udhri wa idtirab al-waqi'*, p. 182.
15. It is in no way intended that these literary works should be reduced to simple formulae; however, I have tried to highlight some of their key unifying components.
16. Al-Batal, *al-Ghazal al-'udhri*, p. 181.
17. Kinany, *The Development of Ghazal in Arabic Literature (Pre-Islamic and Early Islamic Periods)*, p. 258.
18. Jayyusi, 'Umayyad poetry', in Beeston, *Arabic Literature to the End of the Umayyad period*, p. 426.
19. For example, in Sura al-Waqi'ah, the verses describing the situation in heaven read: 'And on couches or thrones, raised high. Verily, We have created them (maidens) of special creation. And made them virgins. Loving (their husbands only), (and) of equal age. For those on the Right Hand'. Al-Waqi'ah (56: 34–38).
20. Jacobi, '*Udhri*', p. 775.
21. Kinany, *The Development of Ghazal in Arabic Literature (Pre-Islamic and Early Islamic Periods)*, p. 266.
22. Majnun Layla, *Diwan Majnun Layla*, p. 134, trans. Khan, *Sexuality and Secrecy in the Medieval Arabic Romance of Majnn Layla*, p. 188.
23. As we shall examine in the last chapter of this study.
24. Johann Christoph Bürgel, 'Love, Lust, and Longing: Eroticism in Early Islam as Reflected in Literary Sources', in al-Sayyid-Marsot, *Society and the Sexes in Medieval Islam*, p. 92.
25. See Miquel's discussion of similar ideas in Miquel, *Majnun Layla wa Tristan*, pp. 81–9.
26. Jacobi, *Die Udhra: Liebe und Tod in der Umayyadenzeit*.
27. This figure is essential to the genre. He or she is the one who blames the lover for his ardent love.
28. See, for example, Majnun, *Diwan*, pp. 179, 184, 190.
29. Hamori, *On the Art of Medieval Arabic Literature*, p. 40.
30. Majnun says: 'they said that I could forget her if I wanted to; I answered them that I did not really want to'. Kinany, *Development*, p. 276.

31. Note, for instance, Jamil's verses:

> I am pleased with very little things accorded to me by Buthaynah
> They are so insignificant
> that if they were known by the man (who spies us)
> he would not be annoyed with my love
> I am pleased even when she says: 'no' or 'I cannot' And when she makes me live on promises
> promises hoped for, but always disappointing
> I am pleased with a quick glance at her,
> and even with spending a whole year without our meeting – neither at the beginning nor at the end

Jamil b. Ma'mar, *Diwan Jamil Buthaynah: Jamil b. Ma'mar* in 'Atawi p. 83, Kinany, *Development*, p. 180 and Kuthayyir 'Azzah, *Diwan Kuthayyir 'Azzah*, Tarad, p. 55.

32. Majnun, for instance, says: 'I cured my suffering from missing Layla by remembering her, just as a drunkard who has no other cure for his pain, but drink.' Kinany, *Development*, p. 281.
33. Kinany, *Development*, p. 253.
34. Ibid., p. 278.
35. Ibid., p. 257 and Jayyusi, *Umayyad Poetry*, p. 425.
36. Kinany, *Development*, p. 289.
37. Dols observes that 'Curiously the *rawis* seem to have done far more in this instance than simply develop a romance'; Dols, *Majnun: the Madman in Medieval Islamic Society*, p. 322. Also, Khairallah notes that 'Ibn Qutaybah presents us with the basic elements of [Majnun's] legend. These elements were later expanded and retold in different variations, but the figure of Majnun was unmistakably drawn by Ibn Qutaybah': Khairallah, *Love, Madness, and Poetry: An Interpretation of the Magnun Legend*, p. 50.
38. This work by al-Isfahani will be the main source of the narratives about *'udhri* poets discussed in this study. Its authenticity will be discussed later in this chapter. The structure of *al-Aghani* will be discussed in the second chapter.
39. Khairallah, *Love*, p. 51.
40. al-Nuwayri, *Nihayat al-arab fi funun al-adab*, vol. 2, p. 184.
41. As observed in classic sources such as al-Isfahani, *Kitab al-Aghani*.
42. Husayn, *Hadith al-arbi'a*, p. 109. However, see al-Hufi's arguments that attempt to controvert Husayn's views, pp. 153–8.

43. Jadidi, *Susyulujya al-ghazal al-'arabi: al-shi'r al-'udhri namudhajan*, pp. 132–7.
44. Kinany, *Development*, p. 262
45. Ibid.
46. Faysal, *Tatawwur al-ghazal bayna al-Jahiliyah wa al-Islam*, p. 235.
47. Ibid., p. 287.
48. Dayf, *al-Hubb al-'udhri*, p. 20.
49. See examples of a similar attitude in al-Nass, *al-Ghazal fi 'asr bani Umayyah*, p. 23 and Sadiq, *al-Ghazal al-'udhri*, p. 10.
50. Al-Tawbah (9: 97).
51. For a detailed discussion on this matter see al-Qitt, *Fi al-shi'r al-Islami wa al-Umawi*, p. 79.
52. Hamori, 'Love Poetry (*Ghazal*)', in Ashtiany, Johnstone, Latham, Serjeant & Smith, *Abbasid Belles-Lettres*, p. 206.
53. Al-Qitt, for instance, argues that religious chastity cannot stand as the only factor to explain the emergence of the *'udhri* phenomenon. He takes into consideration social and political factors: Al-Qitt, *Fi al-shi'r al-Islami*, pp. 109, 130. For similar ideas see also Khulayf, *al-Hubb al-mithali 'ind al-'Arab*, p. 7.
54. Al-Yusuf, *al-Ghazal al-'udhri dirasah fi al-hubb al-maqmu'*, p. 66.
55. Al-Batal, *al-Ghazal al-'udhri*, p. 181.
56. Jamil, *Diwan*, p. 73, Kinany, *Development*, p. 289.
57. Jayyusi, *Umayyad Poetry*, p. 419.
58. Ibid., p. 420.
59. Ibid.
60. Dols, *Majnun*, pp. 321–2.
61. Jayyusi, *Umayyad Poetry*, p. 421.
62. Jacobi, '*Udhri*', p. 775.
63. In an interview, the poet declares: 'When I wrote Majnun's anecdotes I wrote my own anecdotes. The old story does not matter to me as the legend is much more beautiful than the history. Majnun is me, is "us" now. I read Majnun within my contemporary views.' http://www.alwaqt.com/art.phpaid=108245, 11 July 2008.
64. Dols, *Majnun*, p. 331.
65. See Khairallah's discussion of Jami's work in love, *Love*, pp. 97–133.
66. Dols, *Majnun*, p. 324.
67. Ibid.
68. Jacobi, '*Udhri*', p. 775.
69. Al-Isfahani, *al-Aghani*, vol. 2, p. 330.

70. Ibid., p. 333.
71. Ibid.
72. Husayn, *Hadith al-arbiʿa*, p.190.
73. Al-Batal, *al-Ghazal al-ʿudhri*, p. 2.
74. Hilal, *al-Hayah al-ʿatifiyyah bayna al-ʿudhriyyah wa al-sufiyyah: dirasat naqd wa muqaranah hawla mawduʿ Layla wa al-Majnun fi al-adabayn al-ʿarabi wa al-farisi*, p. 49.
75. Al-Qitt, *Fi al-shiʿr al-Islami*, p.109.
76. Al-Jawari, *al-Hubb al-ʿudhri nashatuhu wa tatawwuruhu*, p. 76.
77. Hamori, '*Love Poetry (Ghazal)*', p. 205.
78. Khairallah, *Love*, p. 93.
79. S. P. Stetkevych, *The Mute Immortals Speak: Pre-Islamic Poetry and Poetics of Ritual*, p. 93.
80. Ibn Qutaybah, *al-Shiʿr wa al-shuʿara*, p. 436.
81. Hatum, *al-Ghazal fi al-ʿasr a-lUmawi*, p. 163.
82. Husayn, *Hadith al-arbiʿa*, p. 201.
83. Examples of these studies that tend to follow a repetitive pattern in handling the ʿudhri ghazal are: al-Mukhtar, *Jamil Buthaynah wa al-hubb al-ʿudhri*; Sadiq, *al-Ghazal al-ʿudhri*; Qulaymah, *Jamil Buthaynah raid al-ghazal al-ʿafif*; Najm, *Jamil Buthaynah wa al-hubb al-ʿudhri*; Sabrah, *al-Ghazal al-ʿudhri fi al-asr al-Umawi*; Al-Shibi, *al-Ghazal al-ʿudhri wa makanatuhu al-fikriyyah wa al-diniyyah fi al-ʿasr al-Umawi*; Dayf, *al-Hubb al-ʿudhri*; Al-Ramadi, *Jamil b. Maʿmar shaʿir al-hubb wa ʿashiq Buthaynah*; ʿAyyad, *Jamil Buthaynah imam al-muhbin wa al-Majanin: qiraah mughayirah*. The structure of these works comprises the following: a general introduction to ʿudhri love; stories about ʿudhri poets with special reference to their descent and character; and inclusion of extracts from their poetry, usually without any commentary. In the introductions of these books, the authors discuss love in general: its roots in Arabic literature or, sometimes, world literature, and its characteristics. This is a very generalised and repetitive approach.
84. Jacobi, '*Udhri* poetry', *Encyclopedia of Arabic Literature*, vol. 2, p. 790.
85. Gibb, *Arabic Literature: An Introduction*, p. 45.
86. See, for example, Jacobi, 'Time and Reality in Nasib and *Ghazal*', *Journal of Arabic Literature*, vol. 16, p. 1.
87. Hamori, *Love*, p. 205.
88. Husayn, *Hadith al-arbiʿa*, p. 190.
89. Al-Nass, *al-Ghazal fi ʿasr bani umayyah*, p. 23.

90. For further details, see al-Jahiz, *Kitab al-qiyan (Rasa'il al-Jahiz)*, vol. 2, p. 149.
91. Al-Jawari, *al-Hubb al-'udhri*, p. 51.
92. It is interesting to see that in his article about *'udhri* love, al-Ladhiqi quotes the exact words of Sulayman and al-'Azam without any acknowledgement of their source: al-Ladhiqi, *al-Sharq al-awsat*, 19 September 2003.
93. Al-Jawari's argument appears in several places in his book; see, for instance, pp.13, 64 and 74.
94. Sulayman, *al-Hubb al-'udhri*, p.101.
95. Al-'Azm, *Fi al-hubb wa al-hubb al-'udhri*, p. 81.
96. Al-Shak'ah, *Rihlat al-shi'r min al-Umawiyyah ila al-'Abbasiyyah* and Hatum, *al-Ghazal fi al-'asr al-Umawi*.
97. For instance, he describes Jamil as the leader of romantic poets, not just in his era, but in every era until modern times. He describes Jamil's verse:

> Conversation in their company
> Brings joy,
> But each man who dies in their midst
> Is a martyr

as the most romantic stanza by an Arab poet. Hatum, p. 165.
98. Ibid., pp. 161, 166 and 196.
99. Bakkar, *Ittijāhāt al-ghazāl fi al-qarn al-thani al-hijri*, p. 55.
100. Jadidi, *Susyulujiya al-ghazal al-'Arabi: al-shi'r al-'udhri namudhajan*.
101. Bürgel, 'Love', p. 94.
102. Al-'Aqqad, *Jamil Buthaynah*.
103. Dols considers the early Arabic version of Majnun's romance as well as Nizami's version.
104. Miquel, *Majnun Layla wa Tristan*.
105. Khan, *Sexuality and Secrecy in the Medieval Arabic Romance of Majnun Layla*.
106. Bouhdiba, *Sexuality in Islam*.
107. It was first published in French in 1975, and then translated by Alan Sheridan and published in English in London in 1985. The Arabic translation by Hala al-Ouri appeared first in Cairo in1986 and then in Beirut in 2001.
108. Bouhdiba, *Sexuality*, p. 117.
109. The subject of sensuality in Paradise has been addressed frequently by scholars. Many of them rely heavily on Bouhdiba's analysis. For example, in his essay 'Sexuality, Diversity and Ethics in the Agenda of Progressive Muslims' Scott A. Kugle explains the depiction of Paradise in the Qur'an: '[It] is not just

bodily, but sensually delightful and even sexually blissful'. Kugle, *Sexuality, Diversity and Ethics in the Agenda of Progressive Muslim,* http://www.geocities.com/vidyak1/scottkugledoc.pdf, 5 June 2005.
110. Massad, *Desiring Arabs*, p. 30.
111. Freud, 'Creative Writers and Day Dreaming', in Lodge, *Twentieth Century Literary Criticism*.
112. Bataille, *Erotism: Death and Sensuality*, p. 17.
113. Ibid., p. 20.
114. 'Abdallah, *al-Hubb fi al-turath al-'Arabi*.
115. Salamah stresses this point several times in her study, pp. 53, 80.
116. Lois Anita Giffen, *Theory of Profane Love Among the Arabs: The Development of the Genre*, pp. 99–115.
117. A discussion about the structure of the *Kitab al-Aghani* will be provided in the second chapter.
118. Some of these titles are: the *Kitab al-zahrah* by Abu Bakr Muhammad b. Daud al-Isfahani (d. 297/910), the *Kitab al-muwashsha* by al-Washsha (d. 325/936), *Tawq al-hamamah fi al-ulfah wa al-ullaf* by Ibn Hazm al-Andalusi (d. 456/1064), *Masari' al-'ushshaq* by Abu Ja'far al-Sarraj (d. 500/1106), *Dhamm al-hawa* by Ibn al-Jawzi (d. 597/1200), *Rawdat al-muhibbin wa nuzhat al-mushtaqin* by Ibn Qayyim al-Jawzyyiah (d. 751/135) and *Tazyin al-aswaq bi tafsil ashwaq al-'ushshaq* by Daud al-Antaki (d. 1008/1599).
119. Devin Stewart, *Emory Resources on the Middle East*. www.mesas.emory.edu/gmesc/pdf/10_Love_Theory_Unit_All.pdf, 18 July 2008, pp. 4–5.
120. *Tawq al-hamamah* has been translated into many languages; the English version appeared in 1953, translated by Arberry. It is one of the few Arabic works which, when translated, is attractive to the Western reader.
121. Giffen, *Theory of Profane Love,* pp. 24–5.

2

Reconstructing the Past

Al-ghazal: the Love Poem

During the Umayyad period, for the first time in the history of Arabic literature, the love poem, known as the '*ghazal*', appeared. The *ghazal* is a monothematic poem that is devoted entirely to the erotic theme. Before that time amatory preludes, known as *nasib*, had formed only the opening section of a long poem that praised a patron or tribe or perhaps the poet himself, as well as containing a description of the poet's journey and of his camel or horse and so on. It is still open to discussion 'whether the *ghazal* originated exclusively from the *nasib* or whether other poetic models should be taken into account'.[1] In the first chapter we discussed differing opinions on the main factors behind the development of the Umayyad *ghazal* and the new concept of love arising from it.[2] Jacobi notes that 'the poets of the seventh century introduced new themes and concepts, but they also made use of conventions, sometimes subtly changing their meaning or employing them in unusual combinations'.[3] In any case, when considering the *ghazal*, we should bear in mind that the art of singing contributed to the spread of this kind of poetry. This art was a natural result of prosperity and the availability of leisure time in the Hijaz.[4]

Comparing pre-Islamic love poetry and the Umayyad *ghazal*, Jacobi states:

> When comparing love poetry of the jahiliyya to amatory verses of the first Islamic century, I came to the conclusion that at least some elements of the latter could be derived from a common source, a change in aesthetic consciousness based on two interrelated factors: 1. a new experience of time, 2. a new attitude towards reality.[5]

Even when the Umayyad love poets employed conventional motifs, such as the *atlal* 'ruins', they invented a new ending to the story or connected it with other themes of the poem.[6]

The Roots of the *'Udhri Ghazal*

A group of pre-Islamic poets who had adopted a similar attitude in love and the *ghazal* to the subsequent *'udhri* attitude were referred to as *mutayyamun* (passionate lovers) in classical Arabic literary sources. Examples of these men and the women they loved are al-Muraqqish al-Akbar and Asma, al-Mukhabbal and Mayla, and 'Abdullah b. al-'Ajlan and Hind. This approach to love can be traced back to the pre-Islamic period. Poetry, the creative social expression of the Arab tribes of the desert at that time, voiced this approach,[7] so this expression of love existed in the desert-based nomad societies of the Arabian peninsula before the emergence of Islam. The existence of the pre-Islamic lover-poets is validated by the *'udhri* poets themselves: Qays b. Dharih quotes 'Amr b. 'Ajlan who was killed by his love for Hind[8] and Jamil also quotes him, together with al-Muraqqish, as martyrs of love.[9] However, the amount of poetry that has reached us from such pre-Islamic lovers is scarce in comparison with the *'udhri* poetry we have from the Umayyad period. Hence, although *'udhri* love – as represented in texts – has some roots in the pre-Islamic era, it did not become the marker of a literary genre in its own right until the Umayyad period. Jacobi notes, that 'whereas the pre-Islamic love poetry only knows the hero and heroine as profoundly bound to the collective needs, the new love code of the Umayyad period shows lovers who are individuals, even with an unconventional language'.[10]

Sensual *Ghazal* vs the *'Udhri Ghazal*

Many scholars, such as Taha Husayn and Ghunaymi Hilal, consider *'udhri* poetry to be the opposite of the sensual love poetry known as *al-ghazal al-sarih*, which not only had a place in early Arabic literature but flourished until recent times.

Therefore, love poetry in classical Arab literature, especially during the Umayyad period, has been seen by scholars generally as divided into two main groups: chaste Bedouin (*'udhri*) and sensual urban (*sarih*) poetry. *'Udhri* poets, such as 'Urwah, Jamil and Majnun, are considered the most illustrious poets of the chaste Bedouin genre, and poets from Medina and Mecca, such as 'Umar b. Abi Rabi'ah and al-'Urji, are considered the best in the profane urban genre.[11] Hilal explains that when the Hijaz lost its political prestige, it suffered from a state of isolation, and its poets started to entertain themselves and lead a dissolute life. The best examples are 'Umar b. Abi Rabi'ah and those living in cities where costly facilities and luxuries were available as a result of the Islamic conquests. However, rural poets took their pure love in other directions because they were neither involved in politics nor yearning for a luxurious life. According to Hilal, this dissimilarity can be attributed to the fact that they lived in areas remote from cities and were steeped in Arab traditions and were, therefore, able to preserve Islamic ethics.[12] Yet, as we noted in the first chapter, Hilal's assumption has been challenged[13] and one can argue that some city dwellers were just as surely 'steeped' in Arab traditions.

In any case, according to 'Umar's *ghazal*, the experience of love had become a profane adventure. The lover is presented as the pursuer of women as part of his amorous adventures during the *Hajj* season.[14] 'Umar's description of the beauty of women in his *ghazals* focuses on the sensual side and one single poem might include the names of several women. 'Umar b. Abi Rabi'ah is also famous for the type of *ghazal* that portrays the poet not only as a lover but also as the one being loved and chased by women.[15] His poetry is constructed around dramatic dialogue. His language is simple, tuned with a rhythm adaptable to songs. In addition, 'Umar b. Abi Rabi'ah celebrates his amorous adventures with self-assured and independent women from respectable families. Some of these adventures, as 'Umar's poems show, were initiated by women themselves. Al-Isfahani reports that:

> Hind, the daughter of al-Harith of the Murrah tribe, invited 'Umar b. Abi Rabi'ah to her house one day so that she and her companions could talk to him, saying: 'Oh, oh, 'Umar, listen to this. If only you could have seen me a few days ago when I was with my family! I put my head under my gown and looked at my nakedness and was very desirable. At this I called out: "'Umar, 'Umar" and 'Umar replied: 'I would have called out: 'At your service, at your service'.[16]

As this anecdote and many others of its type show, the kind of love relation that 'Umar's type of *ghazal* presented is a sensual, adventurous love. The beloved in his poetry is portrayed as strong and beautiful, an independent and pleasure-seeking woman. She is also portrayed as the potential companion of a man.

On the other hand, the vow to remain faithful is a leitmotif of the *'udhri ghazal,* as often evidenced in the *diwan* of Jamil. Many of his verses may be understood as allusions to the poet's overwhelming obsession with his beloved. Indeed, a core theme of the *'udhri* tradition presents the lover as being totally preoccupied with the beloved, devoting himself to her and refraining from making love to any other woman.[17] When Jamil found himself presented with seven girls from respectable families, each of them wishing to marry him, he wrote the following poem about Buthaynah:

> Many is the woman who comes to me
> And offers herself in all earnest mixed with jestful words
> I answer her with kindness after hesitating,
> My love for Buthaynah prevents me accepting you. If I had in my heart a
>   fingernail of extra love to give
> I would accept you or I would send you my letters[18] [1]

Jamil, in these verses, is expressing a love that occupies his heart so fully that there is not 'a fingernail of extra love to give' to any woman apart from Buthaynah. Even if other women promised to fulfill his desire, he still cannot think of anyone but his beloved, despite the implication that she does not 'offer herself'.[19] There is a narrative in *al-Aghani* in which Jamil's father tries to dissuade Jamil from pursuing Buthaynah after her marriage, and in so doing he unequivocally states: 'Women are replaceable'. Jamil counters this with the reply that, for him, Buthaynah is not: 'By God, were I able to efface her memory from my heart and to erase her person from my mind's eye, I would have done so but it is impossible [...] indeed this is a trial and affliction.'[20]

From Jamil's perspective, love transcends mundane life and reaches up to the eternal. It is a symbol of the absolute. Love, to him, is the whole of 'being'. Imru' al-Qays and 'Umar b. Abi Rabi'ah, on the other hand, do not love specific women but love instead any woman who provides enjoyment. As for Jamil's love, it is purely personal. He is not interested in an instrument or means, but rather in a single being who is incomparable to any other. This person cannot be substituted by another. Women, from this perspective, seem to be exemplary symbols of desire. The lover finds his ultimate happiness in dreaming about this matchless character and attaining this desire. Thus, he becomes devoted to one woman regardless of whether she marries him or another.[21]

Labib argues that there is a parallel between the concept of monotheism and the unique beloved in the *'udhri* tradition. Islam refuted polytheism by stressing the need to submit to one God alone. Consequently, the concept of monotheism is mirrored in the uniqueness of the beloved from the beginning of the *'udhri* tradition. In Labib's opinion, the theme of *'udhri* poetry is often centred on a woman for whose sake one wishes to die. Moreover, contemplating her love can have a curative effect. Jamil says: 'remembrance of you cures my numb leg'.[22] Sympathising with the lover and supplication to her make the beloved (the woman) an ideal, while the lover (the man) is a human being.[23]

Moreover, the desire is the object itself for *'udhri* lovers. That desire is their only aim even if it ultimately leads to madness and death. That is why Majnun casts himself as the eternally suffering lover:

> She said: you have lost your mind over me
> I said to her:
> Love is greater than what [afflicts] the madmen
> One entrusted with love, the possessor [sahib] of love, Does not recover
>   from it for eternity,
> Whereas the madman is only felled by it for a time[24] [2]

In these verses, Majnun 'nobly privileges his passion for his beloved above all else'.[25] He states that there is no way for the 'possessor of love' to recover from it. Yet 'true love, in contrast to a crazed infatuation, is romanticised as an affliction from which recovery is not only impossible but undesirable'.[26] The motif of the poet's total preoccupation with the beloved was developed and continuously elaborated upon by Umayyad and later by Abbasid poets. 'Abbas b. al-Ahnaf (d. 188/804), for example, devoted a poem to it, describing the loss of all his perceptive faculties. Not even his tongue obeys him any more, but insists on pronouncing the beloved's name. Thus reality has lost its power at last and the lover's mind is entirely dominated by the imagination.[27]

However, in spite of this distinction between the *'udhri* and the *sarih* or 'sensual' *ghazal*, no trace of such a clear division can be found in early texts dealing with the *ghazal* in the Umayyad period. *Al-shi'r wa al-shu'ara* by Ibn Qutaybah (d. 276/899), for instance, is one of the oldest sources to address the *'udhri* poets and their poetry. Ibn Qutaybah did not categorise these poets as one school nor did he place them in the 'opposing' genre of 'sensual love' urban poets. Instead, he just described each of the *'udhri* poets as 'one of the famous Arab lovers (*'ushshaq*)'.[28] Certain modern scholars have also criticised this division, including Salamah, who notes that *'udhri* poets share 'Umar's view of a woman as the potential friend of a man.[29] Some of the urban poets, moreover, such as al-Harith b. Khalid, were themselves proud of being chaste.[30] In addition, Bürgel notes that some *'udhri* elements exist in the love poetry of non-*'udhri* poets such as 'Umar b. Abi Rabi'ah and even in that of the notorious rake Caliph Walid b. Yazid, who boasted of his ability to emulate the *'udhri* style.[31] Therefore, the link between the Bedouin encampment with its chastity, on the one hand, and urban areas full of sensuality on the other, is derived from the emergence of a superficial nostalgia for an imaginary origin, which in this context is represented by the desert. This moral duality of chastity and the profane has been incorrectly applied by scholars in integrated texts of *ghazals* where neither geographic nor tribal belonging seem to be of importance.[32]

Unfulfilled love was also not limited to the Bedouin in the desert. After the time of these bards and their environment, love was expressed in a new milieu in urban areas by poets who were *fuqaha* (scholars of religious sciences) and religious ascetics. One example is 'Ubaydallah b. 'Abdullah b. 'Utbah, who demonstrated his regret for divorcing his spouse by composing poems about her.[33] His story reminds us of the story of the *'udhri* poet, Qays b. Dharih.[34] Among the ascetic poets in Medina was 'Abd al-Rahman al-Jashmi, known as al-Quss, who became infatuated with the songstress Salamah after listening to her singing.[35] Clearly, the bards and *fuqaha* were already rejoicing at love in the Abbasid era when the first compilations of the words of paramours, including *'udhris* and others concerned with love, first began to appear.

The Key Source: the *Kitab al-Aghani*

After the flowering of the *'udhri ghazal* in the Umayyad period and the diffusion of its spirit to *fuqaha* in Medina and Mecca it cannot be traced again as a genre until the Abbasid age, when *'udhri* love became the exalted ideal of courtly society, although the prevailing moral outlook of the latter context clearly differed with respect to the earlier milieu. It was at this time that moving love stories were documented about tragic lovers and when poetry and *akhbar* (historical anecdotes) from prior periods were documented and compiled. The earliest extant version of the romance is to be found in an anthology of Ibn Qutaybah (d. 276/889), who collected the works of major Arab poets.[36] But the most important source of the *'udhri ghazal* is the *Kitab al-Aghani* by Abu al-Faraj al-Isfahni (d. 356/967), the authenticity of which we discussed in the first chapter.[37] However, we still need to know more about the author and his interests, as well as how the work was composed. We also need to look more closely at its structure, in order to understand al-Isfahani's contribution to the *'udhri ghazal*, which became in his period the subject of renewed interest. Abu al-Faraj 'Ali b. al-Husayn al-Isfahani is an ideal scholar to focus on because of his wide range of knowledge, his aristocratic lineage[38] and the fact that he was also a poet. He was of Arab origin, a member of the Quraysh tribe and a lineal descendant of Marwan, the last Umayyad Caliph. He was born in Isfahan and studied grammar, philology, hadith, Qur'anic sciences and history in Baghdad. He was very knowledgeable in the requisites of the convivial companion, such as the narration of anecdotes, fables, poems and biographies, falconry, farriery, medicine, astrology, music and, last but not least, in the preparation of beverages. Al-Isfahani was a man of the world, who was in great demand in aristocratic circles because of his encyclopaedic knowledge.[39]

Al-Isfahani spent fifty years writing his *Kitab al-Aghani*, thanks to the generous patronage system which gave Abbasid scholars the opportunity to work undisturbed by financial concerns.[40] The *Kitab al-Aghani*'s twenty-four volumes (almost 10,000 pages) includes poems and songs from pre-Islamic times to the tenth century; biographies of poets and musicians; and detailed descriptions of literary and music circles. Documenting a song with the name of the poet and composer, along with the modes of rhythm and melody employed, was not enough for al-Isfahani. He gave painstaking descriptions of the context in which a song was composed and performed, believing that the context was extremely important for a proper understanding of the text itself.[41] He also gave copious details of the physical, verbal, and social behaviour of both musicians and audience, the processes of learning, composition and change, the uses and functions of songs, and the cause and nature of textual and musical improvisation. Thus al-Isfahani's work was a precursor of our modern musical anthropology.[42]

Although the greater part of the *akhbar* in *Kitab al-Aghani* was transmitted orally to the author, he also cited written works, noting that 'authors and *ashab adab wa akhbar*' helped to preserve various links of the *isnad*.[43] Kilpatrick notes that al-Isfahani often refers to written materials by using the terms *nasakhtuhu* and *wajadtuhu*.[44] Even so, as Zolondek notes, the written works by these authors are under-represented in the *isnad* of *akhbar* in the *Kitab al-Aghani* and, moreover, we do not know whether these authors showed a significant interest in the subject.[45] This problem applies to the *akhbar* of the poets cited throughout the *Kitab al-Aghani*, including *'udhri* poets. Nevertheless, Zolondek argues, 'it is apparent that Abu al-Faraj had the various transmissions of the "collector sources" in hand and worked systematically from a definite plan as regards both content and the use of the "collector sources" available to him.'[46] Therefore, when addressing the *'udhri ghazal*, it seems that al-Isfahani treats this tradition in the same way as the various other traditions detailed in his enormous work. He reports as much as possible of these poets' *akhbar* and poetry. When he is dealing with a number of reports on a subject and sets out to note their points of divergence, he does not usually follow one main version but integrates the common elements. Even if he does not announce at the beginning that he will mention them, digressions are sometimes made in the course of a *khabar*.[47] One might question here how the stories and narratives about *'udhri* poets, starting with the *Kitab al-Aghani*, gave rise to certain compositions that in effect marked the beginning of a new tradition. This and similar questions will be discussed in the following section.

Reconstructing the Past

How can we explain the retrospective mood of the ninth and tenth centuries that looked back to the *'udhri ghazal* and prompted scholars to collect this poetry and the narratives about *'udhri* poets of the seventh and early eighth centuries? What happened at that time to spark a fresh interest in *'udhri* love almost two centuries after the death of the *'udhri* lover-poets? I would suggest three assumptions to answer these questions. Firstly, when the *'udhri ghazal* was revived as a literary phenomenon in the ninth century it was not with 'new' exponents. Rather, the still living tradition was revived when the poetry was collected and documented and when the stories that somehow fitted with the poetry were collected and retold. Therefore the restoration of the *'udhri* tradition was partly due to the criticism and authorship movement in the Abbasid age. Secondly, foreign influences on Arabic literature, especially from Persia, could also explain the turning back to the *'udhri ghazal*. In particular, the Persian interest in Majnun led to the development of narratives about the Arabic origin of the story and the addition of new Sufi elements to it.[48] Thirdly, concerning moral and ethical issues, the 'profligacy movement' on one hand and the Sufis and asceticism on the other were all instrumental in renewing the interest in the *'udhri ghazal*. I will now discuss these three assumptions in turn.

The period of documentation, criticism and authorship

The interest in the *'udhri ghazal* in the ninth and tenth centuries that is evident in the compilations of *'udhri* poetry, together with biographical details of the poets who wrote it, is not so surprising, as such documentation had already begun in the ninth century with the collection of both pre-Islamic and post-Islamic poetry as well as the related literary material (*akhbar*).[49] Literary criticism also flourished and the Prophet's hadith were collected during the same period. The time lapse, I would argue, between the appearance of *'udhri* poets in the seventh century and the start of writing about them after a gap of about one and a half centuries should not be considered as a real gap when we bear in mind that literature needs a period of fermentation and of bedding down before literary criticism can properly approach it. In fact, an interest in the authors themselves had already been shown at an earlier time, reappearing through slightly later studies and criticism. For example, interest in the stories of *Kalilah wa dimnah*, by Ibn al-Muqaffa' (d. 190/759), which were of Persian and ultimately Indian origin, reignited with Abban b. 'Abd al-Hamid al-Lahiqi (d. 200/815), and interest in al-Jahiz as a personality also resumed in the art of *Al-maqamat*. Therefore, the *'udhri ghazal* returned to captivate the public and scholars alike, alongside every other kind of literary expression. In fact certain figurative elements, such as the wolf for instance, returned to recapture the attention of poets. This animal had figured in Arabic poetry of the pre-Islamic era by al-Muraqqish al-Akbar and al-Shanfara, and reappeared with al-Farazdaq in the Umayyad era and again with al-Buhturi, al-Sharif al-Radhi and others in the Abbasid era.[50]

Hence, it is possible that a literary phenomenon or personality may vanish for a while, and then return in another form. For example, *Al-maqamat* appeared in the fourth century, composed by Badi' al-Zaman al-Hamadhani, before vanishing, only to be reintroduced in the sixth century by al-Hariri and thereafter by al-Suqursuti. Therefore, it can be said that after the invigoration of the *'udhri ghazal* during the Umayyad era, it came back to life again in the Abbasid era. The return of this poetic form is evident in three related areas:

a. Documentation: the collection of anecdotes and biographical details (*akhbar*) and poetry of *'udhri* poets by Abu Bakr Walibi, a collector of Majnun poetry, and by Ibn Qutaybah, who collected numerous anecdotes about *'udhri* poets in his *al-Shi'r wa al-shu'ara'*.

b. Criticism: Arabic criticism before the fourth century was impressionistic and was not aimed at critical intervention as much as it was at demonstrating eloquence. Ibn Qutaybah is considered one of the first critics, establishing rules for literary criticism in his book *al-Shi'r wa al-shu'ara'*.[51] After Ibn Qutaybah came Qudamah b. Ja'far (d. 337/948), whose book *Naqd al-shi'r* (*Criticism of Poetry*) shows the influence of the literary criticism translated into Arabic at that time, particularly Aristotle's *Poetics*. Then two more books on criticism appeared, first that by al-Amidi (d. 371/981), namely *al-Muwazanah bayna al-ta'yyan*, then 'Ali al-Jurjani (d. 392/1002) and his work *al-Wasatah bayna al-Mutanabbi wa khusumuh* (*Mediation between al-Mutanabbi and his opponents*). However, criticism did not fully mature to become methodical until the appearance of Ibn Rashiq al-Qayrawani (d. 456/1064) who penned *al-'Umdah fi sina'at al-shi'r wa naqdih* (*The Pillar in the Creation and Criticism of Poetry*) and al-Hasan al-'Askari with *al-Sina'atayn* (*The Two Industries*). Undoubtedly, this rich period of criticism prompted critics to look at the poetry of previous eras, including *'udhri* poetry.

c. The poetry concerned with courtly love was influenced by the *'udhri ghazal* as we see in its most illustrious exponent, al-'Abbas b. al-Ahnaf (d. 188/804), a poet who is considered by some scholars as the natural heir of *'udhri* poets[52] – even though the love celebrated in his poetry was eventually fulfilled, the beloved here is rather a high-ranking lady of the court. Perhaps it is the themes of long sorrow and cruel fate that link this poetry to *'udhri* poetry.

In the light of the foregoing, we see that a literary style can either vanish or be transformed into something new, and that it can be subject to a phase of documentation, criticism and analysis. So it was with the reappearance of the *'udhri ghazal*. The reasons for the rather changed forms largely reflect the cultural life of the ninth and tenth centuries. At the same time, this mode of poetic expression was also linked to the political and social climate that led to the interest in courtly love (*ghazal*) poetry and to the patronage of scholars and poets. The renewed interest in the *'udhri ghazal* as the poetry of *'udhris* and their stories was part of this cultural revival, constituting rich material for authors writing on the subject of love. First, al-Jahiz (d. 255/868) authored the *Kitab al-qiyan*, his dissertation on female singers and women and especially on passionate love, which was his main theme. He defined it, advocating it as a source of goodness, further drawing an analogy between the mirth of singing and the mirth between lovers, also providing comparisons between men and women.[53] By developing his theories on love, al-Jahiz laid the groundwork for later writers who devoted whole books to the subject.

Subsequently, from the third century entire books were written about lovers who died of unfulfilled love for each other. The *Kitab al-zahrah* by Ibn Dawud al-Antaki (d. 296/909) is one of the most acclaimed works that appeared on the theory of love in the ninth century. It 'initially corresponded to the ideal concepts of Court circles concerning a person of good breeding'.[54] This book makes use of *'udhri* stories and poetry to set a model for 'courtly love'. In this book we read: 'He who wishes to be noble and cultivated must be chaste', and 'It is ignoble to treat the beloved in a contemptuous way by describing her'. In this light, we can understand the emphasis placed on chastity in *'udhri* love. During this period, the idea was remodelled to match the new standards of courtly love.

Another example of this remodelling is found in a book that appeared in the tenth century which set a new standard of morality for the lover using examples from the past, especially from the *'udhri* stories. The book, *al-Muwashsha*, by al-Washsha (d. 325/937), states:

> In the past when a man loved a woman, he did not desert her until death and his heart concerned itself with no other, neither did he endeavour to find consolation elsewhere . . . and the woman behaved in like manner. When one of them died before the other, the partner either took his own life or lived on only in a spirit of love for the one that had been lost; remaining true, and honouring the memory of the partner.[55]

Al-Washsha, in this text, refers to the *'udhri* relationship as a model, and the book is filled with references to *'udhri* poets and with quotations from their poetry. Here we can see the strong influence of these poets, who were much quoted at this time, as well as how their stories were remodelled to match the nature of contemporary society.

In addition, these books introduced a dramatic element to love, as can be seen in titles such as *Masari' al-'ushshaq* (Death of the Passionate Lovers) by al-Sarraj (d. 500/1106), which greatly popularised the theme that passionate love had tragic consequences.[56] Much of the content of *Masari' al-'ushshaq* appears in numerous later works, which use *'udhri* love stories as examples of how love affects its victims and how it often kills them. One of these works, the *Kitab al-wadih al-mubin fi dhikr man istushhida min al-muhbin* by Mughultay (d. 762/1361), is devoted entirely to the martyrs of love. Such drama and death can only be the result of tortured and deprived love. The *'udhri* example is the ultimate one for incarnate fidelity both in love and in separation. Subsequent books on theories of love were suffused with such idealism.

Hence these books emphasised this permanent state of longing and imparted these values to the *'udhri ghazal* in one way or another.

Influence of Sufism and the Persian interest in the 'udhri ghazal

Further interest in the *'udhri ghazal* came from abroad, particularly from Persia, which is closely linked with the Sufi movements that flourished in the Abbasid era. It is well known that the Persians had shown particular interest in the story of Majnun Layla. Their greatest poets, specifically Nizami, re-wrote that story until it took a purely Sufi form with the poet 'Abd al-Rahman Jami. Nizami's narrative poem of approximately 4,600 lines is the third of five long narrative poems knowncollectively as the *Khamsa* (Quintet). Here are some details about his work

> In composing his romance, Nizami used many of the Arabic anecdotes and considered several key elements of the *'udhri* genre. He refers explicitly to his sources seventeen times, at the beginning of each episode, but none of the sources can be identified with certainty: these references are probably a narrative device to emphasize the romance's outlandish origin to his Persian readers. Nizami adds a strong Persian flavor to the legend. For example, the Nawfal episode is developed into a completely different event, hardly resembling the original Arabic account. The Arabic sources portray Nawfal as an official, but Nizami's Nawfal is a chivalrous Persian chieftain (*javanmard*) ready to risk his life to bring the two lovers together. Nizami threads the scattered anecdotes about Majnun's love into a finely woven narrative with a dramatic climax. Persian verse romances are commonly about princes, and characters are usually related to courtly circles. Likewise, Nizami portrays the lovers as aristocrats. He also urbanizes the Bedouin legend: Majnun does not meet Layla in the desert amongst the camels, but at school with other children. Other Persian motifs added to the story are . . . Majnun's supplication to the heavenly bodies and God; his kingship over animals, and his didactic conversations with several characters.[57]

Undoubtedly, these new dimensions given to the story of Majnun heightened the interest in this poetry. Moreover, some scholars, such as Hilal, claim that Sufi love is an *'udhri* love whose evolution was due to specific philosophical and religious factors.[58] Both types were subject to the creed of Islam and the interpretations of its texts. At the same time, neither of these two expressions of love shied away from the physical side and, in the case of Sufi love, contemplating physical beauty was understood as a metaphor of the Sufi's search for God.[59] Hilal also stresses that the Sufis introduced emotional feelings and indeed passion into the anecdotes about Majnun Layla, recounting that he became unconscious for a short time whenever the name of Layla was mentioned. With the Sufis, fainting was accompanied by a frenzy of amorous feeling.[60]

Moral and ethical issues

Although 'diverting entertainment' appeared in Islamic societies from the Umayyad era onwards, as we see for example in the stories about al-Walid b. Yazid, it seems that the 'profligacy movement' known as *mujun*, meaning those who make light of moral values yet also indicating *inter alia* sexual freedom and the consumption of alcohol, became widespread only in the Abbasid era from the third century. Dayf states that two factors contributed to the spread of *mujun* in the third and fourth centuries, firstly the appearance of 'doubters', such as the schools of atheists and *zanadiqah*, and secondly, the popularity of female singers (*al-qiyan*).[61]

The *zanadiqah* (approved sibling marriage) movement, which arose in Persia, was originally influenced by the book known as the *Avesta* attributed to Zoroaster, developed according to tradition by Mani who called upon his followers to lead an ascetic life. The movement continued after the advent of Islam and grew during the Abbasid era, particularly during the days of Caliph al-Mahdi who asked *al-mu'tazilah* and *al-mutakalimah* to respond to the *zanadiqah* by showing their disapproval.[62]

Concerning the female singers, *al-qiyan*, al-Jahiz portrayed their life of singing and seduction through poetry and voice.[63] The *Kitab al-Aghani* also depicts this underside of life which was full of slave girls and female singers, drinking and singing.[64] It seems that this wave of diversions and *mujun* encompassed al-Kufah, according to Mu'ti b. Iyas, Walibah and Hammad 'Ajrad. A portrayal of Basrah at this time by Bashshar b. Burd, who was fond of wine and women (as can be seen in his poetry), reveals that this city was also submerged under the same wave. Moreover, two poets in particular, Abu Nuwas and al-Husayn b. al-Dahhak, depicted widespread profligacy and homosexuality as characteristic of the era.[65] Is it possible that the spread of libertinism in the Abbasid era helped to create a desire to return to the *'udhri ghazal*, which is considered to be the utter opposite of libertinism? Walther claims that the renewed interest in *'udhri* love and in composing books on tragic chaste love came about 'perhaps because people had had enough of the constantly increasing fickleness of erotic relationships'.[66]

However, from my point of view, one should be cautious regarding such interpretations; how do we know that erotic relationships were increasingly fickle?

Perhaps they are represented as such in texts but we cannot assume that this representational history, if it is even borne out by specific examples, bears any relationship to the overall history of lived relationships. *Al-Aghani* contains accounts of *'udhris* and the ascetics. But we also find in *al-Aghani* scores of stories about profligates and a depiction of palace life as one of extravagance and libertinism. This text also depicts the life of poor poets. Moreover, asceticism and Sufism had started to take root in society alongside the alleged emergence of *mujun* and libertinism. Dayf explains that the wave of asceticism in the Abbasid era was not less intense than the wave of *mujun* and may have arrived as a foreign influence from Indian asceticism and Christian monasticism . Abu al-'Atahiyah was perhaps one of the most important ascetic poets, starting life as a *mujun* and ending up by extolling asceticism, death and the grave.[67]

Contradictory Texts on Physicality in the *'Udhri* Tradition

As we have seen from the previous sections, the period of documentation and authorship led to an interest in collecting the poetry and narratives of the *'udhri* poets. Later on, the elements of *'iffah* (chastity) in this tradition were refined. But a close examination reveals inconsistencies about the issue of *'iffah* and physicality in *'udhri* poetry and *akhbar* which appeared in important sources like *al-Aghani*. Perhaps the structure of *al-Aghani* and the way it was composed contributed to this contradiction, as we shall see.

Despite the scholarly emphasis on the *'iffah* of *'udhri* poets, it is a fact that the beloved is noticeably present throughout the genre of the *'udhri ghazal*. The *'udhri* poet celebrates his beloved's corporal beauty in all its glory, and he often refers to his desire for her. Yet he claims that a physical contact with his beloved did not occur. How are we to understand the contradictions found within the *'udhri* tradition regarding physical contact between the lovers? For example, Jamil was reported to have said on his deathbed: 'May Muhammad not be my saviour (in the other world) if my hand ever touched Buthaynah for a suspicious thing. All I used to do is to rest her hand on my heart in order to have some relief'.[68] Is this statement simply due to his piety, or does he imply that the ideal beauty the poetry depicts is unpossessable, even in thought. In Ibn Qutaybah's book *al-Shi'r wa al-shu'ara* we also read: 'Jamil is among those who are content with very little'.[69] He cites these famous verses composed by Jamil:

> I am pleased with very little things accorded to me by Buthaynah
> They are so insignificant
> that if they were known by the man (who spies us)
> he would not be annoyed with my love
> I am pleased even when she says: "no" or "I cannot" And when she makes
>   me live on promises
> promises hoped for, but always disappointing
> I am pleased with a quick glance at her,
> and even with spending a whole year without our meeting –
> neither at the beginning nor at the end.[70]   [3]

In other verses Jamil says:

> I know nothing of what lies beneath her clothes, nor have I ever kissed
>   her,
> I have never touched her.
> We just talked and were lost in each other's eyes.[71]   [4]

Moreover, a number of related themes appear in the passages contained in *al-Aghani*. For instance, Jamil asked Buthaynah during a conversation in her tent one night: 'Would you not like to give me now the reward of all my ardent love for you?' She answered, 'What do you mean?' Said Jamil, 'The thing that normally happens between lovers'. Buthaynah refuses brusquely, saying that she will not see him again should he hint at this ever again. But now Jamil says: 'I only wanted to know your opinion about that. Had you complied with my wish, I would have killed you with my sword immediately, because if you granted it to me, I knew that you would grant it to others too.'[72]

One can easily be captivated by such verses and anecdotes, which can be found in a number of sources that deal with the theme of love within Islamic and Arab history, such as *Masari' al-'ushshaq*, *Rawdat al-muhibbin* and *al-Muwashsha*. Nevertheless, we may observe a striking phenomenon in this tradition at both the poetic and the narrative level. This phenomenon can be traced through the existence of the two contradictory notions in interpretations of one single source. Indeed, as can be seen, if certain narrators have related stories about *'udhri* lovers making a particular claim about them, others relate stories that give the opposite impression. Even with regard to the physical descriptions of the beloved in *'udhri* tradition, different narrators have been inclined to give often incompatible statements. For example, the following episode suggests the ugliness of Buthaynah: Jamil was in a *hammam* in Egypt when an old man observed his beauty and asked him who he was. When he realised that he was Jamil, Buthaynah's famous lover, he said to him: 'What do you like about her? I saw her and I swear that her heel is so sharp that it can be used to slaughter a bird.' Jamil replied: 'Oh sir, if you could just see her through my eyes, you would be happy to commit adultery within the eyes of God.'[73]

One should note the link that Jamil suggested between Buthaynah's beauty and his desire, a desire that was great enough to compel him to use the word adultery. However, in another context, Buthaynah was described by the famous poet 'Umar b. Abi Rabi'ah, after he had had a conversation with her, as a tall and beautiful woman.[74] In *al-Shi'r wa al-shu'ara* a storyteller describes Buthaynah as being like the full moon to indicate her beauty.[75] Likewise, in another passage in *al-Aghani*, Layla asks a woman to scrutinise her (Layla's) body and to report 'whether Majnun lied or told the truth', whereupon the verdict comes: 'No, by God, he spoke the truth'.[76] The notion that Majnun must have really known Layla's body to be able to describe it precisely, as the above anecdote suggests, is at the heart of this account. Moreover, Layla is shown 'pleasurably absorbed in and musing with her friend over the matter of whether the poet-lover has described her physical appearance in a flattering manner, whether his poetry had appealingly mirrored her'.[77] However, Majnun's verses suggest another view regarding Layla's appearance from the point of view of a censurer who associated her with shortness and ugliness, but Majnun insists on his love for her despite the critic's opinion.[78]

As has been seen, these kinds of contradictions in episodes evince confusion over the portrayal of the women that *'udhri* poets loved. Buthaynah's portrayal, for instance, incites Khristu Najm to say:

> Buthaynah's character is excessively ambiguous! She is beautiful and ugly, Bedouin and urban, chaste and profane, she lives in poverty in the desert and in luxury in towns. She was forced marry a Bedouin to remove her disgrace, and then, they consoled her after the death of her lover. She wanders in *'Udhra* faubourg and then appears in the palace of the caliph. She appears as a prodigy of contradiction.[79]

So a single classical Arabic text simultaneously provides contradictory anecdotes, perhaps in an attempt to leave the door open for discussions, probabilities and open-ended predictions. It seems that al-Isfahani was aware of the ambiguity that his anecdotes reflected. Thus he chose a simple strategy: ascribe responsibility to the narrator.[80] By adopting this strategy, *al-Aghani* contains a plethora of contradictory episodes.

This phenomenon is evident throughout *'udhri* poetry and in the anecdotes written about it. Majnun, for instance, says:

> If Layla's husband is among you,
> then I swear by God that I kissed her on the mouth eighty times.
> And I swear by God that I saw her and twenty of her fingers
> were clutching at my back[81]   [5]

Yet he also says:

> When I want to kiss Layla she turns away
> Like a horse with a loud neigh
> And she bites her thumb and nods to say:
> I am afraid that people will see.[82]   [6]

The contexts in which the poet recited these verses differ. He might have said them in different phases of his relationship with Layla, which might have taken various forms. What concerns us here is the contradiction, if we may term it as such, that exists in *'udhri* poetry. This contradiction stresses the ambiguity surrounding the concept of bodily contact between the two lovers.

Yet this ambiguity is not restricted to *'udhri* anecdotes; some of these contradictory anecdotes and verses have been reported about 'Umar b. Abi Rabi'ah, a poet represented by researchers as the antithesis of the *'udhri* tradition, and the leader of a sensual school of Arabic poetry. On the one hand, 'Umar actually confesses that he did everything he described in his poetry, but that he asked God for forgiveness.[83] However, another anecdote reports him saying: 'I swear by God that I never told a woman something she did not want to hear, nor have I touched a woman that I was forbidden to touch.'[84] Hence, this game has long been present in classical Arabic literary texts. Besides the popular anecdotes, there have also been further lesser-known anecdotes that reveal other views on this issue; the only difference is that the other anecdotes are less popular. Occasionally, an episode hints at a different interpretation. For instance, the aforementioned episode in which Jamil asks Buthaynah to reward all his ardent love for her: this was apparently only a test of her purity, and her refusal of his advances was really what he was seeking. This episode shows the *'udhri* couple to be perfectly chaste, but there is a hint in this story that might suggest a different disposition. The rest of the story shows that Buthaynah's father and brother were watching the two with swords under their gowns, and that, after hearing this dialogue, they went away saying to each other: 'We need not hinder this man from meeting her any more'.[85] As Bürgel observes:

> Taking into account the fact that Jamil appears much more active and cunning in the stories than his *'udhrite* colleagues ever do, we may not exclude that in this case he made a serious proposal but sensing either the coy reserve of Buthaynah or the presence of her guardians, or the one as well as the other, he withdrew into the *'udhrite* guise or pose.[86]

Most contemporary Arabic studies try to ignore this contradiction by elevating the status of the texts that emphasise the chastity of the *'udhri* poet.[87] This chastity is usually attributed to the effect of Islamic traditions on the poet's attitude. Other texts that were graphically sensual were rejected and attributed to mistaken ascriptions, but without substantial evidence. Therefore, such studies do not handle *'udhri* love as a well-rounded phenomenon where reality and history intersect with the imaginary, but pick and choose what the researchers fancy, and what they are disposed to believe of the virtue of *'udhri* love.

Therefore, instead of ignoring the contradiction within the poetry and narratives ascribed to *'udhri* poets, one may see it within a duality of both bodily presence and equally bodily absence. It is also valid to assert that the difference between chaste and sensual poetry may be attributed to the mood of a particular poet, or the phase the poet is going through. Or, as 'Abdallah argues, it may be that these differences in contradictory anecdotes about sensual and chaste poetry and narratives within *'udhri* tradition are a result of the different experiences of the young poet and the mature poet.[88] As may be observed, 'Abdallah's opinion in paradoxical anecdotes reported about *'udhri* poets emphasises the element of time, which is a decisive element, and which is important if we are to understand the *'udhri* tradition.

Accordingly, was the *'udhri* poet going through various phases in his relationship with his lover? Or was he playing a game, drawing closer and then withdrawing from his object of desire? Approaching her to satisfy his desire, and departing so as to inflame his love? Obviously, human emotions within love are quite complex and cannot be simply classified into the two categories of chaste and sensual (and these may not necessarily be opposing concepts). This fact gives love poetry a conflicted nature, as the poet's emotions fluctuate between the unattainable glorified image of his lover and his own instinctive desire to unite with her.

Hence, we are not supposed to cut short the historical event, nor should we curtail the text. We should believe first that the phenomenon of the *'udhri ghazal* exists, and that the anecdotes about poets are an essential part of its existence, and then analyse their historical credibility. The role played by storytellers (*ruwah*) should not be neglected here, as they paid special attention to love stories because they were so popular with their audiences. A statement by Ibn Qayyim al-Jawziyyah (d. 751/1349) shows this popularity clearly:

> While the commoner's fame is not comparable with that of a king … he gains his celebrity when he falls in love. He is even mentioned in the presence of kings, caliphs and their successors. His stories are recorded and his poems get recited. Poetry makes his existence eternal. Without love, he would not be mentioned nor would he be able to be paid any attention.[89]

It is plausible to argue that the storytellers tried to please their audiences with details about the meetings and sweet conversations between lovers and, at the same time, they made sure to keep within the bounds of conservative tradition and direct the poets to the right and acceptable path within that tradition. The mainstream inclination towards perpetuating conservative tradition is evident in a narrative about 'Umar b. Abi Rabi'ah. The narrative claims that 'Umar had never acted upon his desire, despite the fact that his poetry abounds in sensual love scenes.[90]

Significantly, these contrasts highlight the latent contradiction in the *'udhri* love tradition, and it could be argued that they show a manifest obsession about physical contact between *'udhri* lovers. Whether the narratives allude to the fact that physical contact took place in their relationships, or claim its absence, the result is still the same. The body lies at the heart of the *'udhri* tradition. The lack of possession/physicality only serves to heighten desire since it only draws more attention to that which is being denied. Hence, this shows us the privileged position of the body by the prominent duality of its presence and absence. The very concept of chastity involves a conscious denial of physical contact, and this consciousness surely implies a strong awareness of physicality.

Notes

1. Jacobi, *'Time and Reality in Nasib and Ghazal'*, p. 1.
2. See Chapter One.
3. Jacobi, *'Time and Reality in Nasib and Ghazal'*, p. 1.
4. For more details see Dayf, *al-Fann wa mathahibuhu fi al-shi'r al-'arabi*, pp. 53–9.
5. Ibid., pp. 1–2.
6. Examples of this variation could be found in the poems of 'Umar b. Abi Rabi'ah and al-Walid b. Yazid. See Jacobi's study of two of their poems: 'Theme and Variations in Umayyad *Ghazal* Poetry', *Journal of Arabic Literature*, vol. 23, No. 2, pp. 111–19.
7. Khulayf, *al-Hubb al-mithali*, p. 57.
8. Qays, *Diwan*, p. 122.
9. Jamil, *Diwan*, p. 32.
10. Jacobi, *Die Udhra: Liebe und Tod in der Umayyadenzeit*.
11. Hilal, *al-Hayah al-'aAtifiyyah*, p. 23.
12. Ibid.
13. See Chapter One.

14. See examples of this in his *diwan*, pp. 150, 371.
15. See examples of this in his *diwan*, pp. 154, 161, 163, 168.
16. Al-Isfahani, *Al-Aghani*, vol. 1, p. 176, trans. Walther, *Women In Islam*, p. 165.
17. Ibn Hazm harshly criticises the idea of having several lovers: 'Herein lies the root of the error which misleads a man into asserting that he loves two persons, or is passionately enamoured of two entirely different individuals. All this is to be explained as springing out of carnal desire, as we have just described; it is called love only metaphorically, and not in the true meaning of the term. As for the true lover, the yearning of his soul is so excessive as to divert him from all his religious and mundane occupations; how then could he have room to busy himself with a second love-affair?' Ibn Hazm, *Tawq al-hamamah fi al-ulfah wa al-ullaf*, p. 58.
18. Jamil, *Diwan*, p. 87.
19. In *al-Shi'r wa al-shu'ra* Ibn Qutaybah provides a similar anecdote about Kuthayyir 'Azzah. 'Aishah bint Talhah invited him to compose poetry about her, instead of 'Azzah, claiming that she was richer and more beautiful. But Kuthayyir replied in verses that showed his devotion to 'Azzah. Ibn Qutaybah, *al-Shi'r wa al-shu'ra*, pp. 508–9.
20. Al-Isfahani, *Al-Aghani*, vol. 8, pp. 314–15.
21. Adunis, *al-Thabit wa al-mutahawil*, vol.1, pp. 299–301.
22. Jamil, *Diwan*, p. 89.
23. Labib, *Susyulujya al-ghazal*, pp. 90–1.
24. Majnun, *Diwan*, p. 217, trans. Khan, *Sexuality and Secrecy*, p. 117.
25. Khan, *Sexuality and Secrecy*, p. 118.
26. Ibid.
27. Jacobi, '*Time and Reality in Nasib and Ghazal*', p. 9.
28. Ibn Qutaybah used this sentence to describe Jamil, *al-Shi'r wa al-shu'ra*, p. 260, Qays b. Dharih, p. 628 and 'Urwah b. Hizam, p. 622.
29. Raja Salamah, *al-'Ishq wa al-kitabah: qira'ah fi al-mawruth*, pp. 356–7.
30. Ibid.
31. Bürgel, '*Love, Lust, and Longing*', p. 94.
32. Salamah, *al-'Ishq wa al-kitabah*, p. 358.
33. Al-Isfahani, *Al-Aghani*, vol. 8, p. 93.
34. See his story in Chapter Five.
35. Al-Isfahani, *Al-Aghani*, vol. 8, p. 6.
36. See Chapter One.
37. See Chapter One.

38. Aristocratic lineage indicates a certain level of studiousness and scholarship, and even access to scholarly books.
39. Sawa, 'The Status and Roles of Secular Musicians in the *Kitāb al-Aghani* (Book of Songs) of Abu al-Faraj al-Isfahani', pp. 69–82 .
40. Jabri, *Dirasat al-aghani*, p. 10.
41. Sawa, 'The Status and Roles of Secular Musicians in the *Kitāb al-Aghani* (Book of Songs) of Abu al-Faraj al-Isfahani', p. 70.
42. Ibid.
43. Zolondek, 'An Approach to the Problem of the Sources of the *kitab al-aghani*', *Journal of Near Eastern Studies*, vol. 19, No. 3, p. 219.
44. Kilpatrick, *Making the Great Book of Songs. Compilation and the Author's Craft in Abu al-Faraj al-Isfahani's Kitab al-aghani*, p. 95.
45. Zolondek, 'An Approach to the Problem of the Sources of the *kitab al-aghani*', *Journal of Near Eastern Studies*, vol. 19, No. 3, p. 219.
46. Ibid., p. 231.
47. Kilpatrick, *Making the Great Book of Songs. Compilation and the Author's Craft in Abu al-Faraj al-Isfahani's Kitab al-aghani*, p. 97.
48. To the present day, three main characters from Arabic literature still exert an influential presence in Persian literature: Majnun, Ali b. Abi Talib and al-Mutanabbi.
49. The book *Tabaqat fuhul al-shu'ara'* (*Categories of Poets*) by Muhammad b. Sallam al-Jumahi (d. 232/846) is considered one of the early books which were devoted to the collection of poetry and the division of poets into categories or classes.
50. For more details on the depiction of the wolf in Arabic literature by different poets from different periods, see al-Tarabulsi, *al-Buna wa al-ru'a*, pp. 35–53.
51. Ibn Qutaybah divided poetry into types: see *al-Shi'r wa al-shu'ara'*, pp. 5–9.
52. Zaki Mubarak studies him along with Jamil and Kuthayyir; see *al-'Ushshaq al-thalathah*. Shawqi Dayf, likewise, considers him as an *'udhri* poet: see *al-Hubb al-'udhri 'ind al-'Arab*.
53. Al-Jahiz, *al-Rasa'il*, p. 166.
54. Walther, *Women in Islam*, p. 159.
55. al-Washsha, Kitab al-Muwashsha pp. 70–1.
56. See my discussion about this book and the theme of tragic love in Chapter Six.
57. Seyed-Gohrab, 'Leyli o Majnun'.
58. Hilal, *al-Hayah al-'Atifiyyah*, p. 38.
59. Ibid.
60. Ibid., p. 91.

61. Dayf, *al-Fann wa madhahibuh*, p.100.
62. Ibid., pp. 109–14.
63. Al-Jahiz, *Risalat al-qiyan*, pp. 9–13.
64. Was it the inclination of Abu al-Faraj al-Isfahani to spread such accounts in order to inform the public of what was going on inside the palaces of their caliphs and princes, including matters which took away their aura of sanctity?
65. Dayf, *al-Fann wa madhahibuh*, p. 103.
66. Walther, *Women in Islam*, pp. 157–8.
67. Dayf, *al-Fann wa madhahibuh*, pp. 114–15.
68. Ibn Qutaybah, al-Shi'r wa al-shu'ara, p. 441, trans. Kinany, *Development*, p. 256.
69. Ibn Qutaybah, *al-Shi'r wa al-shu'ra*, p. 442.
70. Jamil, *Diwan*, p. 83, trans. Kinany, *Development*, p. 180.
71. Jamil, *Diwan*, p. 49.
72. Al-Isfahani, *Al-Aghani*, vol. 8, p. 298, trans. Bürgel, 'Love', p. 93.
73. Manzur, *Mukhtasar tarikh Dimashq*, vol. 6, p. 114.
74. Zakaryyia, *al-Jalis al-salih wa al-anis al-nasih*, p. 452.
75. Ibn Qutaybah, *al-Shi'r wa al-shu'ra*, vol. 2, p. 567.
76. Al-Isfahani, *Al-Aghani*, vol. 2, p. 368, trans. Khairallah, *Love, Madness, and Poetry: An Interpretation of the Magnun Legend*, p. 66.
77. Khan, *Sexuality and Secrecy*, p. 273.
78. Majnun, *Diwan*, p. 252.
79. Najm, *Jamil*, p. 116.
80. This sentence appears frequently in *Al-Aghani*: 'the responsibility lies with the narrator'.
81. Majnun, *Diwan*, p. 237.
82. Majnun, *Diwan*, p. 191.
83. Al-Isfahani, *Al-Aghani*, vol. 1, p. 87.
84. Ibid.
85. Al-Isfahani, *Al-Aghani*, vol 8, p. 298, trans. Bürgel, 'Love', p. 93.
86. Bürgel, 'Love', p. 94.
87. Except for a few studies that led to further discussions on the subject such as al-'Azm's *Fi al-hubb wa al-hubb al-'udhri* and Labib's *Susyulujya al-ghazal al-'Arabi: al-shi'r al-'udhri namudhajan*.
88. 'Abdallah, *al-Hubb*, p. 245.
89. Ibn Qayyim al-Jawziyyah, *Rawdat al-muhibbin wa nuzhat al-mushtaqin*, p. 174.
90. Al-Isfahani, *Al-Aghani*, vol. 1, p. 87.

3

'Udhri Tradition between Chastity and Sensuality

Introduction

This chapter will discuss the concepts of sexuality, marriage and chastity in Islamic discourse, which includes Islamic jurisprudence as well as Islamic culture in general. I will clarify how I use Islamic jurisprudence as a source, in discussing the Islamic emphasis on marriage versus a discernible *'udhri* attitude towards this social institution. The implications of chastity as understood in the stories about *'udhri* poets and theories of love will also be discussed, while taking into consideration the particular context of the ninth and tenth centuries. A problematic relationship exists, however, between the *'udhri* tradition and the prevalent Islamic discourse around sexuality and love. On the one hand, it seems that the *'udhri ghazal* was influenced by several elements brought by the new faith, notably monotheism as well as the description of *hur al-'ayn* (perfect beautiful women in Heaven), which will be discussed in detail later. On the other hand, the *'udhri* tradition moved away from the simple and direct approach of Islamic discourse towards chastity and marriage to create its own models of love and physical union.

Using the term 'chastity' as a translation of the term *'iffah* does not imply that the word 'chastity', as it appears in English discourse, is equivalent to the word *'iffah* as it is used in Arabic and Islamic discourse. Nevertheless, I have chosen to use the term 'chastity' because it is the English word that most closely approximates the Arabic *'iffah*. Both words convey the meaning of restraining oneself from realising certain desires.[1] Other possible words include 'loyalty', which is useful in terms of the *'udhri* poets' attitude towards their beloved; but loyalty does not convey the complexity of attitude and action concerning sexuality and sociality that *'iffah* encompasses. 'Chastity' does imply the complicated relationship between sensuality (seemingly the best translation of the Arabic term *hissiyah*) and *'iffah*, or sexual probity, in Islamic and *'udhri* discourse. This separation of *'iffah* and sensuality is not to deny their close connection; I make it purely for analytic purposes. As we shall see, the two terms are not always opposites. Indeed, in the *'udhri ghazal*, these two terms are complementary.

Sources

'Islamic discourse' cannot be seen as monovocal. Any investigation of sexuality and marriage in discourses associated with Islam should make use of multiple sources, both religious and more broadly cultural. We do not have the scope in this book to elaborate fully the Islamically inflected discussions on these socially central topics, but for contextual purposes we refer to those textual areas closest to the topic at hand. To some extent, poetry and literary prose, which could be defined by the general term *adab*, can offer an insight into the sexual lives of medieval Muslims, although we must always keep in mind the caveats mentioned earlier about conflating textual representations and lived experiences. In this chapter, I will refer to some of this literature, especially that which has appeared in books as collections of anecdotes and poetry about love among Arabs. At the same time, to neglect certain major works and genres of Islamic literature such as the Qur'an, hadith, *tafsir* and *fiqh* would make this image incomplete and incoherent. And thus we must start with the Qur'an.

For example, the *fuqaha* elaborated with ease and comfort on very sensitive issues concerning sexuality. As Maghen observes, 'nor did they feel the need to excuse this explicitness, from which even the *adab* literature largely shied away from, by evoking the merits of reproduction.'[2] There is no feeling of shame in their discourse over this explicitness, however, and they were thus far freer in their treatment of sensitive erotic issues than the early physicians or the poets and *udaba*.[3] 'When proof-texts were needed by the *fuqaha* in the framework of legal debates on *taharah*, scores of anecdotes appeared in which [sexual activities] were ascribed to the Prophet, his wives and his Companions.'[4] Therefore, these religious sources reveal much about how Muslims thought and acted regarding the body, its desires, activities and the rituals related to it. In comparing *adab* and *fiqh*, Maghen states that the

> formulation in *fiqh* may be less fine than that found in *adab* and the descriptions less exciting or adventurous, but those who are interested in discovering as much as possible about the daily dealings of the ordinary Muslim man and woman of other places and times must proceed first to the canon of the establishment. At any rate, they must not limit themselves solely to the canon of the anti-establishment.[5]

Maghen also maintains that the code of purity offers a unique window on gender relations and notions of sensuality at different times and places in Muslim societies.[6] The panorama here is wide and representative. Within this purity code the *fuqaha* saw it as their duty to discover what aroused the majority of people. Therefore jurisprudence is probably the best place to discover what specific Muslim communities, at various times and in various places, found sexually appealing.[7]

The Body in the Qur'an

Not all references to the body in the Qur'an have negative connotations, especially when they are not associated with repression or profanation. In Iqbal 'Urawi's analysis of the Qur'anic view of the body he indicates that the nature and functions of the body prove the truth of monotheism and the greatness of God because he creates them so perfectly. In addition, certain Qur'anic verses refer to particular parts of the body in a way that reveals the omnipotence of God and His miraculous power in creating these parts.[8] Other verses describe the stages of development of the human body from the foetus to the formation of the entire body, again indicating nothing profane:

> Man We did create from a quintessence [of clay]; Then We placed him as [a drop of] sperm in a place of rest, firmly fixed; Then We made the sperm into a clot of congealed blood; then of that clot We made a [foetus] lump; then we made out of that lump bones and clothed the bones with flesh; then we developed out of it another creature. So blessed be God, the best to create.[9]

'Urawi argues that

> The prevalent phenomenon of viewing the body as profane means that women are perceived as concealing evil in their bodies, thereby denigrating the female sex. Thus, linking the above phenomenon to Islam contradicts the actual references to the body in the Qur'an.[10]

In addition, 'Urawi asserts that the body is also presented in the Qur'an as a subject of *zinah* as in the following verse:

> Say: Who hath forbidden the beautiful (gifts) [*zinah*] of God, which He hath produced for His servants, and the things, clean and pure, *tayyibat* (which He hath provided) for sustenance? Say: They are, in the life of this world, for those who believe, (and) purely for them on the Day of Judgment. Thus do We explain the signs in detail for those who understand.[11]

This representation personifies the body as a reflection of all the beauty of nature and the universe. In this case, the body is not necessarily linked to the other *tayyibat*, like food and drink. According to the Qur'an, the body is more than a mere physical necessity, as man is urged to enjoy its beauty. Moreover, the verse does not confine the treatment of the body to *zinah* but extends to a reminder that the body should be counted as one of God's greatest blessings.[12] In addition to the fact that the body is created for a purpose in this life, it will also bring pleasure in the next life. The appearance of believers on the last day is often described as good: '(Other) faces that Day will be joyful, which will neither nourish nor satisfy hunger'.[13] 'God will admit those who believe and work righteous deeds, to Gardens beneath which rivers flow: they shall be adorned therein with bracelets of gold and pearls; and their garments there will be of silk'.[14] 'Urawi concludes by saying that the Qur'anic speech celebrates the body and sets directions not only to purify but also to beautify it.[15] Thus, contrary to the claims of other scholars,[16] 'Urawi affirms that not all references to the body in the Qur'an have negative connotations.

There are many references in the Qur'an to the physical connection between men and women. For example, 'They are your garments and ye are their garments. Allah knoweth what ye used to do secretly among yourselves; but He turned to you and forgave you; so now associate with them, and seek what Allah hath ordained for you.'[17] There are also several Qur'anic verses giving a clear description of the creation of human beings.[18] In fact, the Qur'an 'alludes to the nature of sexual relations as a means of attaining mutual satisfaction, closeness and compassion between a wife and husband.'[19] In the Qur'an, God's creation of mates is considered one of His signs: 'And among His signs is this: that He created for you mates from among yourselves, that you may dwell in tranquillity with them and He has put love and mercy between you; in this are signs for those who reflect.'[20]

Positive Perspectives on Sexuality

It can be observed that Islam 'always took care to admit that sexuality existed as a problematic element in the relationship of the individual and society and never hesitated to leave room for the discussion of approval or disapproval.'[21] It should be noted that the body is given a remarkably high status in Islam. As Bouhdiba claims, Islam:

> in no way tries to depreciate, still less to deny, the sexual. On the contrary, it attributes a sublime significance to the sexual and invests it with such a transcendental quality that any trace of guilt is removed from it.[22]

Although the *'udhri* tradition devotes itself to highlighting marriage by drawing attention to its absence, marriage is strongly recommended in Islam and indeed is regarded as a cornerstone of Islamic belief and practice. The word *nikah* (marriage) appears in the Qur'an twenty-three times.[23] In his extensive study of sexuality in Islam Bouhdiba stresses this point in every way. He quotes many hadiths showing the privileged status of marriage and the unfavourable status of divorce: 'The profound meaning of the institution of *nikah*, an institution given great importance in Islam, lies in the recognition of the harmony of the human couple as an essential ideal of life'.[24] The 'unity based on *nikah* is a creative mission, because it is based on freedom assumed within the framework of life with others'.[25] Therefore, Bouhdiba assumes that this essential intuition makes *nikah* a sacred mission, in which the notions of guilt and sin are absent. It is worth noting that the theme of 'sacred sex' also appears in many other contributions to the subject.[26]

According to many scholars, there is no doubt that Islam strongly favours marriage.[27] It is often mentioned that the Prophet himself 'established marriage and legal sexual intercourse as a general *sunnah*'.[28] Thus, we can find many hadiths dealing with the question of sex and marriage in the *sunnah*:

> O young men, those among you who can support a wife should marry, for it restrains the eyes [from casting evil glances] and preserves one from immorality; but he who cannot afford it should observe a fast, for it is a means of controlling sexual desire.[29]

> Narrated Ibn Masud: We used to fight in the holy battles in the company of the Prophet and we had no wives with us. So we said, "O Allah's Apostle! Shall we get castrated?" The Prophet forbade us to do so.[30]

Hence, scholars have drawn the conclusion from these and other hadiths that Islam views sex in a positive light, as it encourages sexual enjoyment (provided it is within marriage). Also, the Prophet was open to the discussion of this topic with believers: 'Let none of you come upon his wife like an animal, let there be an emissary between them. When asked what the emissary was, he replied, "The kiss and sweet words".'[31]

Bellamy points out that the Prophet's promotion of marriage is used in the argument against celibacy. In addition, his treatment of his wives is given as an example of the fairness due to each of several wives.[32] It seems, then, that strong encouragement of marriage is predominant in Islamic thinking in spite of certain Sufi voices calling for celibacy.[33] It is hard to ignore all the traditions that connect lawful sex and spiritual rewards. When the Prophet stated: 'In the sexual act of each of you there is a *sadaqah*', his companions were astonished, asking: 'Oh Messenger of God! When one of us fulfils his sexual desire, will he be given a [spiritual] reward for that? The prophet explained: 'Do you think that were he to act upon it [lustful desire] unlawfully, he would be sinning? Likewise, if he acts upon it lawfully he will be rewarded.'[34] Furthermore, 'love has its finality in procreation, which is the gift of existence, the promotion to existence of a new being [. . .]. So the act of generation is highly commendable: [Couple and multiply], the prophet was to order.'[35] Accordingly, it is a work of piety to convince others to marry. The Qur'an says explicitly: 'Marry those among you who are single, or the virtuous ones among yourselves, male or female: if they are in poverty, Allah will give them means out of His grace: for Allah encompasseth all, and He knoweth all things.'³⁶ The prophet says: 'To marry is to perform half of one's religious duty'.³⁷ Marriage, then, is half of faith. 'The personality of man finds fulfillment only in the intimacy of the sexes. The unity based on *nikah* is a creative mission, because it is based on a freedom assumed within the framework of life with others'.³⁸

Classical Arabic books on the question of sexuality are numerous. In his work *al-Jins wa 'ulama al-Islam*³⁹ Ibrahim 'Isa states that there are more than a hundred books written by medieval Muslim scholars on this subject. Many of the modern studies devote one or more chapters to a discussion of these medieval sources. For instance, Bouhdiba's work *Sexuality in Islam* includes a chapter entitled 'Erotology', in which the author cites a variety of treatises and books attributed to al-Jahiz, al-Tifashi, al-Nifzawi and many others, all dealing with sexuality. The author also refers to the large volume of this kind of literature.

However, the modern sources that address sexuality and the body in Arab Muslim culture seem to differ in their points of view and in the conclusions they draw. Whereas some sources focus on the concepts of love and sex as they are treated in the Qur'an and hadith, others rely on the interpretations of the *fuqaha*; and yet other focus on history or poetry. Consequently, some sources assert that Islam 'warmy recommend[s] believers to take their share of sexual pleasures, which are an essential prefiguration of the pleasures of Paradise',⁴⁰ whereas others advise sexual repression and the restriction of physical freedom in Islam. Moreover, where some authors are struck by the straightforward language often used to describe the body in Muslim cultures, others highlight its modesty. As this is a huge area of research, however, I shall focus on only the crucial contributions that shed light upon the topics with which I am concerned in this study.

Bouhdiba asserts that in the practice of love the Qur'an describes a balanced approach, but he argues that this has not been translated into social practice. In other words, what was unified in revelation fell apart at the historical level. Bouhdiba also addresses the subject of variations on eroticism: misogyny, mysticism and *mujun*, maintaining that they are three ways of dealing with the single problem: misogyny encloses Muslims in their own empire, *mujun* releases their inhibitions, and mysticism sublimates them.⁴¹ The sensuality of Paradise is also discussed in his chapter 'The Infinite

Orgasm', where Bouhdiba argues that the sensual nature of paradisiacal pleasures means that the physical aspect of the body is not scorned. The author quotes from the Islamic texts that provide details of the infinite pleasure to be had with *houris*. He concludes by addressing the crisis of sexuality and the crisis of faith in contemporary Arab-Muslim society, emphasising the role that colonisation played in the degradation of women.

The subject of sensuality in Paradise has been frequently addressed by scholars, many of them relying heavily on Bouhdiba's analysis. For example, in his essay 'Sexuality, Diversity and Ethics in the Agenda of Progressive Muslims', Scott A. Kugle explains that the depiction of Paradise in the Qur'an 'is not just bodily, but sensually delightful and even sexually blissful'.[42] According to the fifty-fifth chapter of the Qur'an, for the God-fearing are stored up – *inter alia*

> two gardens containing all kinds [of trees and delights] . . . In each [garden] two springs will flow freely . . . In them will be fruits of every kind . . . and in [the gardens] will be chaste maidens, restraining their glances, whom no man or jinn has touched, [whose complexions] will be like unto rubies and coral.[43]

We read elsewhere that:

> the deserving shall lounge on thrones set in lines,[44] wear fine and thick silk,[45] and that round about them shall go ever-blooming youths bearing goblets and ewers, and cups of pure drink. [And there will be] fruits that they choose, and flesh of fowl that they desire, and fair ones with wide, lovely eyes, like unto hidden pearls.[46]

Nevertheless, the sensual nature of paradisiacal recompense is the subject of debate, having been lampooned in the West.[47]

This positive perspective on sexuality infuses the contribution of the famous jurist al-Suyuti (d. 911/1505) to the subject. He wrote many books on it, the best-known one being *al-Idah fi 'ilm al-nikah*, which he begins with what is quite simply a pastiche in rhymed prose of the traditional Friday sermon. Here are a few significant lines from his prelude:

> Laud to the Lord who adorned the virginal bosom with breasts, and who made the thighs of women anvils for the spear handles of men. Whose lance

point devised for attack of clefts and not of throats. Who made the active worker cushioned coynte to correspond with nice fit and perfect measure all the space that lies betwixt the still unstormed-breach, and the maiden-head unreached.[48]

Nevertheless, Kecia Ali argues that 'Muslims have often been self-congratulatory about the heritage of explicit discussion of sex in legal and literary works, without recognising the pervasive nature of the androcentric in those texts.'[49]

Chastity *('Iffah)* between *'Udhri* and Islamic Discourse

While permissible sexual relationships are described in Islamic sources as great wells of love and closeness for the couple involved, prohibitions against adulterous relationships are equally strong. Adultery is strictly and repeatedly forbidden in the Qur'an.

It could be argued that the concept of *'iffah*/chastity, as it appears in the Qur'an and *sunnah*, is rather strict. Here are some relevant quotations:

'Nor come nigh to adultery: for it is a shameful (deed) and an evil, opening the road (to other evils).'[50]

'The woman and the man guilty of adultery or fornication – flog each of them with a hundred stripes: Let not compassion move you in their case, in a matter prescribed by Allah, if ye believe in Allah and the Last Day: and let a party of the Believers witness their punishment.'[51]

'Let those who find not the wherewithal for marriage keep themselves chaste, until Allah gives them means out of His grace. And if any of your slaves ask for a deed in writing (to enable them to earn their freedom for a certain sum), give them such a deed if ye know any good in them: yea, give them something yourselves out of the means which Allah has given to you. But force not your maids to prostitution when they desire chastity, in order that ye may make a gain in the goods of this life. But if anyone compels them, yet, after such compulsion, is Allah, Oft-Forgiving, Most Merciful (to them).'[52]

'The believers must (eventually) win through. Those who humble themselves in their prayers; Who avoid vain talk; Who are active in deeds of charity; Who abstain from sex, Except with those joined to them in the marriage bond, or (the captives) whom their right hands possess, for (in their case) they are free from blame, But those whose desires exceed those limits are transgressors.'[53]

The story of the prophet Joseph and the wife of the governor of Egypt in the Qur'an shows the prophet's high level of chastity and virtue:

> 'The woman whose house it was solicited him. She barred the doors and said: (come over here). He said: (Allah is my refuge! He is my lord and has been good to me with where I live. Those who do wrong will surely not succeed).'[54]
>
> 'He said: (My Lord, the prison is preferable to me than what they call on me to do. Unless you turn their guile away from me, it may well be that I will fall for them) But she in whose house he was, sought to seduce him from his (true) self: she fastened the doors, and said: "Now come, thou (dear one)!" He said: "(Allah) forbid! truly (thy husband) is my lord! he made my sojourn agreeable! truly to no good come those who do wrong!".'[55]

Therefore, any extramarital sexual intercourse, by persons married or unmarried, is punishable and constitutes the offence of *zina*. In the case of unmarried offenders, the punishment is one hundred lashes, while for married offenders it is being stoned to death. However, in general terms, the *shari'ah* doctrine formulates very strict and rigid specifications for the legal evidence required, without which no punishment can be applied.

In the *sunnah* one finds many examples of the strict prohibition of immoral sexuality. Here are some examples from *Sahih al-Bukhari*:

> Narrated 'Abdullah bin 'Umar: 'The Jew brought to the Prophet a man and a woman from amongst them who have committed (adultery) illegal sexual intercourse. He ordered both of them to be stoned (to death), near the place of offering the funeral prayers beside the mosque.'[56]
>
> Narrated Ibn 'Abbas: I have not seen a thing resembling *'lamam'* (minor sins) than what Abu Hurayra 'narrated from the Prophet who said: 'Allah has written for Adam's son his share of adultery which he commits inevitably. The adultery of the eyes is the sight (to gaze at a forbidden thing), the adultery of the tongue is the talk, and the inner self wishes and desires and the private parts testify all this or deny it.'[57]

Looking at this sort of hadith, al-Ghazali compares the gaze to a poisonous arrow and stresses its sinful implications, justifying the Islamic law's condemnation of gazing as a sin when it is coupled with desire.[58] However, there is no contradiction between the positive attitude towards sexuality and the strict code of chastity in Islamic discourse. If we understand the context, we will see that there is room for both. 'An emphasis on modesty does not necessarily go hand in hand with repressed sexuality or a negative attitude to physical intimacy . . . the two tendencies tend to complement one another.'[59] The combination of passion and purity, between the *houris* who are described as 'longing to cohabit with their husbands' and the same *houris* who are also described as 'pure and undefiled . . . whom no man or jinn has touched' is a reconciliation between modesty and carnality that achieved its balance in this Islamic ideal.[60] Maghen states that:

> Vibrant sexuality and elaborate legalism are, at first glance, strange bedfellows. The former is characterised by the shedding of inhibitions and the loss of control; the latter seeks to instill inhibitions and exert control... The jurisprudential component was thoroughly unhampered, and early on managed to spawn a plethora of intricate provisions concerning the ritual effects of divers sexual situations. Passion, for its part... managed to remain lucid and liberated... The texts in which we read about these matters are themselves a symptom of, and a metaphor for, such comfortable coexistence.[61]

On the other hand, an examination of the concept of chastity/*'iffah* as it appears in *'udhri* tradition suggests a different definition from that which appears in the Qur'an and *sunnah*. As discussed in the first chapter, the *'udhri* poets lived during the Umayyad period; but the *'udhri* tradition was crystallised later on when the collections of *'udhri* poetry were gathered and when the books about the lovers among the Arabs (*'ushshaq al-'Arab*) were produced. Although these books are devoted mainly to *'udhri* love, they are not actually confined to the poets' stories, as narratives about other lovers from different periods are also included. As Jacobi explains:

> In a more realistic strand, *'udhri* love is not so much an emotion or state of mind, but a code of behaviour among lovers. It can be associated with

the literary and social ideal of (*zarif*) refinement, described in detail by al-Washsha'(d. 325/936) in his *kitab al-Muwashsha*.[62]

By examining the *'udhri* poetry and the narratives that appear in *al-Muwashsha* and many other collections of love stories, which all stress the chastity of the lovers, one will find a special concept of chastity that is not necessarily purely Islamic. On a poetic level, the desire to obtain the object of love is expressed repeatedly. Certain characteristic terminology strikes the reader of *'udhri* poetry, such as thirst, nights, touch, saliva, beds, longing, kissing, embrace, appointments and so on. It is irrelevant whether this desire has been satisfied or not as that question belongs to the historical contexts, which is not our concern here. Rather, we are examining the literary context. The poets' expression of their desire and longing for physical contact with the beloved is extreme. For example, Jamil wishes he could spend one night with Buthaynah, talking and kissing:

> Ah me! Shall we ever spend another night like our night until we see the
>   rising of the dawn;
> She showering her words upon me,
> and oft times showering her saliva upon me from her mouth?[63]   [1]

In other verses he shows his readiness to fight Buthaynah's people who were angry when he spent the night with her.

> And I can never forget her family when they came with their swords and
>   surrounded us and said: Jamil has spent the night with her in the camp.
> And they unsheathed their swords and stood there.
> But in the house was I the forest lion,
> and were it not for fear for the soul of Juml [Buthaynah]
> and fear of God they would have been given bloody noses[64]   [2]

He always expresses his longing for his beloved's kisses:

> Do you not know –
> You who have sweet saliva –
> That I shall remain thirsty
> Until I have tasted your sweet?[65]   [3]

He tells Buthaynah:

> And if a skin that is
> not yours touched me
> under my garments
> I will get a rash[66]   [4]

Moreover, he wishes:

> O I wish (though wishes are not enough)
> that I had met with her after the watchmen were asleep.
> How welcome you are as a shawl for a cold lad to make his garment when
>   he fears the chill and the cold[67]   [5]

Such verses and allusions to physicality between the two lovers incited a contemporary scholar to suggest that the marriage union had actually taken place in Jamil's story: Fatmah Tajwar, in her study *al-Marah fi al-shi'r al-Umawi*, argues that Jamil's sensual verses – like the ones quoted above – suggest a marital bond between him and Buthaynah. For example, she cites the verse where the two lovers ask someone from their families to judge and resolve the disagreement between them. Tajwar wonders:

> If the relationship was not public, as in a marital form, would Buthaynah have asked a member of her family to sit in judgment? [She would have been too ashamed to ask a relative if the relationship had not been a marital one]. Would it have been acceptable for a female to make such a request had it only been an affair?[68]

However, in my view, the sensual allusions in Jamil's love poetry do not necessarily indicate his marital union with Buthaynah. We may rather see them in the light of the desire that the poet expressed towards his beloved. Moreover, such allusions are not confined to Jamil, as all the *'udhri* poets express similar wishes, so were they all engaged in a marital union with their beloved? Majnun, for instance, depicts his longing for Layla using several images:

> I see Layla's slip and I envy it – the slip,
> for what it contains, is the object of my envy[69]   [6]

A similar image is found in 'Urwah's poem:

> I wished, out of my passion for 'Afra',[70]
> that I was her Yemeni slip under her chemise   [7]

Qays draws a link between his longing for Lubna and the prophet Idris longing for paradise:

> I long for the perfume of her bosom
> Just as [Prophet] Idris longed for Paradise[71]   [8]

The longing for the beloved to quench the poet's thirst involves poetic images such as thirsty birds and the thirsty fasting person.[72] Qays' verses elaborating on his longing for Lubna are worth examining here:

> See the parched birds which circle round the water night
> and day, but for fear of being beaten never drink their fill
> or come close to the cool ponds
> They see the froth of the water and death together
> and are attentive to the voices of the water bearers
> They are no more afflicted than I am
> with the heat of longing and ardour
> but the enemy has hindered me[73]   [9]

The birds represent the poet himself, or the external equivalent of his desire. These verses contain remarkable terms as they picture the interplay between two contrasting forces: the motivating force (towards water, life and woman) and the force of the resisting obstacle. The birds' persistence in gazing at water that is inaccessible is a metaphor of the poet's persistence in trying to reach the object of his desire, the woman. 'The voices of the water bearers' evokes the sense of deprivation felt by the birds and by their emotional counterpart, the poet. For the poet to reach the life-giving water, he must, paradoxically, cross the terrifying bridge of death.

Majnun states that his remedy is to embrace his beloved.[74] He longs for her to the extent that he wishes to be part of her clothes.[75] One will notice the use of terms such as 'privacy at night' and 'bedfellow'. Qays describes Lubna saying:

> O most perfect of people from head to toe,
> and most beautiful of people clothed or unclothed
> Oh how wonderful you are as a bedfellow just after sleep
> as I pull you towards me full of sleep and wakefulness![76]   [10]

Here, then, the *'udhri* concept of love clearly involves the concept of bodily desire. Similarly, Majnun addresses Layla:

> Ah me! Shall I ever spend a night
> where my beloved sleeps comfortably?[77]   [11]

Yet contemporary scholars such as Ghunaymi Hilal compare the perspective of *'udhri* poets to that of chaste religious people, such as the prophet Joseph who resisted being seduced by the wife of the governor of Egypt.[78] However, those *'udhri* songs about the craving for physical contact with the beloved are, one could argue, far away from the strict concept of chastity as articulated in Joseph's attitude. He prefers to be jailed rather than succumb to the desire of the seductress.

On a narrative level there are several accounts that imply physical contact between *'udhri* lovers, some which have already been mentioned. In one account, for instance, Jamil visited Buthaynah in secret and she hid him for three nights in her home.[79] In any case, it seems that a specific concept of chastity emerged later on in the corpus written about love in general and *'udhri* love in particular.[80] This concept divides the body of a woman into the upper and lower parts. The lover should attain the pleasures of love by captivating the upper part of his beloved, not the lower.[81]

These traditions in love were crystallised later in the ninth and tenth centuries when the books that were concerned with courtly love, and which set the norms for lovers, appeared. Although the tales are set mainly in cities and courts, and the lovers were usually much more refined than the earlier Bedouins, these stories are full of echoes from the early Bedouin lovers, especially *'udhri* ones. Their stories were polished and reproduced in the form of courtly love. The book *al-Muwashsha* is a good example of this genre. Washsha, the author, 'sets forth what the cultivated man, the *zarif* or the *adib* should know [. . .] This *Zarf/adab* ideal sets standards for good manners and decent behaviour in courtship. An integral part of these codes are the concepts of idealised and chaste *'udhri* love.'[82] Within this concept of chaste love the author of *al-Muwashsha* writes:

> To love is to kiss, to touch hand or arm, or to send letters whose spells are stronger than witchcraft. Love is nothing but this: when lovers sleep together, love perishes. The unchaste are only interested in having children.[83]

Likewise, in his treatise on love, where 'he deals with *'ishq* as a universal principle',[84] Ibn Sina states:

> If the purpose of kissing and embracing is to get close to and become one with the lover, these actions are not shunned because one desires to acquire his beloved by touching after gazing at her. Thus, the lover desires to embrace and kiss his beloved. However, if embracing and kissing are followed by sexual intercourse, they are to be refrained from.[85]

Interestingly, this special understanding of *'iffah* appears even in the books written by famous jurists (*fuqaha*) like Ibn Qayyim al-Jawziyyah. In his *Rawdat al-muhibbin* he states that:

> They (the jurists) have made a kiss permissible for one who otherwise fears death saying that not to do so might lead to death, a kiss being a small thing compared to death which is a great thing. When someone becomes ill with two diseases the most serious illness is treated first and there is no danger greater than death. They have even made it mandatory for the beloved to accede to such a thing if it is known that it might otherwise lead to death.[86]

Ibn Qayyim al-Jawziyyah also provides several related anecdotes that show that for someone truly in love, to kiss or embrace is semi-legal, or at least only the kind of minor sin called *lamam*:

> Abu al-Hasan al-Mada'ini said: 'A Muslim once fell in love with a girl in Mecca and desired her but she refused so he said in the words of 'Ata b. Abi Ribah the jurist: 'I asked the Meccan jurist whether there was any sin in the embrace and kiss of one whose heart yearned'. He said: 'God forbid that piety should be taken away by an embrace between two wounded hearts'. She said: 'By God, you asked about 'Ata that and he said you can do this?'

> He said: 'Yes, by God'. So she visited him and said: 'Woe betide you if you go beyond the ruling of 'Ata!'.[87]

Thus it seems that support from jurists for the lovers to reach a certain point in their physical union is forthcoming:

> Al-Zubayr b. Bakkar related from 'Abd al-Malik b. 'Abd al-'Aziz who said: 'Muhammad b. al-Munkadir recited the saying of Waddah al-Yemen: 'She did not yield until I humbled myself in front of her and made her read what God has made allowable regarding derangement *lamam*'. Muhammad laughed and said: 'Waddah was a jurist in his own right!'.[88]

Furthermore, the *'udhri* concept of chastity is clearly declared by a man who was asked: 'Would you like to have your lover tonight?' He said: 'Yes'. He was asked: 'So what would you do?' He said: 'I would obey love by kissing her and disobey Satan by not sinning with her.'[89]

Nevertheless, some theorists draw more flexible boundaries, as does al-Jahiz in *Risalat al-Qiyan*. Ibn Hazm, in his famous eleventh-century love treatise, *Tawq al-Hamamah (The Ring of the Dove)*, expresses puzzlement over why Bedouin tales show the women as being fond of publicity while they have a reputation for chastity:

> I have read in some Bedouin tales that their women-folk do not feel satisfied and convinced that a man is really in love with them until his romantic feelings become public knowledge and are completely divulged; he must advertise and broadcast his attachment, and sing their praises for all to hear. I know not what to make of that, considering they have such a reputation for chastity: what chastity does a woman in fact possess, if her greatest desire and joy is to be notorious after this fashion?[90]

In this passage, Khan notes, a woman 'is portrayed as allowing her name to be appropriated by a male poet in return for a kind of stardom or renown which in turn confers upon her an aesthetic and erotic value prized in courtship rituals'.[91]

Paradoxically, the *'udhri* model in love, and its special treatment of the question of physical contact between the lovers, differs from the strict teaching of Islam on the subject. Islamic teaching highlights the preference for marriage, which the *'udhri* tradition challenges, as will be discussed in the following sections.

Marriage in the *'Udhri* Tradition

Despite all the Islamic encouragement of marriage, it seems that the *'udhri* attitude to it moves in another direction. It is not that the poets fail to express their desire to marry their beloved, but rather, they show the impossibility of its realisation. It seems that the *'udhri* love tale resists the expected and accepted happy ending, simply because the enactment of it will mean the end of the story itself, and, more dangerously, the end of the poetry. If the poet lover did not suffer, he would not compose poetry.[92] Therefore, the resistance, on a narrative level, to marriage between the lovers is understandable in this light.[93]

Considering the *'udhri* corpus, there were, in fact, no real obstacles to marriage between the lovers as they were usually cousins from the same tribe, equal in wealth and social status. In the tale, however, all kinds of difficulties make the marriage impossible. Sometimes the tale claims that the poetry the poet composes about his love prevents him from making his wish come true. Paradoxically, in other contexts, when a poet writes poetry about a woman, her father rewards him. But in the *'udhri* context poetry was considered to be the cause of the lovers' misery. Moreover, whenever the story moves towards union between the lovers, new obstacles appear. This factor helps explain why all the offers from noble people to unite the lovers by marriage always fail. For example, the following narrative is told about Majnun:

> Nawfal (ibn Musahiq)[94] asked him: (Is it love that has brought you to this state?) (Yes) said Majnun, (and it will bring me to a worse state than this). Nawfal asked: (Would you like me to help you marry her?) (Yes) replied Majnun, (is there any possibility of that?) Nawfal replied: (Come with me, I will bring you to her and arrange your engagement to her, making you desirable to her people by [paying her father] your marriage gift. (Will you really do it?) asked Majnun, and Nawfal said: (Yes). Majnun said: (Mark what you are saying). (I will make it my duty to do this for you), said Nawfal. So Nawfal went off with him, and then sent for some clothes. Majnun put them on and went with him like the soundest of companions,

> talking with him and reciting poetry. The news reached Layla's family; they came to meet them with arms and said to Nawfal: (By God, O son of Musahiq, we would die before Majnun enters our house; the Sultan has allowed us to shed his blood with impunity). Nawfal tried his best to persuade them, but they refused. When Nawfal realized that, he told Majnun to go away. Majnun said: (By God, you have not kept your word!). Nawfal answered: (Your departure is easier for me than bloodshed). So he [Majnun] went away.⁹⁵

As can be seen, Nawfal represents authority in this narrative, for he came to collect the alms tax. He met Majnun, empathised with him and tried to help him marry. Nevertheless, a higher authority, in the form of the Sultan, was then introduced into the narrative to prevent Nawfal from achieving his aim. The Sultan permitted others to shed Majnun's blood with impunity. The narrative shows that by choosing matrimonial union, Majnun actually chose death. His own blood stands between him and his beloved.⁹⁶

The *'udhri* narratives go beyond preventing lovers from getting married, indeed even mocking the notion of matrimony itself. In all the *'udhri* stories, the beloved marries a man other than her love. This marriage usually takes place in the first half or middle of the story. Yet 'the love relation does not simply fade or disappear after the time of the marriage. On the contrary, it is itself opposed to the matrimonial bond. The tension between the two relationships – marital and amorous – is, therefore, a crucial factor (in *'udhri* romance)'.⁹⁷ The narratives state that the poet-lover continues to visit his beloved after the marriage, showing no respect for the matrimonial bond. The citation below reveals how Majnun persists in visiting Layla after her marriage takes place:

> Layla's husband and her father departed due to a matter that took the tribe away to Mecca during the night. Then Layla sent her slave-girl to Majnun to extend an invitation to him. So he stayed at her place for a night and she made him leave at daybreak, saying to him: Come to me each night as long as the tribe is away. He [regularly] came to her place until they [father and husband] returned. Concerning the last night of their tryst, when she bade him farewell, he recited:
>
> Enjoy Layla, indeed you are an owl . . .

That each day draws nearer to its death.
Enjoy until the riders return, [for] when they return,
Forbidden to you is her speech.[98]

Likewise, Jamil is reported visiting Buthaynah even after her marriage:

> [Jamil used] to come to her secretly and then she was married. Thereafter, he used to visit her in her husband's house clandestinely until Dajajah b. Rib'iy was appointed governor over the Wadi al-Qur. They complained about [Jamil] to him and he ordered him not to visit her at her home and empowered them to shed his blood with impunity if he resumed visiting her.[99]

Respectively, the episodes quoted above, as Khan points out, 'suggest that the beloved in question voluntarily engages in a consensual bond with her lover. She receives her lover of her own free will even after marriage.'[100] Although *'udhri* love is not a courtly love, one may apply to it what Lewis said about courtly love in mediaeval Europe: 'the poet normally addresses another man's wife and the situation is so carelessly accepted that he seldom concerns himself much with her husband.'[101]

Moreover, it seems that the *'udhri* tradition tends to treat 'husbands' ironically. Certainly, the husband is, like the beloved herself, a victim of social *mores* and customs. He proposes to a certain girl to obtain a normal married life, but then he has to face all the difficulties of being married to the beloved of a poet, while the poetry spreads far and wide the poet's own feelings about her. Yet the narratives do not empathise with the husband as he is often portrayed as an outsider who separates the lovers. Although he lives in an Islamic society where he is supposed to have power and rights, he actually occupies the weakest position in the story. Al-Isfahani states that people in Madinah were singing Qays' poetry about Lubna. So her husband admonished her. She became so angry with him that she told him:

> By God, I did not marry you because I wanted you [...]. I got married because the Sultan would have shed Qays' blood if he came near my tribe, so I wanted to protect him from being murdered by marrying another man. If you want to do so, set me free. I do not need you.

Her husband, al-Isfahani continues, tried to placate her by inviting singers to sing Qays' poetry to her![102]

Consequently, the *'udhri* tradition is not in favour of marriage, in spite of all the virtues that marriage has in Islamic society. Could it be argued that 'the love which is to be the source of all that is beautiful in life and manners must be the reward freely given by the lady, and only our superiors can reward. But a wife is not a superior'?[103] The narratives ensure that the lovers are kept away from the idea of marriage, and, moreover, if the lovers ever did get married, the story would be sure to separate them for one reason or another. The story of Qays and Lubna is typical in this regard. In fact, their love story starts at the moment of separation, when their desperate longing for each other begins. At the same time, the beloved always marries another man, not her lover, and the husband invariably appears as a pathetic and dislikeable character, as mentioned above.

Between Platonic and *'Udhri* Love

The term 'platonic love' seems to take on somewhat different shades of meaning when used in different contexts. Initially, I am citing here two definitions from the *Oxford English Dictionary*, both with a number of examples:

1. Of love, affection, or friendship: intimate and affectionate but not sexual; spiritual rather than physical. Now usually with lower-case initial. 1678 J. NORRIS *Coll. Misc.* (1699) 355 Platonic Love is the Love of Beauty abstracted from all sensual Applications, and desire of Corporal Contact. 1995 *Daily Express* 17 March 29/2 If you have a physical attraction, who wants to remain platonic friends? But if you get into sex, the friendship goes.
2. Of a person: that feels or professes platonic love; that has a non-sexual relationship. 1709 R. STEELE *Tatler* No. 32. 3 This Order of Platonick Ladies are to be dealt with in a peculiar Manner from all the rest of the Sex.

Thus, the popular understanding of platonic love 'is a non-sexual affectionate relationship. A simple example of platonic relationships is a deep, non-sexual friendship, not subject to gender pairings and including close relatives.'[104]

However, this interpretation shows a misunderstanding of the true nature of the platonic ideal of love that, from its origin, was that of a chaste but strong love, that was believed to be elevated above sex.[105] In his book about platonic love, Gould argues that Plato assumes love to be the key to civilisation, art, justice and all great, brave acts in the world, while the Christians and Romantics, in different ways, thought that love destroyed society or was an effort to escape from it.[106] Moreover, love is the key to everything important in life. Without it, neither thought nor activity is profitable or possible.[107] Gould adds that platonic love could not find fulfillment solely in physical pleasures.[108]

Several scholars use the term 'platonic love' to describe *'udhri* love. For example, Massignon, in the first edition of the *Encyclopedia of Islam,* claims that *''udhri* love is related to the platonic love of the Greeks from which it is derived';[109] and Kinany says that *'udhri* love is a sort of platonic love.[110] Likewise, Grunebaum pointed to close parallels between *'udhri* and Greek love poems and apparently saw the root of *'udhri* behaviour in a Greek influence.[111]

However, *'udhri* love as presented in poetry and stories ascribed to or told about *'udhri* poets is far removed from the concept of platonic love. This idea has not escaped the notice of many scholars who have, in fact, challenged the concept of *'udhri* love as platonic love. In the new edition of the *Encyclopedia of Islam*, for example, Renate Jacobi writes: *''udhri* love in the seventh century is neither platonic nor courtly, not even sentimental'.[112] Al-Jawari, likewise, dedicates numerous pages in his book to making a clear distinction between *'udhri* love and platonic love. His argument relies on various facts, such as the Arabs being unaware of Greek philosophy when *'udhri* love appeared among them. Also, *'udhri* love emerged in the desert among Bedouin, far away from the intellectual influence that was present in towns and cities. Moreover, *'udhri* love is a poetic expression, while platonic love is a philosophical idea.[113] Likewise, Sulayman lists various factors that distinguish *'udhri* love from platonic love. He argues that platonic love is a means towards creation and creativity. Thus, it is not an end in itself. On the other hand, *'udhri* love is indeed an end in itself. In platonic love, you must have someone to guide you and show you goodness and beauty. However, you will not realise absolute beauty until you are literally burned with the fire of knowledge, in order to fully appreciate art and to gain wisdom. Nothing of that sort exists in ʿudhri love. Also, platonic love has a final aim, which is God or absolute beauty, whereas ʿudhri love is all about lovers.[114]

Conclusion

In this chapter I have studied the association of ʿudhri love with chastity by exploring the concept of chastity in Islamic discourse on the one hand and the representation of this concept in the ʿudhri tradition on the other. Evidently, the view of chastity as it appears in the Qurʾan and *sunnah* is rather strict and it establishes a high standard of virtue. Nonetheless, ʿudhri theory and practice, as crystallised in ʿudhri poetry and books that have dealt with the ʿudhri phenomenon, suggest a different view of chastity. It could be argued that this view divides the body of a woman into the upper and lower parts. The lover should obtain the pleasures of love by captivating the upper part of his beloved, not the lower. It seems that ʿudhri poets – according to the ʿudhri corpus – were distanced from the notion of marriage in direct contrast to the encouragement of marriage that Islam favours. As we have discussed, Islamic discourse around marriage is positive, marriage being highly favoured among Muslims. The Prophet's hadiths and his personal life are good examples of this view. But the entire ʿudhri tradition challenged the possibility of a marital bond between ʿudhri lovers. Even if they were married, like Qays and Lubna, the narratives would separate them in order to inflame their yearning, which is, after all, the main theme of ʿudhri poetry. Moreover, the poets continued to visit their beloved, in spite of the fact that they were married to other men and the beloved's husband is always treated unsympathetically, making him appear pathetic and hateful. In addition, while the Islamic attitude emphasises the aspect of reproduction as the result of sexual enjoyment, the ʿudhri tradition provides no trace of children. Indeed, the beloved is usually depicted in an ethereal manner with no hint of potential motherhood, as will be seen in the next chapter.

Notes

1. In the *OED* these definitions are provided for chastity: 1) Purity from unlawful sexual intercourse; continence. 2) Abstinence from all sexual intercourse;

virginity, celibacy. 3) Exclusion of meretricious ornament; purity of style, modesty, chasteness. On the other hand, in *Lisan al-'Arab*, *'iffah* it is defined as: refraining from all that is forbidden. To refrain oneself from greed and what is forbidden by religion. A chaste woman: a woman who protects her private parts. As we can see, the first definition of chastity is very close to the definition of *'iffah*.

2. Maghen, *Virtues of the Flesh – Passion and Purity in Early Islamic Jurisprudence*, p. 119.
3. Ibid.
4. Ibid., pp. 120–5. There are many examples of these anecdotes and a number of them were quoted by Maghen and ascribed to Muslim women like Umm Sulaym, who made this statement during her inquiry to the Prophet about a sensitive issue: 'God is not embarrassed by the truth'.
5. Ibid., p. 129.
6. Ibid., p. 133.
7. Ibid.
8. Al-Balad (90:9), Al-Infitar (82:6–8).
9. Al-Mu'minun (23:12–14).
10. 'Urawi, 'Mustawayat hudur al-Jasad fi al-khitab al-qur'ani', *'Alam al-fikr* (37:4), p. 17.
11. Al-A'raf (8:32).
12. 'Urawi, *'Mustawayat'*, pp. 17–21.
13. Al-Ghashiyah (88:7–8).
14. Al-Hajj (22:23).
15. 'Urawi, *'Mustawayat'*, p. 29.
16. The question of the body in Islam is mishandled in Fuad Khuri's contribution on this subject. In his book *The Body in Islamic Culture*, he tackles the question of the body in Islam from too narrow a perspective. For instance, he examines the Qur'anic verses only superficially, ignoring their various interpretations. He claims that the same anecdote about Adam and Eve occurs in both the Old Testament and the Qur'an. However, it is clearly stated in the Old Testament that is was Eve who was tempted by Satan to eat the forbidden fruit, and that she, in turn, tempted Adam to eat it, while the Qur'an states that both Adam and Eve were tempted by Satan. Satan, trying to seduce him [Adam], said: '"Do you want me to show you the Tree of Eternity and the Everlasting Kingdom?" Adam and his wife [Eve] ate [the fruit] from the tree and found themselves naked. Then they began to cover themselves with the leaves from

the Garden. Adam disobeyed his Lord and went astray. His Lord accepted his repentance, forgave him and gave him guidance.' (20:120–122). Moreover, the notion of the essential impurity of women is rejected in Islam. Nevertheless, to support his idea of the preference for virgin brides in Islam, Khuri quotes certain verses from the Qur'an, apparently without realising that they refer to *al-hūr al-'ayn* in Paradise, not to earthly women. On the same page, he quotes the following hadith: 'A woman is contracted in marriage for her looks, wealth, or noble origin.' However, he neglects to complete this hadith: 'So try to obtain one who is religious, may your hand be besmeared with dust [may you enjoy the benefits]'. These omissions and misreading betray a bias or blind spot in Khuri's interpretation of Islamic discourse around sexuality.

17. Al-Baqarah (2:183–7).
18. Al-Mu'minun (23:12–17).
19. *An Islamic Perspective on Sexuality*, by the Muslim Women's League, http://www.mwlusa.org/topics/sexuality/sexuality_pos.htmlH, 5 November 2007.
20. Al-Rum (30:21).
21. Franz Rosenthal, 'Fiction and Reality: Sources of the Role of Sex in Medieval Muslim Society', in al-Sayyid-Marsot, *Society and the Sexes in Medieval Islam*, p. 4.
22. Bouhdiba, *Sexuality in Islam*, p. 6. This, of course, reflects Bouhdiba's personal interpretation of Islam.
23. See, for example, Al-Nisa' (3: 22), Al-Nur (24: 32).
24. Bouhdiba, *Sexuality*, pp. 90–1.
25. Ibid., p.91.
26. See, for instance, Kamal, *Islam and Sacred Sexuality*, www.gaia.web.org.waia-wicca , 12 June 2006.
27. The acceptance of sexuality as a healthy aspect of life is a decisive cultural difference between Arabic and Western religious thinking, also reflected in their different versions of Paradise. See Behrens-Abouseif, *Beauty in Arabic Culture*, p. 70.
28. James A. Bellamy, 'Sex and Society in Islamic Popular Literature', in al-Sayyid-Marsot, *Society and the Sexes in Medieval Islam*, p. 32.
29. Al-Qushayri, *Sahih Muslim*, Vol. 2, Book 5, No. 3231, p. 703.
30. Al-Bukhari, *Sahih al-Bukhari*.
31. Al-Ghazali, *Ihya 'ulum al-din*, p. 86.
32. Bellamy, 'Sex and Society', p. 30.
33. In the early period of Islam, Bellamy says, there was a movement in favour of

celibacy. He quotes the following hadith: 'Abdullah b. 'Umar related that once they were on a raid and had no means [of sexual gratification]. They asked: "Why do we not castrate ourselves?" But the Prophet forbade that.' He argues that centuries later, celibacy reappeared among the Sufis. He highlights the attitude of some of the later Sufis such as Ibrahim b. Adham and Bishr al-Hafi, the latter fearing that he would be an executioner on the bridge if he had a family. In general, they worried about being distracted by worldly concerns from the worship of God. The same point is made by al-Ghazali, who recommended the Sufi murid to avoid marriage at the beginning of his career. For more details see Bellamy, 'Sex and Society', pp. 32–4.
34. Al-Qushayri, *Sahih Muslim*, Vol. 2, Book 5, No. 2198, p. 482.
35. Bouhdiba, *Sexuality*, pp. 12–13.
36. Al-Nur (24:32).
37. Al-Bayhaqi, *Kitab shu'ab al-'iman*, http://www.ahlalhdeeth.com/vb/show thread.php?t=23108, 14 January 2009.
38. Bouhdiba, *Sexuality*, p. 91.
39. 'Issa, *Al-jins wa 'ulama al-Islam*.
40. Ibid., p. 104.
41. Bouhdiba, *Sexuality*, p. 117.
42. Kugle, *Sexuality, Diversity and Ethics in the Agenda of Progressive Muslims*, http://www.geocities.com/vidyak1/scottkugledoc.pdf, 5 June 2005.
43. Al-Rahman (55:46–58).
44. Al-Ttur (52:20).
45. Al-Dukhan (44:54).
46. Al-Waqi'ah (56:17–23).
47. The Muslim attribution of this worldly voluptuousness to the other world (the *akhirah*) provoked an uncharacteristically violent outburst from the Jewish *mutakallim* Moses Maimonides. About a century after Maimonides, a text known as *The Travels of Sir John Mandeville* – while actually praising many Muslim beliefs and institutions – describes the Islamic notion of paradise with an unmistakable hint of derision. For more details see Maghen, *Virtues*, pp. 6–7. However, we should note that the travels have long been recognised as spurious and later than they purport to be.
48. Al-Suyuti, *The Book of Exposition*, pp. 1–2. Note that parts of this translation are grammatically and idiomatically nonsensical.
49. Ali, *Sexual Ethics and Islam. Feminist Reflections on Qur'an, Hadith, and Jurisprudence*, p. xxxvi.

50. Al-Isra' (17:32).
51. Al-Nur (24:2). Harsh modern commentators are often quick to note that the punishment prescribed for adultery is mitigated by the impracticality of meeting its requirement for being applied: the testimonies of four eyewitnesses to the act (24:13). Many today consider this to mean it is an almost purely symbolic way of denoting the severity of the offence, while others consider it a legally required punishment.
52. Al-Nur (24:33).
53. Al-Mu'minun (23:1–7).
54. Yusuf (12:23).
55. Ibid.
56. Al-Bukhari, *Sahih al-Bukhari*, Vol. 2, Book 23, No. 413.
57. Ibid., Vol. 8, Book 74, No. 260.
58. Al-Ghazali, *The Alchemy of Happiness*, p. 97.
59. Maghen, *Virtues,* p. 112.
60. Ibid.
61. Ibid., p. 281.
62. Jacobi, ''Udhri', p. 776.
63. Jamil, *Diwan*, p. 38.
64. Ibid., p. 59.
65. Ibid., p. 107. See also p. 24. Yet some contemporary scholars, such as Faysal, warn us not to have any ill thoughts about this verse: Faysal, *Tatawwur al-ghazal*, p. 287.
66. Ibid., p. 20.
67. Ibid., p. 118.
68. Fatmah Tajwar, *al-Marah fi al-shi'r al-Umawi*, p. 131.
69. Majnun, *Diwan*, p. 71.
70. 'Urwah, *Diwan*, p. 51.
71. Qays, *Diwan*, p. 124.
72. Majnun, *Diwan*, pp. 170, 182.
73. Qays, *Diwan*, p. 155. Qays used the word '*haimat*', which can mean either birds or camels. However, I chose to interpret it as birds.
74. Majnun, *Diwan*, p. 163.
75. Ibid., p. 76
76. Qays, *Diwan*, p. 109.
77. Majnun, *Diwan*, p. 140.
78. Hilal, *al-Hayah al-'atifiyyah*, pp. 34–5.

79. See more examples about Jamil's and Buthaynah's relationship in al-Isfahani, *Al-Aghani*, Vol. 8, pp. 300, 304, 305.
80. I am referring particularly to *Rawdat al-muhibbin* pp. 210–14 and *al-Muwashsha* pp. 125–9.
81. Al-Ibshihi, *al-Mustatraf fi kull fann mustadhraf*, p. 402.
82. Giffen, *Theory of Profane Love*, p. 14.
83. Washsha, *al-Muwashsha*, p. 209.
84. Giffen, *Theory of Profane Love*, p. 146.
85. Ibn Sina, cited in al-Hufi, *al-Ghazal*, p. 148.
86. Ibn Qayyim, *Rawdat*, pp. 129–30.
87. Ibid., p. 329. The same verses appear in *Tazyin al-aswaq*, although the Meccan jurist refers to al-Shafi'i. An interpretation is provided there to the verses: a newly married man asks whether or not he can embrace his wife during Ramadan while he is fasting.
88. Ibid.
89. Ibid. Likewise, Ibn Hazm's *Tawq* contains much evidence that stolen glances and even stolen pleasures were fairly common among 'good' people. See pp. 183–8 of his book.
90. Ibn Hazm, *Tawq*, p. 86.
91. Khan, *Sexuality and Secrecy*, p. 266.
92. The link between composing poetry and an unattainable beloved will be discussed in detail in Chapter Seven.
93. On the other context, considering western courtly love, Lewis states that: 'courtly love excludes love from the marriage relation'. *The Allegory Of Love. A Study In Medieval Tradition*.
94. He came to the tribe to collect the alms tax.
95. Ibn Qutaybah, *al-Shi'r wa al-shu'ara*, Vol. 2, p. 565, trans. Khairallah, *Love*, p. 137.
96. In Ahmad Shawqi's treatment of the Majnun legend in his modern poetic play *Majnun Layla*, he portrays Nawfal trying to help Majnun by conversing with Layla's people, but her people were armed and ready to take Majnun's life. They did not listen to Nawfal, and they wanted to marry off Layla to another man called Ward. Interestingly, Shawqi makes Majnun's *ghazal* for Layla the chief motivation that persuaded Ward to propose to her. Nevertheless, according to the play, Layla remained a virgin after her marriage as Majnun's strong presence stood between her and her husband. See Shawqi, *Majnun Layla*.
97. Khan, *Sexuality and Secrecy*, p. 278.

98. Al-Isfahani, *Al-Aghani*, Vol. 2, p. 376, trans. Khan, *Sexuality and Secrecy*, pp. 303–4.
99. Al-Isfahani, *Al-Aghani*, Vol. 8, p. 300, trans. Khan, *Sexuality and Secrecy*, p. 305.
100. Khan, *Sexuality and Secrecy*, p. 305.
101. Lewis, *Allegory Of Love*, pp. 2–3.
102. Al-Isfahani, *Al-Aghani*, Vol. 9, p. 143.
103. Lewis, *Allegory Of Love*, p. 36.
104. http://en.wikipedia.org/wiki/Platonic_love. 3 March 2010.
105. Ibid.
106. Gould, *Platonic Love*, p. 23.
107. Ibid., p. 47.
108. Ibid., p. 56.
109. Massignon, '*Udhri*', *Encyclopedia of Islam*, p. 990.
110. Kinany, *Development*, p. 7.
111. Grunebaum in Bürgel, '*Love*', p. 92.
112. Jacobi, '*Udhri*', p. 776.
113. Al-Jawari, *al-Hubb al-'udhri*, p. 64.
114. Sulayman, *al-Hubb al-'udhri*, pp. 58, 59. See the similar argument by Ihsan al-Nass, *al-Ghazal*, p. 26.

4

The Representation of the Beloved's Body

Introduction

Studying the *'udhri ghazal* reveals that the body enjoys a prominent and significant position in it and involves both the beloved and the lover. This chapter will concentrate on the depiction of the beloved's body. Certainly, focusing on the bodily presence in *'udhri* poetry does not imply a denial of intellectual aspects, but the discussion of those aspects is beyond the purpose of this chapter. This is not to say that the intellectual aspects of *'udhri* poetry will be set aside. In fact, it can be argued that studying the body provokes a challenge to the classical distinction in Islamic culture between the body and the soul. This distinction can be found particularly in Sufi discourse, where the flesh is afflicted and thus the subject seeks an escape from this world and its material rewards and pleasures. Al-Ghazali, for example, clearly distinguishes between the body (*badan*) and the soul (*nafs*) in his refutation of the philosophers' statement that it is impossible for human souls to undergo annihilation after having come into existence.[1] According to the Persian mystic Farid al-Din 'Attar, the body is the soul's cage; in the hereafter the body will become soul, and one must prepare for it in this world.[2] Ibn al-Nafis, the physician and theologian, says: 'Man is composed of body and soul: the body is this thing which can be perceived, but the soul is that to which one refers when one says: "I".'[3]

However, salient aspects of the religious system, as Maghen argues, limited the extent and effect of Sufi preaching that separated and subordinated the body. One of these factors was the pervasive Islamic outlook reflected in Qur'anic statements such as: 'O you who believe! Do not prohibit the good things which God has permitted you'.[4] Another factor was the blatantly sensual nature of paradise, and the third was *taharah*, the deeply entrenched and omnipresent Islamic code of ritual purity.⁵

The symbolic body will receive discussion in Chapter Five. In this chapter I will focus only on the depiction of the body of the beloved. I will begin by examining the images used to portray female beauty in the *'udhri ghazal*, with the link between this portrayal and the conventional pattern of female beauty as suggested throughout classical Arabic poetry in general. Next, I will look at the question of the stereotypical image of female beauty in both Arabic poetry and Persian paintings; hence, I will provide a comparison between Layla's physical portrayal in Majnun's poetry and later Persian painting. This will lead me to investigate the stereotypical image of the desirable woman in classical Arabic literature in general, and in the *'udhri ghazal* in particular: the image of a corpulent woman. Thus I intend to discuss this desirable image of a woman in the light of its origins in ancient Arab culture. Although the *'udhri ghazal* makes use of tropes and metaphors that were inherited from the pre-Islamic period, nevertheless it moves away from the old tradition by emphasising the ethereal aspect of female beauty. Therefore, I will look at the notion of sublimated beauty in the *'udhri ghazal* and its link with the notion of time, eternal beauty, and love. I will end by examining the theme of the beauty of the beloved that leads to the death of the lover.

The Conventional Model of Female Beauty, with Special Reference to Pre-Islamic Literature

The importance of the body in classical Arabic literary discourse is undoubted. Common themes found in this discourse include such topics as sexuality and eroticism, the feminine ideal, the concept of virility, and so on.⁶ A specialised sub-set of literature developed around describing female beauty:

> Human beauty was a major topic in Arabic aesthetic discourse, and the only subject besides calligraphy of which aesthetic canons were compiled. A special literature deals with female beauty, describing in detail its types, forms, colours, and proportions, and setting criteria for perfection. It also includes a discussion of the tastes and predilections of religious and historic

persons for certain women. A large variety of terms were used to describe types of female beauty and grades of beauty and sex appeal.[7]

Therefore, this literature governed the conventional desirable elements of female beauty and defined it within certain parameters. The general criteria of beauty remain almost the same in both the pre-Islamic and early Islamic periods. The later depiction of this beauty was derived from the inherited depiction found in pre-Islamic literature.

Figurative language associated with female beauty involves metaphors based upon the oryx and the doe, ivory, silver, pure water, sand dunes, grapes, wine, the sun, the moon, and so on. It is significant, however, that these metaphorical possibilities are not limited to poetry. In fact, one of the oldest passages describing the female body – attributed to the pre-Islamic period – appeared in prose form. This passage is attributed to a woman who was sent to observe another woman's body in order to describe it to the king of the Kindah tribe, 'Amr b. Hijr, the grandfather of the famous poet Imru' al-Qays. The king wanted to marry the daughter of 'Awf b. Mihlam al-Shaybani. 'Awf's daughter was called Umm-Iyas, a brilliant and very beautiful girl. 'Amr b. Hijr sent a clever woman called 'Isam to observe Umm-Iyas so that she could describe her to him and report whether what he had heard about her beauty was accurate or not. Hence, 'Isam went there and saw Umm-Iyas, then returned to the King and described what she had seen. Her discourse recorded the criteria for female beauty. I am quoting 'Isam's description of Umm-Iyas at length in order to show how significant and comprehensive this text is in terms of representing female beauty:

> Umm-Iyas's forehead is as clear and beautiful as a gleaming mirror covered with completely dark hair just like that of a braided horse tail; her black tresses appear like chains, and when she combs them, they look like clusters of grapes washed by heavy rain. Moreover, her eyebrows are very well-designed as if they were drawn by a pen, and dark as if they were coloured by carbon. They are curved around her beautiful eyes which look like the eyes of a beautiful bird. Umm-Iyas's nose which is neither long nor short is as sharp as the blade of a beautiful polished sword. Furthermore, her cheeks are a purplish colour and snow-white as pearls. She has a wonderful

small mouth with a charming smile, cheerful prominent white incisors and pearl-like teeth; in addition, her saliva smells like wine and tastes like honey; let alone her lips which are red like flowers. She is eloquent, clever and quick-witted and she has a beautiful neck which is like a jug made of silver. She has fleshy arms which make you think that they are boneless and have no veins; additionally, she has soft hands and her breasts are just like two pomegranates. Besides, her abdomen is neither fat nor thin and is rolled up like folded compacted cobatti.[8] She also has a navel like a shining piece of ivory that is used for painting. Further, her back is like a stream of water which ends at a fascinating waist. Beneath it there are rumps which force her to sit when she tries to get up, and make her look as if she is standing when she sits. Her rumps are like a little heap of soil matted by drizzle and they are carried by rounded thighs which look like tiered palm pith, and the thighs are carried by fleshy shanks with dark hair. All these parts are carried by two arrowheads like small feet. May God bless them, how can they tolerate all of that weight? Finally, I do not want to describe the rest of it;[9] however, it is more beautiful than any description – whether in prose or in poetry.[10] [1]

Consequently, 'Amr b. Hijr immediately proposed to Umm-Iyas.

This precise description of the female body is almost the same description that we encounter in the poets' portrayal of their beloveds. This woman, Umm-Iyas, has certain elements of beauty that Imru' al-Qays' Fatimah has, or al-A'sha's Hurayrah has, and so on. The description begins from top to toe, from what is seen and known (such as the face) to what is unseen (such as the private parts). The woman who describes the body draws a parallel between it and certain natural elements. Her report goes much further than mere observation and is enhanced by her claims about the sweet taste of Umm-Iyas's saliva. Therefore, 'Isam is seeing Umm-Iyas with masculine eyes, rather than with her own, through her detailed description of Umm-Iyas' physical beauty. Her description indicates the overwhelming influence of the prevailing discourse at that time on classical Arabic culture.[11]

In the light of this, one can understand the power that the desirable image of the female body has over literary expression. The following verses from pre-Islamic poetry present the authoritative image of an attractive woman:

> She shows you when you enter privily with her
> And she is secure from the eyes of the hateful foemen (…)
> A soft breast like a casket of ivory
> Chastely guarded from adventurous fingers,
> The flanks of a lithe, long, tender body,
> Buttocks oppressed by their ponderous cargo[12] [2]

As we can see, these classical verses reflect the dominant concepts of female beauty. The breast shines like 'ivory', the body is 'tender', buttocks 'oppressed by their ponderous cargo', and so on. In Imru' al-Qays' *Mu'allaqah* similar elements appear in depicting his woman:

> I twisted her side-tresses to me, and she leaned over me; Slender-waisted
>   she was, and tenderly plump her ankles,
> Shapely and taut her belly, white-fleshed, not the least flabby,
> Polished the lie of her breast bones, smooth as a burnished mirror…
> She turns away, to show a soft cheek, and wards me off
> With the glance of a wild deer of *Wajra*, a shy gazelle with its fawn;
> She shows me a throat like the throat of an antelope not ungainly when
>   she lifts it upwards, neither naked of ornament[13] [3]

Once again, the whiteness of the skin, softness of the body, slenderness of waist, and a general resemblance to deer and antelope are emphasised. 'The names vary but it is, from top to toe, always the same woman: all pampered softness, languor, plenitude.'[14] Moving to the early Islamic period, the *nasib*[15] celebrates the same image of a desirable woman:

> On the morning of
> departure when her tribe set out
> Su'ad was but a bleating antelope
> with languid gaze and kohl-lined eye…
> When she smiles she flashes
> side teeth wet
> as if with a first draught of wine
> or with a second,
> mixed with cool water from a *wadi*'s bend…[16] [4]

So, it is not an individual – whether she be Su'ad or Fatimah or 'Ablah – who emerges, but rather it is the perfect image of a beautiful woman that we see. These previously cited verses and many others indicate that the '[poem] has less to do perhaps with the poet's experience than with the audience's expectations',[17] as it provides the stereotype of female beauty and establishes a poetic figurative language to represent it.

Moving to the *'udhri ghazal*, some motifs in the poem are developed in various aspects beyond what they were in the poems just mentioned. Before the Umayyad age, the *nasib* used to be the prelude, or the opening section, of every poem. Poets would begin their poems by expressing their longing for a woman, describing her beauty, and crying at her campsite ruin. Then the poems would move onto different themes such as eulogies and satire. However, in the Umayyad age love poetry in the form of the *ghazal* emerges as an independent genre among *'udhri* and other poets who dedicated their poetry to love, such as 'Umar b. Abi Rabi'ah. Therefore, in the *'udhri* tradition the *ghazal* is not just the opening section of a poem (the *nasib* of a *qasidah*) any more, but it becomes an independent *qasidah* itself, and the entire poem addresses the theme of love. Apart from Kuthayyir, who was often with the caliph and composed praise poems to him, *'udhri* poets also limited their poetry to the theme of love and they never composed eulogies. Furthermore, their intentions differed from those of previous poets; their motives for composing love poetry were not just aesthetic but also psychological or emotional.[18]

'Udhri poets add several elements to the *ghazal*. These elements include themes such as devotion in love. They abandon the motif of halting at the ruined campsite. They also include the use of simple language and their dedication to only one subject instead of many.[19] Nonetheless, when it comes to depicting the beloved's beauty, these poets adopted a similar image to what had been established since the pre-Islamic *nasib*. Therefore, the physical descriptions of Layla, Lubna, Buthaynah, 'Afra and 'Azzah are very much the same as the description of Fatimah and 'Ablah from the *Mu'allaqat*. It is always the same features that are stressed: tallness, whiteness, big eyes, long neck, ample bosom, slender waist, heavy hips and plump legs. 'There are a multitude of such poetic descriptions, differing little in content, the pre-Islamic pattern having been for centuries copied without much variation.'[20]

The following section will discuss in detail the depiction of the beloved's body in the *'udhri ghazal* and will illustrate how this depiction resembles the old poetic norms. However, the following discussion will also show that there is an attempt by *'udhri* poets to distinguish themselves from the previous poets by stressing the ethereal nature of their beloved's beauty. This phenomenon gives the *'udhri ghazal* its own distinctive nature among other classical *ghazal*s in spite of their similar depictions of the female body.

Corporeal Representation: the Physical Description of the Beloved's Body

By its focus on corporeal representation, the *'udhri* poem celebrates the beloved's beauty in all its glory, as will be described in detail. Thus, the reader of *'udhri* poetry will encounter a plethora of detailed description about the beloved's desirable body. This section will further examine this motif through highlighting several aspects of the beloved's beauty, as shown in *'udhri* poetry, such as her glow, face, scent and figure.

It will also explore the metaphoric image of the beloved as a 'gazelle' along with its mythic associations.

The glow of the beloved

The verses of Majnun, Qays, Jamil and Kuthayyir depict the beloved as a resplendent beauty with a white, unblemished face like the full moon. This face is not only dazzling like the moon;[21] moreover, and more frequently, it is bright like the sun.[22] On the one hand, the beloved's resplendence resembles the moon or the sun, on the other hand, the moon and sun themselves are incapable of emulating her brilliant light. She makes them feel shy in her presence. Majnun declares:

> I was poured a drink by a sun whose light put the full moon to shame
> and who outshone the lightning when it flashes[23]   [5]

Yet the fullest moon would be eclipsed by the light of her presence.[24] In comparison with pre-Islamic poetry, the theme of the woman's glow and her resemblance to objects such as a beacon, a lamp and the sun often appears in the pre-Islamic *ghazal*.[25] For example, when Imru' al-Qays describes his beloved's face he says:

> In the evening she lights up the darkness
> As though she were the light in the place
> Where the hermit performs his eventide devotions[26]   [6]

However, the *'udhri* poets do not simply link the pure hue of their beloveds' faces with the light of sun as Tarafah, for instance, does in his *mu'allaqah*.[27] *'Udhri* poets go further in the comparison between the beloved and the sun. Kuthayyir even places 'Azzah in a situation of going to court, so that the judge Muwaffaq should state who is the more beautiful: 'Azzah or the sun?[28]

The contest between Layla on the one hand, and the sun and the moon on the other, is always won by Layla's beauty:[29]

> Illuminate the world instead of the moon when it
> declines, and play the role of the sun whenever the dawn is
> late, because you have the radiance of the sun,
> and the sun does not have your beautiful mouth
> and your charming smile,
> You have the sparkling moonlight
> but the moon does not have your gorgeous breasts,
> and your attractive upper chest,
> The shining sun in the forenoon
> can neither have eyes full of pathos, eyes darkened with kohl,
> nor Layla's special charming characteristics,
> The sun cannot also appear like Layla,
> who looks like a frightened oryx,
> when she bows because of her coquetry[30]   [7]

Using the words 'moon', 'dawn', 'sun' (*badr, fajr, shams*) reveals a tendency to abstract the beloved from her physical attributes by making her resemble ephemeral elements such as light. The eyes of the lover see the beloved with a shining face whose eyes are filled with light to such an extent that these eyes are more glittering and shining than sunlight itself. Thus, the body of the beloved is not perceived in concrete terms like other elements in life, but as glittering and soft as light. Majnun states:

They said: where does she live?
Who is she?
I said: she is the sun, the sky is her home[31] [8]

The sun is a key source of life on earth. Majnun realises the power of the sun and its high state. No one can reach it, while it can reach every thing on earth. Therefore, depicting Layla as the sun is a theme repeated in many verses composed by Majnun:

I say to my companions:
'She is the sun – her light is close but she is too distant to touch'[32] [9]

'Ali al-Batal argues that the resemblance between the sun and woman in classical Arabic poetry has its roots in ancient Arab mythology. The sun was one of the gods that used to be worshipped by the ancient Arabs. They ascribed characteristics of motherhood to the sun, conceiving it as the Mother god, which is why the sun is referred to as being female. Therefore, a woman described as a sun in Arabic poetry is evidence of this link.[33] However, in Islamic poetry these religious images were transferred to artistic models, so that the sun-woman metaphor was removed from its ancient mythic setting to a new rational setting, in which the sun is not the Mother god that gives life, but resembles the woman in her aloofness and radiance.[34] This can be seen clearly when Majnun says to his friends that she (Layla) is the sun; her light is visible while her actual figure is not palpable.[35]

It is clear, moreover, that this insistence on the beloved's light complexion is meant to reflect her interior serenity. Jamil compares Buthaynah's luminescence with the light that illuminates everything around her.[36] The lucent face could indicate one's inner peacefulness. The tradition that demonstrates that a beautiful believer is the utmost perfection and an ugly unbeliever is the utmost ugliness,[37] or the saying that beautiful people are auspicious,[38] should not escape our notice here.

The beloved and the metaphor of the gazelle in 'udhri *poetry*

The beloved's eyes shoot darts and wound the heart not the skin.[39] Beautiful eyes are described as big and black with brilliant whites, *hawra* and *najla*.[40]

Qays refers to these eyes as drowsy and says they pose a possible threat to his own life:

> Proclaim for my blood, if I die
> From a maiden who has languid and drowsy eyes[41] [10]

Nevertheless, the most significant fact about the depiction of the beloved's eyes is their resemblance to those of a deer and doe.[42] Majnun states that Layla's eyes, while gazing at him, are more beautiful than a deer's black doting eyes whilst looking after its fawn.[43] Jamil, likewise, sometimes describes Buthaynah's eyes as white antelope's eyes, and as brocket's eyes on other occasions.[44]

In fact, the comparison of the beloved with a gazelle is one of the major topoi of classical Arabic love poetry. In his long description of the beauty of his beloved, Imru' al-Qays uses this comparison, as we have seen in his aforementioned verses.[45] The image of a lonely frightened deer left behind with her little fawn becomes a parallel image to that of the beloved, who is described as having the same big dark eyes and the same long neck. This is an important theme within *'udhri* poetry, as Jamil repeats this image three or four times[46], and Majnun adopts it as a core motif of the similes in his poetry. Layla is often portrayed as a gazelle in Majnun's verses; he even declares that the gazelle is almost Layla herself, except of course, for the antlers.[47] Layla's neck, in particular, is depicted like the neck of a gazelle.[48] Kuthayyir offers a series of images in order to achieve the position where the beloved is as beautiful as, or more than, a doe:

> The white-breasted shining-backed gazelle,
> who takes her young to the cool of the shade
> and scratches with her horns the fruit of an Arak tree
> and reaches with her hooves if the branches are high,
> is no more beautiful of eye or neck or throat than she
> when she wears her finery[49] [11]

He also says:

> She captured me with the eyes of a gazelle
> who is accompanied by her white new-born to the Arak trees

in the bend of the *wadi* of Bisha
where the plaintive doves sing;
as if those doves who called loudly in the morning
become at noon chanting songstresses for wine-drinkers[50]   [12]

This doe is usually a white deer (*rim*). Once again, whiteness is stressed in the *'udhri ghazal*. Reading Sells' analysis of some classical Arabic poems, I would also argue that in these verses quoted above, the poet 'set up a descriptive point only to be overrun through the semantic overflow of the passage. The movement of the poem continually overflows the descriptive points the simile poses.'[51] The metaphor introduced here is that of the beloved as a doe. Kuthayyir introduces the doe apparently as a metaphor for the beloved by saying: 'she captured me with a doe's eyes'. Nevertheless, the poet becomes preoccupied with the depiction of the doe and forgets his original motivation: a description of the beloved. The doe is shaking Arak berries. In the other verses the doe is following her fawn to Arak, where the doves are singing. Then, again, Kuthayyir leaves the doe that he is describing and becomes preoccupied with the description of the doves. The doves are like beautiful singers in a drinking gathering. As Sells observes:

> [The metaphor of the doe] reveals a poetics that is far removed from the simple substitution of gazelle for beloved. The gazelle imagery and that of the beloved are developed synchronically. It becomes difficult to tell whether the object of description is the beloved or the gazelle.[52]

At a superficial level, the gazelle is a metaphor of the beloved in that they share beautiful features like stunning eyes and sleek, aesthetically pleasing contours of the body. Al-Dughli claims that Arab poets portray their beloveds as gazelles because their desert environment was poor and they could not find other metaphors to describe them.[53] I disagree with this assertion, and I would rather see this metaphor in a different light. As argued by Khan, especially for Majnun, 'gazelles are generally considered among the most serene of animals, their presence lends a pastoral air to his wildness'.[54] There is also another suggestion regarding the gazelle used as a trope, which connects with mythology. The gazelle was considered sacred and Arabs would allow them to go free instead of killing them.[55] An anecdote states that a gazelle was caught by a group of hunters and Majnun bought the gazelle and set it free: 'It ran away when I set it free. O, gazelle, you owe your freedom to Layla'.[56] Bürgel demonstrates that 'sparing or freeing a gazelle out of a certain feeling or affection for a person it resembled was a literary topos already in early Islamic times.'[57] In another anecdote, Majnun killed a wolf which killed a deer and then he buried the deer and burnt the cadaver of the wolf.[58] Thus, the 'gazelles are so placed in this narrative (Majnun's) precisely because they lend a sentimental, romantic cast to the poet-lover's state of wildness.'[59]

Moreover, the emphasis on the image of a deer with its fawn could be understood in the light of the woman who has become sacred through motherhood. This process has its roots in ancient Arab religious belief, which used to worship the goddess-mother. The ancient Arabs portrayed her as a mother-deer and a mother-oryx.[60] It seems that the poets simply inherited this image and they applied it to their beloveds. However, the *'udhri* poets used these images without seeing their beloveds in term of motherhood.

The face of the beloved

The face of the beloved is the prime focus of *'udhri* poets. Every single feature of it is celebrated in generous description. The poets clearly realise the importance and status of the face as a centre of one's beauty and associate with it the roles of communication and seduction.

With regard to the beloved's hair, *'udhri* poetry defines attractive feminine hair as black, thick, fragrant and especially perfumed with ambergris and basil.[61] It is usually falling in waves and sometimes also with curls. Kuthayyir describes 'Azzah's hair as dark tresses clustering down her back like bunches of grapes.[62]

Moving to the beloved's cheeks, they are portrayed as glowing and amazingly soft.[63] In fact, the stress on softness is recurrent in *'udhri* poems. The beloved appears in them as a highly sensitive woman. Her body is so tender that an insect's minute wing would make it bleed.[64] Moreover, Buthaynah's skin is so soft that whenever she has a bath the water almost injures her skin[65] and Layla's finger is described as being of pure silk.[66] 'Afra' is depicted as a woman who is completely enveloped with down (*muna'ammah*) and all of her fingertips are tinted.[67] The exaggeration of describing the tenderness of the beloved in so far that the smallest of ants walking on her skin would make it bleed, persuades the author of *al-Zahrah* to write about it. He cites many verses with such images and criticises them as extreme exaggeration (*sarfun shadid*).[68] In my view, they are extreme, but this highlights an image of the beloved seen by the lover as being synonymous with such softer elements as water and light.

As for the mouth of the beloved, this feature assumes the utmost significance within ʿudhri poetry and the poets provide a series of similes to celebrate it. The mouth is given a great deal of attention due to a number of reasons. First, it is considered as a basic aspect of the beauty of the beloved. Second, it is the place for kisses and pleasurable contact. Third, it is the part of the body for speaking and the source of beautiful words and discourse. The adjectives given to the mouth in the *ʿudhri ghazal* concentrate on describing the mouth's aromatic smell. The smell is described as musk[69] and the poet draws a link between the mouth's perfumed smell and its pretty smile, so the poet's beloved smiles often and 'when she smiles, some parts of her beautiful teeth appear'.[70] These beautiful teeth have spaces between them.[71] The attention given to the smell of the mouth and its shape is incomparable with that given to its taste. The *ʿudhri* poets attribute large parts of their poems to describe how amazing is the taste of the beloved's mouth, how sweet her saliva.

> As if her mouth is full of the essence of carnation, and musk;
> early morning clouds' raindrops are in her mouth[72]   [13]

This image of the beloved's mouth scented with a good smell and full of raindrops is very similar to certain poetic images in pre-Islamic poetry. For instance, Imruʾ al-Qays says:

> Wine and recent
> rain, blossom, incense smoke
> Cool from her mouth I kissed
> In the soaring song of dawn[73]   [14]

Jamil also describes Buthaynah's saliva by saying that it is a mixture of raindrops, wine and scent:

> She captivated me with her beautiful
> mouth, whose straight teeth appear when she smiles

> and her mouth has a fascinating smell and cold saliva,
> As if vintage wine is mixed with her saliva
> and early pure raindrops mixed with honey[74]　　　　　　　　　　[15]

The significant word here is 'captivated' because her beautiful mouth is one of the first things that seduced him. While Jamil refers occasionally to the beloved's saliva as wine, Majnun talks in detail about this 'wine'. He describes its production process and how it was fermented in *Hawran*[75] with bottles of wine that were kept for a period of time so that its value would increase:

> Not even a protected fermented wine in *Hawran*
> which emits sparks when it is poured from its bottle,
> And which is surrounded by other similar bottles of wine
> which the sellers have kept for sale,
> Is better than the taste of her mouth
> which if its saliva is mixed with musk at night,
> will water a cloud that is heavily raining
> with no lightning and thunder[76]　　　　　　　　　　　　　　[16]

It could be argued that the poet includes the storage and protection of the wine in order to make an indirect reference to the difficulty and the time involved to reach his beloved to kiss her. Majnun's image of a fermented wine, which the sellers have kept for future sale for a long time, as used to describe the beloved's saliva, recalls a similar image in the pre-Islamic *ghazal*. Al-Muraqqish al-Asghar starts his verses with the exact phrase: 'Not even a fermented wine', and then he goes on to describe the unique treatment that this wine has received. It has been protected for twenty years and kept for later sale. After this description of this special wine, al-Muraqqish says: 'It is better than the taste of her mouth when I come to visit her [his beloved] at night.'[77] Undoubtedly, Majnun's image is derived from al-Muraqqish.

It could be argued that the description of the beloved's saliva as raindrops and wine suggests a link between her and sacred objects. Rain is a primary source for water; a verse in the Qur'an reads 'we made from water every living thing'.[78] Wine also carries certain religious meanings. As shown by pre-Islamic poetry, wine was an important component in some religious rituals. Wine was considered as the sacred liquid of the gods, giving them their extraordinary powers.[79] In spite of the prohibition of wine in Islam poets continue to refer to it, although without reference to sacred rituals. In Majnun's poem cited above, the description of the wine that resembles his beloved's saliva appears in great detail. In other verses Majnun insists on the sweetness of Layla's mouth while claiming that he has not tasted it in reality. He reports having stared at her mouth the way people stare at clouds and perceive the sweetness of their raindrops.[80] However, if Majnun avoids saying that he had really tasted the wine of his beloved's mouth, Kuthayyir refers to this directly and says that the honey of her mouth is tasted only by her bedfellow and that other people are prohibited from doing so. Let us follow the succession of these descriptions:

> The sweet saliva of her mouth
> which has bevelled teeth in the late night
> became like honey that is mixed with cold raindrops
> of early morning clouds in *majadih*[81]
> those who cannot obtain her mouth enjoy looking at its beauty
> and she waters her bedfellow from her sweet mouth
> when he kisses her suddenly
> she cleans her snow-white teeth at dawn,
> by a green *miswak*[82] from *Nu'man*
> every creditor was repaid except the poet
> As 'Azzah does not achieve his wish
> so he remains thirsty for her [83]   [17]

To symbolise their agony in love and distance from the beloved, *'udhri* poets use themes such as 'the late night', 'the creditor' and 'a thirsty person'. Kuthayyir states that his thirst for his beloved is not slaked while all other creditors get repaid. Talking about the description of the mouth and thirst is so important because the beloved's saliva is not just a delicious honey but also water that quenches the thirst. The lover's passion for this water always makes him very thirsty, and we will talk about this in detail later. Finally, the beloved's saliva is reported to be a cure for sick people and also said to bring dead people to life again when they taste it.[84] In addition, the beloved's smiling and sweet mouth is described as a source for beautiful words. Beautiful words and discourse are an image for beauty itself.[85]

The scent of the beloved

The sweet scent of the beloved is also celebrated in *'udhri* poetry. The smell of musk emanates from her body[86] and diffuses itself about her. When the lover visits her during the night, he smells the sweet scent of a mixture of wine, musk and ambergris.[87] Lavender and musk perfume her clothes.[88] Her hair breathes sweet basil and ambergris.[89] Her aroma is sweeter than the aroma of greensward.[90] Jamil says:

> It is as if the particles of pure-fragranced
> musk with which she perfumes her sleeves and
> elbows rise when she rises from her bed
> and will be passed to whoever embraces her[91] [18]

Moreover, Majnun declares:

> If we travel at night, and you are in
> front of us merely your sweet aroma
> will guide our she-camels[92] [19]

Here, the scent is not just enjoyment, is not simply a scent to remember and enjoy.[93] It is not only a guide but a beacon for anyone who travels during the night. Its aroma is not only effective in the human world; it also has power in the non-human world: that of our she-camels. In the above-cited verse the beloved's scent is a beacon for both the human and non-human worlds.

The form of the beloved

The *'udhri* poet also represents the whole figure of his beloved. There are certain elements in this figure that appear frequently in the poems. The poet's lady is plumpish. Buthaynah's bosom shines like gallipots of silver.[94] It is clear, bright and white. Its ampleness is stressed again when Jamil says:

> Her breasts and behind prevent her chemise
> from touching her belly or from touching her back[95] [20]

In *'udhri* poetry, as in pre-Islamic poetry, the beloved's curved body is celebrated in several images. According to Jamil,[96] Majnun[97] and Kuthayyir[98] she has tenderly plump ankles. Her appendages are plump (*khudl*).[99] Her legs are smooth of shank and soft of thigh.[100] The most crucial denominator of the beloved's body is her plump buttocks. This feature attracts the poets' attention, and they celebrate it using several similes. The favorite simile for heavy hips in *'udhri* poetry is moistened sand, and the rump-curve is likened to a sand dune. 'Urwah describes 'Afra by saying that there are two sand dunes under her waist, over which a rain shower falls:

> And underneath the two (breasts) are two compacted sand dunes
> which have been struck by droplets of rain from Gemini[101]   [21]

Likewise, Majnun, Jamil and Kuthayyir compose verses describing their beloved's buttocks as a soft dune.[102] She is often portrayed as a woman proud of her shape. She would feel happy if the wind blew and wrapped her clothes around her tightly, showing off her voluptuous body.[103] Moreover, the beloved's buttocks weigh her down so heavily that she can barely walk. The image of the woman tired from walking is often repeated in the *'udhri ghazal*.[104] Kuthayyir compares 'Azzah's walk to a torrential stream (*sayl*) that is obstructed by the curve of the *wadi*, so that it runs very slowly.[105] Although the woman in these poems cannot walk well because of her rotund body, her slender waist is just like a ben's[106] bough. Qays describes Lubna:

> Whenever she walks a span of earth,
> She drags her feet, panting, so she doesn't go more than a span
> She has a behind which shakes when she walks
> and a lean-waisted body like the branch of the ben tree[107]   [22]

The slight waist of the beloved is described also by Jamil in several verses: 'she is lithe-waisted, just like *al-Sabiriyyah*'.[108] The poets usually link the slender waist with heavy hips beneath and plump breasts above.[109]

Comparing these compositions to pre-Islamic poetry, one will find similar images of a woman who can barely walk, or who has a slender waist and plump buttocks.[110] Moreover, some phrases from pre-Islamic poetry are re-used in *'udhri* poetry, almost verbatim. For example, Ka'b b. Zuhayr says:

> She has a lithe waist, plump buttocks,
> She is neither short, nor tall[111]

And Jamil says:

> She has a lithe waist, plump buttocks,
> She is perfect, with no defect or drawback in her body.[112]

Imru' al-Qays says:

> She shows me a throat like the throat of a (white) antelope, not ungainly
> When she lifts it upwards, neither naked of ornament.[113]

And Kuthayyir says:

> She shows me a throat like the throat of a (white)
> antelope, naked of ornament, but decorated and adorned
> with pendulous, long, thick hair.[114]

As seen in these verses, there is a direct reference to previous traditions, not just in images, but also in literal phrases such as: she has a lithe waist, plump buttocks and a throat like the throat of a (white) antelope.[115]

The Portrayal of Layla in Persian Book Painting

We have seen how the popular notion of classical Arabic ideal beauty has been applied to the portrayal of the beloved in *'udhri* poetry; several unchanging elements characterise such portrayals. However, if we were to examine the depiction of the beloved in the legend based on *'udhri* love stories that appeared centuries later in Persia we would discover a completely different portrayal. Yet the influence of the fashion of any given era on the representation of an object is common in art. Therefore, my justification for making this comparison between Layla's portrayal in Majnun's poetry and her portrayal in later Persian paintings, which are based on the Majnun legend, is to examine the influence of fashion on different forms of art.

There are numerous extant manuscripts that contain paintings illustrating versions of the love story of Majnun and Layla, most of them from the *Khamsa*, written by Nizami (1150–1214), the great Persian poet.[116] The details of the various manuscripts are not my prime focus here. I will merely concentrate on the paintings in order to evaluate how Layla is depicted. It is noticeable, however, that the image of Layla in these Persian paintings suggests another depiction of the beloved, one that differs substantially from that offered by Majnun's poetry. While she is presented in Majnun's verses as an ideal of Arabian desirable beauty, where big black eyes, ample bosom, slender waist, plump legs and heavy hips are celebrated, Layla is very differently imagined in these Persian paintings. In one painting, which shows Layla receiving Majnun in her tent, Layla is illustrated as an exceptionally thin young maiden. There is no trace of a bosom, nor are there any rounded parts on her body. She is shown with a round face, 'Chinese' eyes, a tiny mouth and arched eyebrows. This painting occurs in an illustrated version of Nizami's *Khamsa*, dated 1444, and belongs to the Shiraz school of miniature painting.[117] In another painting Majnun is depicted speaking with an elderly man in a date grove some distance from Layla, who is seated.[118] Layla is illustrated as a sad young woman, putting her hand on her cheek. The most apparent aspects of her figure are her moon face and her arched eyebrows. Likewise, in a painting showing Majnun and Layla fainting,[119] Layla appears as a thin maiden, with arched eyebrows meeting on her forehead and a flat chest. In another painting, Layla looks upset while slapping her husband. Her face has the same fine features, and 'Chinese' eyes. She is portrayed in a sitting position and is given a slim body. Her raised hand is nothing like the plump arm that has been described in Majnun's verses.[120] It must be noted that most of these paintings were accomplished in the fifteenth century. During that time, features such as the moon face, 'Chinese' eyes, a tiny mouth and arched eyebrows became the usual cliché for beautiful young people, both male and female. The beloved is moon-faced and likened to Buddha.[121]

However, several illustrations of Nizami's *Khamsa* present different perspectives and aspects of the story. Some painters focus on Majnun, or Layla, some on the animals surrounding them, and some painters focus on the Sufi imagery of the story. For example, one painting shows Majnun dying on Layla's tomb, and no one around him seems to care.[122] This painting alludes to a very important Sufi theme. Within some Sufi traditions the way to achieve ultimate truth or love is gained by the suffering of the soul, totally alone, without any support. As mentioned earlier, my only interest is a specific aspect of this: the depiction of the beloved through these images.[123] Subsequently, it seems, through this brief review, that Layla's portrayal is influenced by the fashionable style of a given era and not by any close attention to how the text describes her beauty. Clearly her depiction in Arabic poetry varies greatly from her depiction within Persian paintings. Nonetheless, although substantial differences are obvious, Layla's portrayal is enacted through a stereotyped image, in both Arabic poetry and Persian paintings.

The Desirable Image of a Corpulent Female Body

We have seen how these bodily descriptions are similar to those with which the Arab poets since pre-Islamic times used to describe their ladies. But let us consider in a little more detail the figure of a desirable woman as corpulent. Bodily descriptions take on erotic characteristics when concentrating on the shape and form of the female body. Indeed, 'several round images, such as the egg and the pearl, are used in the classical *qasidah* in symbolic association with the beloved'.[124] If a bosom is *mu'id*, that means that it fills one's hand, and if it is *nair*, that means that it fills one's eyes.[125] In addition, the description of a woman who does not have heavy hips as *rasha* and *zala* codes her appearance through negative adjectives that indicate she is not a desirable woman. Jamil makes a comparison between Buthaynah, who would feel happy if the wind blew and wrapped her clothes around her, showing off her voluptuous body, with the *zul* women (who do not have heavy hips), so they try to avoid the wind as they do not have anything to show off.[126] The use of this lexicon indicates a general tendency towards sensuality and suggests a highly tactile relationship.

In the following section I will examine an argument about the preference for a corpulent woman among Arabs after the pre-Islamic period, provided by a contemporary author, Khalil 'Abd al-Karim, in his book entitled: *Al-'Arab wa al-marah hafriyyah fi al-istir al-mukhayim*: *The Arab Concept of Women*.[127] His argument is based on a study of several Arabic lexicons and therefore seems to have influenced other relevant writings in the field.[128] I will summarise his argument for the purpose of analysing it and to set up my own position challenging his assertions.

Attempting to explain the Arab preference for corpulent women,[129] 'Abd al-Karim claims that it is because Arabs, in the period when this literature flourished and lexicons for describing female bodies were developed, lived with camels and horses, depending completely upon them for their lives, and they viewed women within the same framework through which they viewed their horses and camels. His study includes an investigation of Arabic dictionaries that reveals that the roots of words referring to women and animals have much in common. Hence 'Abd al-Karim argues that the Arabic words to describe women are derived from the same linguistic roots as those used to describe camels and horses. According to him, Arabs prefer a fat camel (*kinaz*), and a horse with big hips and plump thighs (*hirkulah*). The more a woman is similar to the *kinaz* camel or the *hirkulah* horse, the more preferable she becomes.[130] He also claims that camel-raising is an economic and social custom among the Arabs. The geographical environment imposes a strong bond between the Arab and his camel and owning a camel is also an indication of a high social position within the tribe. Therefore, this association makes the camel a measure or norm for women as well.[131] 'Abd al-Karim provides a series of instances from Arabic dictionaries to support his assertion. For example, *dahuh* could be used for a woman and a she-camel alike. *Damkhaj* means a large she-camel and a large woman.

Sani'ah means both a good she-camel and a beautiful woman, and so on.[132] Since Arab men preferred strong animals with large features, they use the same language to depict the preferred type of woman, that is, one with similar features. Moreover, 'Abd al-Karim claims that women were, like animals, used for enjoyment, domestic service and the preservation of the community. Therefore, so runs his argument, it is no wonder that Arab men used much the same vocabulary to refer to women as to their camels and horses. From 'Abd al-Karim's perspective, that indicates the low status of women in Arab culture. 'If Arabic contains such crude vocabulary to describe the intimate relationship between a man and a woman, how can one proclaim that it is a poetic or beautiful language?'[133] 'Abd al-Karim emphasises that the hard life of the Bedouin had a strong and lasting influence on the Arabic lexicon. This, in turn, he claims, has influenced other nations that adopted the Arabic language later. That means that the Arabic language changed the status of women, in the nations that adopted it, from high to low.[134]

These are the main threads of 'Abd al-Karim's study, which create a link between the Arab concept of women as revealed by the Arabic language and their Bedouin life which depends upon animals such as camels and horses. However, I would like to challenge 'Abd al-Karim's assertions. I maintain that he takes an extremely critical and reductive view of the subject. Many of his conclusions are open to further discussion, especially the link suggested by the author between the language used by the Bedouin and women's status in Muslim culture in general. Moreover, the equine lexicon and similar linguistic roots to describe a woman and a she-camel do not mean necessarily that they are in the same state, or that the Arabs could not distinguish between human and animal beauty. In many languages, it could be argued, there is an exchange between semantic fields. The shared stems for words imply richness and a derivative capacity that is inherent in the language rather than a lack of creative similes and imagination. Not only in Arabic. In English, for example, a slang word to describe an attractive young unmarried woman is 'filly' (a young mare or female horse). Other colloquial words describe girls as 'chicks' and 'birds'. One might note here that these terms all reflect a masculine point of view. What 'Abd al-Karim criticises as crude vocabulary to describe the intimate relationship between a man and a woman exists, in fact, in other languages. For instance, in Shakespeare's *Othello*, Iago informs Brabantio, Desdemona's father, of Desdemona's elopement with Othello: 'Even now, very now, an old black ram is tupping your white ewe.'[135] Moreover, associating the desirable figure of a woman with the fine figure of a horse is open to more than one interpretation, for the Arab horse is certainly not built like a cart horse, rather it has elegant and slender features.

'Ali al-Batal advances yet another rationale that appears more convincing than 'Abd al-Karim's assertion. He suggests that the image of the corpulent woman is inherited from ancient religious belief. The Mother Goddess was one of the deities that were worshipped by the ancient Arabs. Her corpulent body symbolises fertility and motherhood. Motherhood is a principal function of the Mother Goddess, who gives life, enriches the tribe of warriors and preserves the human race.[136] It is essential that a god is depicted with all the characteristics for which he is being worshipped.[137] Therefore, when an Arab poet portrays a woman as fat and comments that she 'hardly walked' this is because he has in mind, perhaps unconsciously, the perfect image of a sacred woman. It is sacred particularly because of her sexual fertility that leads to motherhood. Through the worship of the Mother Goddess and her association with the sun and its associated images such as a gazelle and a palm tree, this leads to the predominant image of the desirable woman. Al-Batal argues that the motifs that usually constitute this image indicate that classical

Arabic poetry used earlier metaphors, yet at the same time lost an association with the ancient religion, which worshipped the sun-mother and its associated images such as the gazelle and the palm tree.[138] His suggestion is based on the idea that religious sanctity was ascribed to women in ancient ages, but the religious associations were lost over time. The later poet preserved the image of the female corpulent body, but removed the ancient pagan religious associations from it. Therefore, this image became a model of desirable female beauty, whilst moving away from its possible ancient roots.

While the above cited theory is persuasive, I would also propose that in ancient Arabic culture a woman's corpulence and her ample hips would be seen as a sign of her prosperity and wealth, leading one to assume her to be of a high class and of noble origin – and someone whose family was always able to feed her well. It also implies that she did no physical work. It goes without saying that attaining such a woman of noble birth requires great courage and capability on the part of the poet.[139] However, while that might be the case for the pre-Islamic poet, for the *'udhri* poet the beloved is usually portrayed as a cousin or at least one as of his relatives. Thus, there is no need at all to show his courage. He is rather describing her beauty within the favourite motifs of preceding traditions, which were inherited from the predominant poetic themes of pre-Islamic times.

However, a slow evolution in the standard portrayal of beauty would eventually lead to the preference for *al-majdulah*, which is classified by al-Jahiz:

> Most people who know about women, most experts on the subject, agree in preferring the *majdula*, that is to say the type of woman intermediate between fat and thin. Her figure must be elegant and shapely, her shoulders symmetrical and her back straight; her bones must be well covered, and she must be neither too plump nor too skinny. The word *majdula* conveys the notion of tautness, of firm flesh without superfluous fat. A graceful walk is the most beautiful thing about a woman, and she cannot walk gracefully if she is portly, fat and overburdened with flesh. Indeed a *majdula* is more often slim, and her slenderness is her best known feature [. . .] A *majdula* is described in prose by the words: the upper part of her body is a stem and the lower part a sand-dune.[140]

Al-Jahiz shows the different attitudes that had an effect on aesthetic taste in his own time. The model of beauty was developed according to the development of other forms of knowledge. The social, cultural and ethnic structure had changed and transformed the notions about body and beauty. The new society, in the Abbasid period, was a cosmopolitan one that brought together people from Persia, Turkey, Ethiopia, India and many other regions. These included slave girls who brought new standards of beauty. Their beauty was varied and, moreover, associated with cultural functions such as music and singing.[141] Slowly, the poet's taste moved towards a shapely woman instead of a portly one. Al-Jahiz calls her *al-majdulah* and emphasises the fact that she is not too plump. He even makes a contrast with the preferred image drawn from earlier poetry of a woman who walks with difficulty because of her great weight. However, his insistence on her litheness does not prevent him from noting the heaviness of the lower part of her body, so he uses the old poetic simile of the sand dune. Moreover, the old norms and descriptions of female beauty were criticised by al-Jahiz in *Kitab al-Nisa*. He asserts that a beautiful woman is, obviously, more beautiful than an oryx and a doe, and more beautiful than anything people may compare her to.[142] However, in spite of al-Jahiz's critique, poets continued to use similar figurative language to depict their women. There are endless examples of subsequent poets such as al-Mutanabbi[143] and Abu Tammam[144] describing beautiful women as gazelles, and portraying particular parts of their bodies as sand dunes and so on.

The *'Udhri Ghazal*: More than Imitation

The beloved, then, in these poems, is represented similarly to the beloved in the pre-Islamic ode. She appears within traditional beauty standards as established or at least confirmed by both Arabic poetry and prose since the pre-Islamic epoch. However, does that really mean that the *'udhri* poet is just imitating the old model of personifying female beauty?

And does that mean that poetic tradition has more influence within *'udhri* poetry than the experience of devoted love, which is dedicated to one individual beloved and describes her unique individual beauty, which is supposed to have its own features? The poetic tradition of describing the female body has existed for a long time. We must remember that the perception of poetry in the early Islamic period relied on how closely the poem resembled or catered to the established taste in receiving poetry. Hence, 'the poet was expected to work within the framework of the literary tradition [. . .] the ideas were measured by their transmission of ancient established common sense.'[145] We might recall a famous critical opinion, from Ibn Qutaybah, which appeared later and stressed this connection:

> The later poets should not deviate from what the preceding ones were doing. They should neither stop at inhabited houses to recall their memories and write their poems, nor lament beside settled houses because the preceding poets did that at ruined and obliterated dwellings. Since the earlier poets travelled by camels and described them in their poems, the later poets should not travel by donkeys or mules and do the same. Later poets are not to stop to drink at sweet streaming water for the reason that the earlier poets stopped at turbidity ponds. The later poets ought not to pass by myrtle, daffodil and flowers on their way to the praised person because the preceding poets passed by wormwood and '*ararah*[146] on their way to the praised person.[147]

Nevertheless, in spite of the potential weight of literary tradition, another conclusion may be reached. The bodily image of the woman is governed by the one who describes her, who usually confines himself to certain criteria of beauty pertaining to his Eve. Alternatively, it is governed by the lover's preeminence that transfers everything about his beloved into beauty. For this very reason, it could be argued that the *'udhri* imitation of the older norms does not mean that they do not see their beloveds with their own eyes. Kinany claims that:

> The *'udhri* poets frequently used old clichés to express their new, intense, and rich feelings, so that they put new wine into old bottles, and did not realize that an old cliché even when used to express new sentiment has a limited and established power of expression, and that it could not suggest anything more than a very conventionalized and therefore restricted sentiment and thought.[148]

I would rather suggest that the *'udhri* lover sees his beloved through his own passionate eyes, which incline to idealise the object of his love. Therefore, the *'udhri* poet stipulates that the boundaries of ideal beauty – as defined in Arabic poems – apply to his own, unique beloved. He tends to idealise her and thus to obtain his image of the ideal woman. Hence, he sees and describes his beloved in terms affected by his cultural and aesthetic inheritance. She herself becomes, through his loving eyes, the very archetype of ideal beauty. No one can replace her, even the literary model of beauty. She becomes the model. She becomes the archetype, illuminated and illustrated with all the necessary and desirable colours and contours of beauty. That is what a lover poet did: he made his beloved the ideal. Al-'Aqqad declares:

> Art is concerned with eternal images and everlasting models, not with creatures that appear once in life and then disappear. What concerns the artist with beauty is its ability to be a general model for many individuals or to all species.[149]

This is well articulated in an essential statement ascribed to Buthaynah: 'He (Jamil) sees me with the eyes that are not in your head!'[150] stated in an answer to the enquiry of Caliph 'Abd al-Malik b. Marwan of her: 'What did Jamil see in you, to compose such beautiful poetry about you?' Buthaynah's response to 'Abd al-Malik resorts to the lover's eyes and the poet's imagination, rather than to ordinary eyes or reality. Reality does not matter in the realm of the poetic lover. We might remember here the anecdotes that insist on Buthaynah's ordinary appearance.[151] It is the authority of love that transfers every aspect of the beloved's body into perfect and beautiful detail, and personifies her as the imagined model of the ideal woman. This model is now firmly engraved into collective consciousness and literary tradition. The common features of the cultural background do not contrast with the originality in feeling. In spite of this, *'udhri* poetry has its own individuality, as we shall see in the following section.

The Ethereal Nature of Beauty

Although the *'udhri ghazal* makes use of tropes and metaphors that were inherited from the pre-Islamic period, there is an additional element that distinguishes it from the previous tradition and gives it its special elements. The *'udhri* poet's imitation of older forms and notions in his descriptive verses addressing his beloved's beauty is combined with an attempt to idealise her. He does not want her beauty to be compared to or derived from other women's beauty, even though their beauty is the perfect pattern of female beauty. This is observed from the poet's insistence that his beloved is the most beautiful creature. Comparative phrases are frequent in the *'udhri ghazal*, so as to imply that the beloved is incomparable with any other elements in nature or humanity. When the poem portrays the beloved as a special animal such as a deer or an oryx, it implies that the beloved is more beautiful than either of them.[152]

Likewise, the poem often stresses the higher position of the beloved compared with natural elements such as the sun and moon.[153] The moon and sun themselves are incapable of emulating her brilliant light.[154] Comparative phrases are also used to emphasise the unique beauty of the beloved among other women. Jamil asserts: 'Her eye and neck are the most beautiful among all creatures'.[155] If she is the most beautiful among all creatures (*khalq Allah*), she is necessarily the most beautiful woman in the world. Her stunning beauty is definitely not contending with any sort of beauty.[156] Qays declares that Lubna is the most perfect human from top to toe:

> O most perfect of people from head to toe,
> And most beautiful of people clothed or unclothed[157]   [23]

The beloved surpasses other women in everything; Jamil portrays Buthaynah as the moon whereas other women are merely minor stars:

> She is the full moon,
> whereas the other women are [merely minor] stars
> And what a great distance between them
> She is superior in beauty to other people,
> just as the Night of Qadr is preferred
> over one thousand months[158]   [24]

Her body has its own value, so her own natural beauty is its decoration and adornment.[159] This beauty is independent of outside influences, just like the poet's independence of any form of beauty, any human or any companion. Therefore, he does away with people, does not enjoy their company and, even more, he hates any speech that is not hers and any scene from which she is absent:

> After her, it is as though the
> people I love are the sap of the split bitter apple tree;
> for after her, my eyes detest every sight,
> and after her, my ears detest every speech[160] [25]

Consequently, it could be argued that although there are several evident erotic elements depicting female beauty in the *'udhri ghazal*, it is also the case that the description and feeling of this beauty is not always purely erotic or sensual. Of course, sensual feeling runs through many images in this *ghazal*, and influences its descriptive language, especially while imitating the older norms and patterns.

Nonetheless, the *'udhri ghazal*, in many cases, evaluates beauty and sublimates it to worlds that transcend human ones. This was shown when we discussed the issue of the *'udhri* poet's persistence in describing the light of his beloved and her status beyond that of the moon and sun. Jamil compares Buthaynah's luminescence with the light that illuminates every thing around her.[161] Hence, the body of the beloved is perceived as glittering and soft as light.

Furthermore, the beloved's beauty in the *'udhri ghazal* is beyond nature and associated with many extraordinary effects. For example, one effect is the impossibility for even the most virtuous of people to resist her beauty:

> Monks of Midian,
> and those I know weep from the fear of the torment while seated
> But had they heard as I have heard her speech,
> they would fall down to 'Azza bowing and prostrating
> The dead is resurrected when she touches his bones
> and become immortal when they see her[162] [26]

Ibn Qayyim al-Jawziyah ascribes to a person from the *'Udhrah* tribe this passage: 'If you, men from Banu Fizarh, see the women of our tribe, you would take them as Allat and al-'Uzza[163] and leave Islam behind you!'[164] Preternatural effects are associated with *'udhri* beauty to the extent that they affect people in the way that usually only religion can. One may observe this semantic exchange between religion and love. As Hamori puts it: 'The poaching of religious language is meant in the *'udhri* lyric to express the extent of this dangerous devotion'.[165] Majnun clearly says:

> When I pray I turn my face towards
> her place though the right direction is the opposite one
> I do not do that through polytheism,
> but because my lovesickness resisted the cure of the doctor[166]   [27]

Small wonder that the language of love converges with religious language, as the poet's admiration of beauty resembles religious belief. In many cases, the beloved's beauty surpasses human beauty and there are more astonishing effects attributed to it. The woe is gone because of Layla's face, and rain is falling because of Layla's face.[167] Her saliva is a nostrum for dead people, causing them to rise up from their graves.[168] If a poison mixes with her saliva, it will be quenched when the poet drinks it.[169] Hence, the *'udhri ghazal* draws a parallel between extraordinary effects attributed to beauty and extraordinary effects attributed to prophets, saints and *hur al-'ayn* (the women of Paradise). One might remember here the hadiths that attributed great light to *hur al-'ain*. For example:

> It is on record on the authority of Ibn Mas'ud that he said: 'the Apostle of God – God bless him and his family and give them peace – said that [when] God created the Garden of Eden, He summoned Jibrail – upon him be peace – departed and went around throughout the Garden. One of the dark-eyed maidens looked down on him from one of the palaces there and she smiled at Jibrail – upon him be peace. As a result, the Garden of Eden became illumined by the radiance of her teeth. Jibrail – upon him be peace – fell down prostrate, believing that this was from the radiance of the Lord of Might Himself. Then the maiden called out [to him], 'O faithful one of God, raise your head'. He did so and looked at her. Then he said: 'Praise be to God Who created you'. The maiden replied: 'O faithful one of God, do you know for whom I was created?' [He replied 'no']. She said, 'God created me [for him who] preferred seeking the pleasure of God Most High to the desires of his own heart.'[170]

This great light attributed to *hur al-'ayn* could be applied somehow to the *'udhri* poetic imagination while portraying the beloveds. The light of the beloved, as the light of *hur al-'ayn,* is greater than any other light. According to Majnun, she [Layla] is the sun whose light puts the full moon to shame, and who outshone the lightning when it flashes.[171]

The lover looks to his beloved as the only person capable of bestowing happiness on him, as illustrated in this statement from Majnun:

> You are the only person who if you want
> Could make me either happy or miserable[172]   [28]

The supplicatory language, then, is dominant in *'udhri* discourse to the extent that the poet could not talk to his beloved directly since she was imagined as a sacred and venerated person:

> When I suddenly met her I became confounded
> Nothing right or wrong could I find to say[173]   [29]

It is understandable that the beloved's physical beauty is associated with such preternatural effects, as it is free from the notion of time. This beauty goes beyond time itself. It is timeless beauty and eternally youthful. Jamil points out:

> Buthaynah said,
> when she saw
> locks of red hair (on my head)
> Oh Jamil, You become older and your youth's gone.
> I said,
> O please stop it, Buthaynah
> Have you forgotten our times at Liwa and Ajfari?
> When my locks were (black) just like a crow's wing,
> Daubed with Musk and ambergris
> Your youth will never fade as
> you are a precious pearl We
> are from the same time,
> So how can I have grown old while you have not?[174]   [30]

There are two time frames in Jamil's poem: his time and Buthaynah's time. His time is affected by age and vicissitude, while Buthaynah's time is constant and does not change. Buthaynah, in Jamil's poem, has no past, she does not change, she is always in the present. Her beauty remains the same: yesterday, today and tomorrow.[175] She is the source of all good qualities, as she is identified with the perfect, eternal and immutable. She is removed from time altogether by the image of eternal youth that designates her omnipotence.[176]

When the beloved's body surmounts time, this implies its perfection and immortality. It is an immortal body that ascends to the level of worshipped statues and images. I would maintain that there is a link between the beloved's body and that of worshipped idols as it appears in the *'udhri ghazal*. Worshipped idols and the beloved share a common aloofness and do not respond directly to those worshipping them. Let us consider Kuthayyir's verses:

> When she left me she did not heed me, I
> called to her, but she was silent as a rock so smooth
> that gazelles, would slip if they walked there
> Reluctant she was, and always cruel;
> and if I tired of such behavior, she wearied also[177] [31]

And Jamil's verse:

> Do you not know, O mother of Dhil-Wad',
> that I jest with your memories while you are impermeable[178] [32]

Jamil also declares:

> I await what you promised me,
> as the poor man awaits the rich man
> counting his debts but does not fulfil a promise to us
> and is not impoverished
> You and your promises are like nought,
> but the thundercloud which does not rain[179] [33]

Thus, she is a rock, reluctant (*summ, safuh, salud*), she does not respond, or she is beyond response, just like a statue. Nevertheless, she deserves, like the image, to be worshipped. The image of the beloved is derived from the image of stubborn rocks, and also from the image of a statue, which is worshipped even though it gives no response. However, we should bear in mind that despite the *'udhri* poet's comparing his beloved to a solid rock, and the inanimate nature which that implies, he does not lose hope in what his worshipped love might give him in return. Worshippers of idols used to await their idols' response in spite of their apparent silence. They also presented the idols with sacrifices, as they believed the idols were capable of bringing good and turning away harm, along with providing rain and fertility. Although the *'udhri* poet claims that his love goes beyond the notion of taking and giving, and although he addresses his beloved when saying 'do harm or good to me, no reproach', he implies often that he nevertheless anticipates that she will be ever-giving. He is as the thirsty man to whom the water is unreachable; the debtor whose loans cannot be repaid.

Kuthayyir says:

> By Allah, every time I came near her
> She went far away, and when I spoke at length
> She said little[180]   [34]

So devotion goes beyond reason and is regardless of the behaviour of the beloved. Even if the aloofness of the beloved leads the poet to death, he should embrace his destiny:

> O when will my tortured heart be cured (of
> your love) The arrows of death are between me and
> seeing thee Despite the exile, the pain, the longing, the
> shivering You don't come closer but I don't go further away
> I am like a bird within the swinging palms of a child
> The bird suffers death and the child enjoys the game
> The child is too young to feel for the bird
> And the bird has no feathers to fly away[181]   [35]

The bird in these verses is represented as being in a weak, surrendering condition so as to signify the weakness of the poet towards his love. Here, love is destiny and its powerful effect is comparable to exile, pain, longing and to death itself. Yet there is no choice. The bird, signifying the poet, has no feathers to fly away. It should be clear, however, that this theme has nothing to do with the theme of unrequited love. In fact, I disagree with scholars like Kinany who define *'udhri* love as unrequited love by arguing that 'the *'udhri* lovers suffered indeed tremendously from all the pangs of unrequited love'.[182] An examination of *'udhri* poetry reveals that the beloved always plays an active part in the romance. In *Diwan Jamil* there are several verses that suggest long conversations between him and Buthaynah, in which they both express their longing to each other. For example, he says:

> I was patient as I left in the evening and she was
> sorrowful complaining to me of an ardent love
> Saying: 'Spend a night with me,
> may I be your ransom, I will complain to you, for that is easy[183]   [36]

In these verses Buthaynah is complaining to her lover, the poet. She is even inviting him to spend the night with her. Another poem reveals a long conversation between Jamil and Buthaynah in which she asked him to conceal his love because she is afraid that their enemies might hurt him.[184] Another poem hints that Buthaynah shows her love to the poet, but she is frightened by gossip (*al-wushah*).[185] Therefore, the complaint about the beloved's aloofness is rather to praise her, as Arabs used to praise difficult women, and to stress the poet's devotion for her regardless of her response to him. Jamil addresses Buthaynah:

> And you were not fair
> As for (other) women, they are hateful to me now,
> and as for that which is proper, she withholds[186]   [37]

And Kuthayyir addresses 'Azzah:

> Do me good or do me harm, I shall not blame you,
> Nor hate you, even when you make yourself hateful[187]   [38]

When 'Azzah met the caliph 'Abd al-Malik, she was proud of Kuthayyir's verse on her in which he described her as a rock.[188]

The immortality of the body is also related to the immortality of soul. The *'udhri* poet suggests that his love began before he was created, and would last after his death: 'My soul became attached to hers before we were formed'.[189] Consequently, it becomes valid for the *'udhri* poet to talk about eternal love, as even death will not end their mutual love. Addressing Buthaynah, Jamil sang:

> My heart will love you, as long as I live;
> And when I die my echo will follow your echo between the tombs[190]   [39]

'Urwah also claims:

> I love the day of Judgment since I have been told
> That I shall meet her there[191] [40]

Conclusion

To sum up, in this chapter I show how the beloved's body is depicted in the *'udhri ghazal*. There are certain elements in this depiction that make use of many images and metaphors inherited from the literature of the previous period. This led to the discussion of the desirable image of a corpulent female body and its connection with ancient religious belief in which a corpulent body symbolises fertility and motherhood; motherhood is a principal function of the Mother Goddess. In addition, I made a comparison between Layla's image in Arabic poetry and her image in later Persian paintings. In both forms of art the beloved is portrayed in an almost stereotypical way, which is influenced by the fashionable style of the era. However, the *'udhri ghazal*, in my opinion, offers more than an imitation and moves away from the previous tradition by emphasising the ethereal aspect of female beauty and ascribing extraordinary effects to it. Hence, I examine themes such as the beloved's eternal youth, her omnipotence and the devotion for her that goes beyond reason. As a result, this should lead us to think about symbolising the body and associating it with nature, which will be the main theme of my next chapter.

Notes

1. Al-Ghazali, *The Incoherence of the Philosophers*, p. 205.
2. As cited in Michael Winter, 'Islamic Attitudes Toward the Human Body', in Law, *Religious Reflections on the Human Body*, p. 42.
3. Ibid.
4. Al-Ma'idah (5:87).
5. Maghen, *Virtues*, pp. 4–7.
6. This literature includes many motifs. For example, in defining the feminine ideal, motifs such as how to examine a *jariyah* (female slave) are found. The concept of virility includes motifs such as medicine that promotes virility.
7. Behrens-Abouseif, *Beauty in Arabic Culture*, p. 56.
8. Arabic plural noun of clothes made of linen from Egypt.

9. She means Umm-Iyas' pudenda.
10. Al-Andalusi, *al-'Iqd al-farid*, Vol. 7, pp. 121–2.
11. Al-Zahi, *al-Jasad wa al-surah wa al-muqaddas fi al-Islam*, p. 75.
12. 'Amr b. Kulthum, 'Mu'allaqah', in Arberry, *The Seven Odes: the First Chapter of Arabic Literature*, p. 204.
13. Al-Qays, 'Mu'allaqah', trans. Arberry, p. 63.
14. Hamori, *'Love Poetry (Ghazal)'*, p. 204.
15. It is crucial to distinguish between the *nasib* and the *ghazal*. The *nasib* is the lyrical-elegiac opening section of the *qasidah*, while the *ghazal* is independent love poetry.
16. Zuhayr, *Banat Su'ad*, trans. Pinckney Stetkevych, 'Pre-Islamic Panegyric and the Poetics of Redemption', in Pinckney Stetkevych, *Reorientations: Arabic and Persian Poetry*, p. 24.
17. Hamori, *'Love Poetry (Ghazal)'*, p. 204.
18. Sabrah, *al-Ghazal al-'udhri*, p. 209.
19. Except for a few examples, especially with Kuthayyir.
20. Behrens-Abouseif, *Beauty*, p. 57.
21. Jamil, *Diwan*, pp. 37–8; Majnun, *Diwan*, p. 83.
22. Qays, *Diwan*, p. 81; Majnun, *Diwan*, p. 77.
23. Majnun, *Diwan*, p. 160.
24. Ibid., p. 115.
25. Al-Hufi, *al-Ghazal*, p. 42.
26. Al-Qays, in Jones, *Early Arabic Poetry, Volume Two: Select Odes (Edition, Translation and Commentary)*, p. 69.
27. Tarafah's verse reads: 'A face as though the sun had loosed his mantle upon it, pure of hue, with not a wrinkle to mar it' (trans. Arberry, *The Seven Odes*, p. 83).
28. Kuthayyir, *Diwan*, p. 153.
29. It is significant that, afterwards, the notion of the sun and the moon feeling shy in the presence of a beautiful woman or man becomes a frequent theme in Arabic literature. For example, al-Sahib (d. 385/969) says: 'He almost put the morning sun to shame' (in al-Tha'alibi, *Yatimat al-dahr*, p. 284). See more examples in al-Muhibbi's *Nafht al-rihanah*, pp. 190, 300, and in al-'Imad al-Isfahani's *Kharidat al-qasr*, p. 107. All the references are from www.alwaraq.net, 5 June 2007. Moreover, we can find this theme later on in other Eastern poetry, such as the one written by Rahman Baba, the Pukhtun poet. For instance, one of his verses reads: 'At dawn the moon feels ashamed before your

face, and must live in the pitch-dark'. See Baba, *The Poetry of Rahman Baba: Poet of the Pukhtuns*, p. 141.
30. Majnun, *Diwan*, pp. 91–2.
31. Ibid., p. 21.
32. Ibid., p. 67.
33. Al-Batal, *al-Surah fi al-shi'r al-'arabi hatta akhir al-qarn al-thani al-hijri*, p. 57.
34. Ibid., p. 109.
35. Majnun, *Diwan*, p. 67.
36. Jamil, *Diwan*, p. 111.
37. Al-Jawziyyah, *Rawdat al-muhibbin*, p. 217.
38. Ibid., p. 117.
39. Jamil, *Diwan*, p. 23.
40. Kuthayyir, *Diwan*, p. 181; Jamil, *Diwan*, p. 38.
41. Qays, *Diwan*, p. 46.
42. There are various terms referring to the deer in the *'udhri ghazal*. According to Badwi, these terms are: *ghazal, shadin, tafl, jidayah, rasha, khashf, tila, aghann, rashih, adma, rim, khadhul* and *zabyah*. See Badawi, *al-Alfaz al-dallah 'la al-husn wa al-qubh fi al-Shi'r al-'udhri*.
43. Majnun, *Diwan*, p. 108.
44. Jamil, *Diwan*, pp. 59, 85.
45. See earlier in this chapter.
46. See earlier in this chapter.
47. Majnun, *Diwan*, p. 217.
48. Ibid., p. 176.
49. Kuthayyir, *Diwan*, p. 153. Interestingly, another Umayyad poet, 'Umar b. Abi Rabi'ah, devoted the following verses to the difference between a girl and a gazelle:

> A young gazelle grazing upon a meadow high
> On even hills reminds me of the Taymite's daughter
> I said to it/her, feeling some apprehension in my heart— For I had never seen such a similarity –
> How you resemble her! But for the leanness of your legs,
> And that your flanks are not like hers, That you are bare and naked while she is Not naked, nor are her hands bare.
> And that you have no hair, whilst hers
> Is blackest flood upon her shoulders clothing her.

('Umar b. Abi Rabi'ah, cited and translated by Bürgel, 'The Lady Gazelle and Her Murderous Glances', *Journal of Arabic Literature*, Vol. 20, No. 1, pp. 1–2).
50. Kuthayyir, *Diwan*, p. 70.
51. Michael A. Sells, 'Guises of the *Ghul*. Dissembling Simile and Semantic Overflow in the Classical Arabic Nasib', in Pinckney Stetkevych, *Reorientations: Arabic and Persian Poetry*, p. 141.
52. Ibid., p. 143.
53. Al-Dughli, *Ahadith ghazilah fi al-ghazalayn al-'udhri wa al-'umari wa imtidadatuhuma fi al-ghazal al-'arabi*, p. 75.
54. Khan, *Sexuality and Secrecy*, p. 95.
55. Ibid. See also al-Jihad's statement that: 'Arabs name the sun "gazelle" for its core resemblance to a gazelle ...while for the Arabs the oryx symbolises immortality and pleasure', *Jamaliyyat al-shi'r al-'arabi. Dirash fi falsafat al-jamal fi al-wa'i al-shi'ri al-jahili*, p. 286.
56. Kinany, *Development*, p. 283.
57. Bürgel, 'The Lady Gazelle and Her Murderous Glances', p. 4. There is also a detailed discussion of the magical and numinous background of the gazelle metaphor on pp. 6–10.
58. Al-Isfahani, *Al-Aghani*, Vol. 2, p. 377. W. Robertson Smith discusses the south Arabian tribe called the Banu Harith 'among whom if a dead gazelle was found it was solemnly buried, and the whole tribe mourned for it seven days', Smith, *Kinship and Marriage in Early Arabia*, p. 227.
59. Khan, *Sexuality and Secrecy*, p. 96.
60. Al-Batal, *al-Surah*, p. 95.
61. Majnun, *Diwan*, p. 85.
62. Kuthayyir, *Diwan*, p. 197.
63. Majnun, *Diwan*, p. 72.
64. Jamil, *Diwan*, p. 112.
65. Ibid., p. 30.
66. Majnun, *Diwan*, p. 52.
67. 'Urwah, *Diwan*, pp. 25, 46.
68. Ibn Daud, *al-Zahrah*, p. 135.
69. Jamil, *Diwan*, pp. 18, 122; Majnun, *Diwan*, p. 36.
70. Jamil, *Diwan*, p. 111.
71. Kuthayyir, *Diwan*, p. 70; Majnun, *Diwan*, pp. 115, 120; Jamil, *Diwan*, p. 67.
72. Majnun, *Diwan*, p. 222.

73. Al-Kindi, *Diwan Imru' al-Qays*, p. 156, in Tuetey, *Imrulkais of Kinda, Poet (The Poems-the Life-the Background)*, p. 41.
74. Jamil, *Diwan*, p. 120.
75. An area in Syria, known for its good wine at that time.
76. Majnun, *Diwan*, pp. 106–7.
77. Al-Muraqqish al-Asghar, in al-Qurashi, *Jamharat ash'ar al-'arab*, p. 200.
78. Al-Anbiya' (21:30).
79. Al-Batal, *al-Surah*, pp. 74–5.
80. Majnun, *Diwan*, p. 156.
81. An ancient Arab device for mixing wine.
82. Tooth stick with a beautiful smell.
83. Kuthayyir, *Diwan*, pp. 70–1.
84. Jamil, *Diwan*, p. 38.
85. This study will elaborate later on the role of conversations in the *'udhri ghazal*.
86. Jamil, *Diwan*, p. 68.
87. Ibid., p. 39.
88. Ibid,. p. 113.
89. Majnun, *Diwan*, p. 85.
90. Kuthayyir, *Diwan*, p. 110.
91. Jamil, *Diwan*, p. 68.
92. Majnun, *Diwan*, p. 230.
93. As 'Umar b. Abi Rabi'ah, for instance, defines his beloved's smell in his famous poem about Nu'm, see his *Diwan*, p. 101.
94. Jamil, *Diwan*, p. 27.
95. Ibid., p. 51.
96. Ibid., p.117.
97. Majnun, *Diwan*, p. 115.
98. Kuthayyir, *Diwan*, p. 197.
99. Jamil, *Diwan*, p. 71.
100. Ibid., p. 122.
101. 'Urwah, *Diwan*, p. 47.
102. Majnun, *Diwan*, p. 106; Kuthayyir, *Diwan*, p. 106; Jamil, *Diwan*, p. 112.
103. Jamil, *Diwan*, p. 113; Kuthayyir, *Diwan*, p. 197.
104. Jamil, *Diwan*, p. 113; Qays, *Diwan*, p. 52, Majnun, *Diwan*, p. 60.
105. Kuthayyir, *Diwan*, p. 144.
106. The ben tree (*Moringa*).
107. Qays, *Diwan*, p. 52.

108. Jamil, *Diwan*, p. 59; *al-Sabiriyyah* is a soft kind of cloth. It has been used since the pre-Islamic period to describe a woman's belly. 'Antarah, for instance, says: '[her] belly is soft like *al-Sabiryyiah*', *Diwan*, p. 110.
109. For more instances see Jamil, *Diwan*, pp. 37, 45, 59, 71; Majnun, *Diwan*, p. 115; Kuthayyir, *Diwan*, pp. 40, 124.
110. See, for example, al-A'sha's poem: 'bid farewell to Hurayrah as her people depart' in his *Diwan*, p. 144.
111. Zuhayr, *Diwan*, p. 46.
112. Jamil, *Diwan*, p. 117.
113. Al-Qays, '*Mu'allaqah*', Arberry, *The Seven Odes*, p. 63.
114. Kuthayyir, *Diwan*, p. 106.
115. Robert Hillenbrand relates the women described in poetry to Umayyad paintings and sculptures. For example, the women depicted at Qusair 'Amra, Qasr al-Hair al-Gharbi, Mshatta and Khirbat. These women have abundant folds of flesh. Hillenbrand, 'La dolce vita in early Islamic Syria: the evidence of later Umayyad palaces', *Art History* Vol. 1 (1982).
116. The treatment of the Majnun love legend appeared first in the form of the *mathnawi* in Persia. Nizami's *Khamsa* has strongly influenced subsequent writers of the subject. However, the transfer of the Majnun legend from Arabic to Persian literature, and the new elements that were added to it, is beyond the scope of this chapter.
117. Shiraz school of miniature painting, 'Layla receiving Majnun in her tent', 1444, Aqqoyunlu dynasty, in *Art and Culture Magazine*, winter 2003, Issue 7.
118. Shiraz school of miniature painting, 'Majnun speaks with an elderly man in a date grove apart from Layla, who is sitting at a distance', c.1480, *Khamsa* of Nizami, Aqqoyunlu dynasty, Library of Topkapı Museum, Istanbul, H.761, f.133b.
119. 'Layla and Majnun fainting', in Lentz and Glenn Lowry, *Timur and the Princely Vision. Persian Art and Culture in the Fifteenth Century*, p. 274.
120. Ivan Stchoukine, *Les peintures des manuscrits timurides*, pl. Xa, *Khamsa* of Nizami, dated 846/1442, f.170.
121. I gained this information from a meeting with Professor Robert Hillenbrand on 20 March 2007.
122. 'Majnun dies on Layla's Tomb', in Pinder-Wilson, *Persian Painting of the Fifteenth Century*, pp. 20–1.
123. I need not outline here the differences between these versions of the one image.
124. Sells, '*Guises of the Ghul*', p. 133.

125. 'Abd al-Karim, *al-'Arab wa al-marah*, p. 211.
126. Jamil, *Diwan*, p. 21. 'Umar b. Abi Rabi'ah went so far as wishing that slim women (*rashawat*) should be isolated and put into exile. See his *Diwan*, p.11.
127. The author provides this title to his book in English, along with the Arabic title.
128. See 'Abd al-Nur Idris, *Rihlat al-Muanath fi wijdan al-shi'r al-'arabi*, www.alwatanvoice.com\pulpit, 3 February 2006.
129. Although the author mainly focuses on Arabs of the early or pre-Islamic period, his book includes many references to contemporary Arabs, especially from the Arabian Peninsula.
130. 'Abd al-Karim, *al-'Arab wa al-marah*, p. 8.
131. Ibid., p. 36.
132. Ibid., pp. 39–41.
133. For further details, ibid., p. 184.
134. Ibid., p. 229.
135. Shakespeare, *Othello*, I, i.
136. Al-Batal, *al-Surah*, p. 61.
137. Ibid., p. 58.
138. Ibid., p. 70.
139. 'Idris, *Rihlat al-muanath*, p. 2.
140. Al-Jahiz, 'Kitab al-qiyan', in Pellat, *The Life and Works of Jahiz*, p. 259.
141. Al-Jahiz, 'Kitab al-Nisa', in *al-Rasail al-kalamiyyah*, p. 85.
142. Ibid., p. 102.
143. Al-Mutanabbi, *Diwan, Sharh Abu al-Baqa al-'Ukburi*, Vol. 3, p. 194.
144. Abu Tammam Habib b. Aws al-Ta'i, *Diwan Abi Tammam bi sharh al-Khatib al-Tabrizi*, Vol. 4, pp. 166, 176, 184, 203, 208, 268.
145. Behrens-Abouseif, *Beauty*, p. 100.
146. This is an Arabic name for a type of small tree with a very nice smell.
147. Ibn Qutaybah, *al-Shi'r wa al-shu'ra*, pp. 76–7.
148. Kinany, *Development*, p. 285.
149. Al-'Aqqad, *Jamil Buthaynah*, p. 17.
150. Al-Abshihi, *al-Mustatraf fi kull fanin mustadzraf*, Vol. 2, p. 220.
151. Al-Ifriqi, *Mukhtasar tarikh Dimashq*, Vol. 6, p. 114.
152. Majnun, *Diwan*, p. 217; Kuthayyir, *Diwan*, p. 153.
153. Kuthayyir, *Diwan*, p. 153.
154. Majnun, *Diwan*, pp. 115, 160.
155. Jamil, *Diwan*, p. 85.
156. Georges Bataille states that 'beauty is its meaning, what gives it its value, and

indeed the elements that make it desirable', *Erotism, Death, and Sensuality*, p. 142.
157. Qays, *Diwan*, p.109.
158. Jamil, *Diwan*, p. 37.
159. See for instance Kuthayyir, *Diwan*, p. 106 and Jamil, *Diwan*, p. 111.
160. Qays, *Diwan*, p. 84.
161. Jamil, *Diwan*, p. 111.
162. Kuthayyir, *Diwan*, p. 76.
163. Allat and al-'Uzza were two important pagan deities that people worshipped before Islam.
164. Ibn Qayyim al-Jawziyah, *Rawdat al-muhibbin*, p. 337.
165. Hamori, '*Love Poetry (Ghazal)*', p. 206.
166. Majnun, *Diwan*, p. 228, in Kinany, *Development*, p. 298.
167. Majnun, *Diwan*, p. 92.
168. Majnun, *Diwan*, p. 120; Jamil, *Diwan*, p. 38. A similar image can be found in the pre-Islamic *ghazal*, though it is very rare. For example, in his amatory prelude (Kinany, *Development*, p. 92), A'sha Qays declares:

> If she placed a dead man on her neck
> He would come to life again
> There would be then no need
> To carry him to a cemetery.

169. Majnun, *Diwan*, p. 55.
170. Al-Samarqandi, *Qurrat al-'uyun*, in Macdonald, 'Paradise', in *Islam Studies*, 5, p. 354.
171. Majnun, *Diwan*, p. 160.
172. Majnun, *Diwan*, p. 229, in Kinany, *Development*, p. 271.
173. 'Urwah, *Diwan*, p. 22, in Kinany, *Development*, p. 271.
174. Jamil, *Diwan*, p. 44.
175. Adonis, *al-Thabit wa al-mutahawwil*, p. 289.
176. A similar idea appears in the troubadour love lyric. See Gross, '*Loc Aizi/Anima Mundi*: Being, Time, and Desire in the Troubadour Love Lyric', in Paxson and Gravelee, *Desiring Discourse. The Literature of Love, Ovid through Chaucer*, p. 114.
177. Kuthayyir, *Diwan*, p. 55, in Kinany, *Development*, p. 290.
178. Jamil, *Diwan*, p. 28.
179. Ibid., p. 40.

180. Kuthayyir, *Diwan*, p. 56, in Kinany, *Development*, p. 291.
181. Majnun, *Diwan*, pp. 22–3.
182. Kinany, *Development*, p. 257.
183. Jamil, *Diwan*, p. 45.
184. Ibid., pp. 41–2.
185. Ibid., pp. 122–3. See more instances on pp. 45, 113.
186. Ibid., p. 28.
187. Kuthayyir, *Diwan*, p. 57, in Kinany, *Development*, p. 291.
188. See the whole story in Al-Isfahani, *Al-Aghani*, Vol. 9, p. 21. See also Vol. 1, p. 336 about Layla's love for Majnun.
189. Jamil, *Diwan*, p. 29, in Hamori, p. 34.
190. Jamil, *Diwan*, p. 40, in Bürgel, p. 116.
191. 'Urwah, *Diwan*, p. 41, in Kinany, *Development*, p. 300.

Plate 1 Layla and Majnun fainting. A lion attacking a person, *Khamsa* of Nizami, Herat. 1494–5. © British Library.

Plate 2 Majnun brought to Layla's tent, *Khamsa* of Nizami, Tabri. 1539–43. © British Library.

Plate 3 Majnun dies on the grave of Layla, *Khamsa* of Nizami, Iran. Timurid Dynasty. 1431. The State Hermitage Museum, St Petersburg. Photograph © The State Hermitage Museum; photo by Vladimir Terebenin.

Plate 4 Majnun at the Ka' ba, *Khamsa* of Nizami, Iran. Timurid Dynasty. 1431. The State Hermitage Museum, St Petersburg. Photograph © The State Hermitage Museum; photo by Vladimir Terebenin.

Plate 5 Layla in the palm grove, *Khamsa* of Nizami, Iran. Timurid Dynasty. 1431. The State Hermitage Museum, St Petersburg. Photograph © The State Hermitage Museum; photo by Vladimir Terebenin.

5

Present and Absent Bodies of the Beloved

Introduction

In the previous chapter we have seen how the *'udhri* poets depicted the body of their beloved as a model of ideal beauty. In their poetry they present her concrete, corporeal body. Nevertheless, the bodily presence in the *'udhri ghazal* does not always take the form of a physical body – sometimes it also appears symbolically, alongside a physical depiction, thereby expressing the idea of both the present and the absent beloved. The present form can be observed in gestures and speech. Gestures or intimate body language such as glances, gazes, sighs and smells are all illustrated in the *'udhri ghazal*, indicating the physical presence of the beloved, depicting communication, a kind of *wisal*, amorous union, between the lovers at the same time. In addition, speech has always been associated with love in the *'udhri* tradition. The beloved's speech is a characteristic of her bodily presence.

Moreover, the absence of the beloved is often presented symbolically in the form of her phantom or her being in a location inaccessible to the lover. These images are substitutes for her actual presence and a means of keeping her in her lover's mind. Her pure absence is expressed by the poet's longing for the place where she is, as well as by the phantom. Therefore, the phantom of the beloved and her location act as symbols for her absence.

The third aspect in the *'udhri ghazal* that I aim to examine in this chapter is that of presence through absence; the beloved who is present in the natural world in some metaphorical sense but still physically absent. The omnipresence of Layla in nature, as reflected in the mind of Majnun, and his ability to see the signs of his love within nature, will be discussed in detail.

Bodily Presence

Glances and other signs

I will examine below the role of physical gestures in the *'udhri ghazal*,[1] 'which expressively hovers between act and language, foregrounds language, self-division between muteness and communication, errancy and truth, unmeaning and meaning.'[2] Glances, sighs and smells are frequently depicted as channels of communication between the lovers. The Arabic treatises on love identify both the idea of longing looks that lead to love in the first place, and also gestures that are essential for communication between the lovers. At the same time, the question of the theological legality of looking at women was not forgotten in such discussions. In his attempt to define the conversation and glances between men and women, al-Jahiz provides many anecdotes to show that it was not shameful for women to converse with men or to exchange glances. All his examples, he says, give the lie to the tradition reported by *hashwiyah*, the literalists, according to which the first glance is licit but the second is illicit.[3] To support his view, al-Jahiz says:

> Up to our day, women who are daughters or mothers of the caliph or even of less exalted rank perform the circumambulation of the Ka'bah with their faces uncovered and that condition must be fulfilled in order that the pilgrimage be complete.[4]

However, those who took a stricter attitude referred to the Qur'anic verse enjoining men and women to behave modestly and chastely and included the advice that they 'cast down their eyes'.[5] Ibn Qayyim al-Jawziyyah explains that 'what the heart did not intend [the first glance, which occurs without any intention] is not subject to punishment. But, if the person takes a second look [at a woman] by intent, he sins.'[6]

Not surprisingly then, in the typical *adab* books on love, the subject is seasoned with piety. 'The authors do not trouble themselves over the battle against desire [*hawa*] and the terrible consequences of looking [. . .]. They are doubtless in the habit of thinking of the positive spiritual potentialities of human love.'[7] Authors such as Ibn Da'ud and Ibn Hazm tackle the issue of glances as a profound question in both causing and increasing love. In *Kitab al-zahrah* glances are treated by Ibn Da'ud as the first cause of love; the first chapter of *Kitab al-zahrah* is entitled 'he whose glances are many, his woes last long'. In *The Ring of the Dove*, Ibn Hazm demonstrates that glances play an honorable part and achieve remarkable results in one chapter entitled 'of hinting with the eyes'. He states that 'by means of a glance, the lover can be dismissed, admitted, promised, threatened, upbraided, cheered, commanded or forbidden.'⁸ Ibn Hazm then describes how even the most ordinary glances are forms of expression. He also emphasises the function of the eye as a messenger:

> You should realize that the eye takes the place of a messenger, and that with its aid all the beloved's intention can be apprehended. The four senses besides are also gateways of the heart, and passages giving admission to the soul; the eye is however the most eloquent, the most expressive, and the most efficient of them all. The eye is the true outrider and faithful guide of the soul; it is the soul's well-polished mirror, by means of which it comprehends all truths, attains all qualities, and understands all sensible phenomena.⁹

Regarding the *'udhri ghazal*, it is stated in Majnun's romance that 'In the beginning of his affair, Majnun used to see Layla and frequent her company as well as have close ties with her. Then she was made to disappear from his gaze.'¹⁰ This text, by al-Isfahani, uses the word '*nazirihi*' for 'his gaze'. So, the first stage in this text is *nazar*, then *nazar* becomes *ru'yah*, and then, as the rest of the text suggests, it became *ru'ya* when Majnun reached the state of madness and *huyam*. The writer implies here that Majnun's love for Layla was caused by their visual communication and conversation. 'His intimacy with her is deviant. Since the origin of this intimacy lies in his image of her through his eyes, her image must be made to vanish from his gaze', from his *nazar*, but it did not vanish from his heart when *ru'yah* was transformed into *ru'ya*, which is the stage of his suffering.

It was this specific part of the conversation and glances in Majnun's romance which incited some authors, such as Ibn al-Jawzi, to criticise Majnun and take him as an example of the dangers which lie in the glances between men and women as well as in their conversation. Ibn al-Jawzi argues that this practice 'worked insidious harm to Majnun and others like him, driving them mad and destroying them in the end. They erred, he says, in that such behavior is against both human nature and the sacred law.'[11]

However, in Majnun's poetry, looking and glances function in several ways; sometimes they relieved the tortured heart:

> Were our eyes to meet then all would be well
> And the troubles would be lifted from my heart[12]   [1]

He also says:

> I gave her a look that I would not exchange
> For all the red and black camels of the land[13]   [2]

When the lovers' eyes meet they magically cure each other's troubled hearts. A kind of *wisal*[14] is reached. Hence, those precious glances are more valuable to Majnun than anything else, even 'the red or black camels'. Glances could also be a suitable channel of communication between the lovers in a society full of blamers:

> When she looks my way her eyes
> speak to me and my eyes reply while we
> remain silent
> One of them tells me I will meet her
> while the other almost leaves me dead[15]   [3]

Glances could express great contrasts of meaning in these 'visual conversations'. Although their tongues were silent, the outer angle of her eye would 'speak' and his would 'answer'. One glance is promising and it announces a meeting, another might lead to death. The role played by the eyes in Majnun's poetry is pivotal, so some of his verses read:

> I was prevented from greeting her the day of her
> departure, so I saw her off with the angle of my eye which
> was in tears And I was speechless to answer her
> Who has ever seen a lover in tears bidding farewell to his heart[16]   [4]

Here, the gaze functions as an index in a system of gestural codes. It is not just Majnun, but his beloved, Layla herself, who is said to have recited the following verses to him:

> Both of us appear in front of people
> To hate each other
> And yet each is entrenched with his friend
> The secrets of the glances are not hidden
> If the eyes disclose what he conceals[17] [5]

Similarly, Jamil's glances convey messages between himself and Buthaynah:

> But the glances we exchanged were as messengers,
> which conveyed what our hearts conceal[18] [6]

So here, the two lovers rely upon the gesture of looking to conceal as well as to reveal. Furthermore, 'love has involved the composition of demeanour to mislead others, turning facial expression into a misleading sign written upon the body itself.'[19] Jamil says:

> When you come to me then control your eyes
> For our love is obvious to one who has vision
> And turn away if you meet an eye you fear
> And exhibit hate – that is more secret
> But when you come you always move your eyes towards me,
> So that your love nearly becomes manifest[20] [7]

'Just as the corporeal image of holding the tongue metaphorises the suppression of speech, the gestures and movement of the eyes represent expression of speech.'[21] Kuthayyir declares:

> So I swore never to forget 'Azza's glance;
> I almost exposed my stammering passion on the night
> when their eyes were upon us
> and she gave me a sign with her hand that I must not speak[22] [8]

It is noteworthy in all these verses by *'udhri* poets cited above that the eyes function as a metaphor for language. Khan notes that Majnun's romance

> rehearses for us how the body (eyes) functions as metaphor for language: the imaging (secreting) and conveying (revealing) of the lover's desire that occurs through the eyes metaphorises language's capacity for constituting and conducting desire. Majnun's glances at Layla generate desire in him yet

his eyes also betray to others his infatuation for her. Language and gaze are both causes and stages of the love-quest. In the medieval Arabic discourse on love, the glance (*lahza*) could actually be interpreted as a metaphor for word or expression (*lafza*). Both words and glances have the same function in that they generate desirable images in the mind.[23]

The sudden glimpse of the beloved could have a great effect on the lover. 'Urwah expresses his feelings in such a situation:

> It is just that, as soon as I see her,
> unexpectedly, I am struck dumb, so that I can
> hardly answer;
> I abandon any ideas that I might have had before
> and forget whatever I had resolved when she was absent.
> My heart shows to me her excuse and assists her
> against myself: I am no longer master over my heart[24]   [9]

Once again, glances are a substitution for conversation. So 'Urwah 'can hardly answer'. He is moved by the sight of his beloved to the extent that he forgets whatever he 'had resolved when she was absent'. This scene of desire and destruction in these verses is caused entirely by his gaze. It is the gaze of the lover at the beloved that smites his own heart;[25] he is no longer master of his heart. Thus, it could be argued that in the *'udhri* tradition the representation of the lover's gaze can be the subject or the object between male and female characters.[26] Moreover, keeping the aforementioned verses by Jamil and Kuthayyir in mind, the interchange occurs as a shared gaze between the two lovers.

Glances relate to the poetic image of piercing. The eye of the beloved reaches the lover's and reaches his heart through a glance. There is a familiar conceit in the Arabic *ghazal*: the lover's or the beloved's gaze that penetrates as an arrow, through the eye, to wound the heart.[27] This conceit establishes the link between gazes and death. Abu al-Tayyib al-Mutanabbi's verse reads:

> It is I whose eye's outer angle evoked fatality,
> Thus, who is the enquirer, when the victim is the killer?[28]   [10]

Khalil al-Safadi in *Sharh lamiyyat al-'Ajam* says, commenting on al-Mutanabbi's verse:

Hence, look at how Abu al-Tayyib claimed that the eye is behind the evocation of fatality. According to all poets, it is the eye which is guilty, because, with its capacity of seeing, the eye leads to the annihilation of the heart. Poetry books, however, are full of such meaning and it is well-known enough and needs no more quotations to prove it.[29]

Indeed, as al-Safadi declares, poetry books are full of such meaning. Imru' al-Qays, for example, says:

> Your eyes only shed those tears so as to strike and pierce
> With those two shafts of theirs the fragments of a ruined heart[30] [11]

The famous verses of the poet Jarir read:

> The eyes whose corners are white have slain us
> And then do not bring our dead to life again
> They fell the man of wit and leave him motionless,
> While they are the weakest of God's creation[31] [12]

The *'udhri* poet Qays Lubna declares, moreover:

> If I die, then seek blood requital from every virgin girl
> With languid eyelids and listless eyes[32] [13]

The murderous glance is associated with the image of the beloved as a gazelle in several lines of classical Arabic poetry. For example, al-'Abbas b. al-Ahnaf says:

> A fawn (*rim*) shot with its eyeballs, aiming at my heart,
> my heart's hunter, whose ransom and protector I am[33] [14]

In another verse by the same poet the mere appearance of the gazelle makes the hunter die:

> How could a man as powerless as the like of me hunt
> a gazelle which kills those who behold her[34] [15]

Regarding the connotations of the metaphor of the female gazelle and her 'murderous glances', Bürgel explains that this animal can 'evoke an uncanny feeling, due to its close links with the realm of fairies and demons.'[35] Through several examples he shows how the gazelle was sacred among ancient Arabs, the image traditionally holding a sense of magic and numinosity. Indeed, this reminds us of the magical power ascribed to the beloved, especially in Majnun's poetry. Therefore, the gazelle metaphor 'expresses the strange mixture of fear and fascination evoked by the irritating fusion of weakness and power in woman.'[36] Bürgel maintains that love poetry

> created a realm where woman existed not only unsubdued but ruling, even tyrannically, and yet adored. This realm is that of an ideal love, somewhat crazy, somewhat perverse, it is true, but with all the features of an elaborate system like a philosophy and indeed a religion, the religion of love, in which man adores a Lady Gazelle and willingly submits to her whims, even to the extent of being killed by her murderous glances.[37]

In a previous chapter the significance of the beloved's smell as shown in the *'udhri ghazal* was noted.[38] Here, however, I would argue that this odour, carried by the zephyrs, is also depicted in *'udhri* poetry as a channel to communicate with the beloved. Kuthayyir declares:

> The east wind brings her scent to me every night
> And we are together in our dreams wherever we sleep[39]   [16]

Majnun also says:

> If ever riders come from near his land he breathes
> in seeking relief from the scent of the riders[40]   [17]

The smell, even from the beloved's land or direction, is depicted as a cure for the agony of ardent love. Therefore, the body of the beloved is presented in the *'udhri ghazal* through symbolic channels both of gestures and smell. Its presence is also depicted through speech, as we shall see in the following section.

Speech

Jamil's famous verse reads:

> Women's converse is real bliss (*bashashah*)
> And women's victims are martyrs[41]   [18]

In this verse, Jamil signifies the importance of the conversation with the beloved in the *'udhri ghazal*. His use of the word '*bashashah*' is significant as it alludes to joy and happiness. In another verse he says, addressing Buthaynah:

> She is beautiful, smiling,
> Her speech resembles a string of pearls, unloosed and scattered[42] [19]

Here, Jamil uses the metaphor 'a string of pearls, unloosed and scattered' to describe the beauty of Buthaynah's speech. 'This metaphor is a play upon that term often employed by medieval Arab critics in describing poetry as "a string of pearls".'[43] It is perhaps not surprising that we find so many allusions in the *'udhri ghazal* to women's speech and the joy of conversation between women and their lovers. Al-Jahiz states clearly that this kind of conversation was common among Bedouin men and women:

> Among Bedouin men and women there was no veiling of women; yet in spite of the absence of the veil, they disapproved of sly glances and secret ogling. Nevertheless, they were accustomed to foregather for conversation and evening parties, and might pair off for whispering and joking (the man who was addicted to this being termed *Zir*, [a word] derived from [the verb meaning] to visit). All this will take place under the eyes of the women's guardians or in the presence of her husband, without these taking exception to conduct not in itself exceptionable, provided they felt secure against any misbehaviour occurring.[44]

Moreover, he also states that such conversations were the cause of the passion between *'udhri* lovers:

> Men continued to hold converse with women both in pre-Islam and [in the beginning of] Islam, up to the time when the veil was imposed as a particular duty on the wives of the prophet. Such converse was the cause of the association between Jamil and Buthaynah, 'Afra and 'Urwah, Kuthayyir and 'Azzah, Qays and Lubna, Asma' and Muraqqish, Abdallah b. 'Ajlan and Hind. Moreover, noble ladies used to sit and talk to men, and for them to look at each other was neither shameful in pre-Islam nor illicit in Islam.[45]

In Ibn Qutaybah's '*Uyun al-akhbar* a chapter is devoted to 'the discourse of women', in which the author presents an abundance of romanticised tropes to describe the words of women as they appear in Arabic poetry. For example, Ibn Qutaybah quotes Ibn al-'Arabi's verse:

> Her speech is like a shower of saving rain heard by a shepherd
> After long years of drought
> Who faints wishing to live and out of joy says 'more, O Lord'.[46] [20]

And he also quotes Bashshar b. Burd's verses:

> As Harut delivers his magic in her tongue
> And her speech is like flowers in verdant meadows[47] [21]

Therefore, women's words are like 'a flow of clouds' and 'flowers in verdant meadows'. In other verses that Ibn Qutaybah provides, women's words are like 'the glitter of gold and silver', 'a string of pearls, unloosed and scattered' and 'honeyed wine'.[48] Khan argues that:

> Women's words, like their bodies, are objectified as ornaments of seduction and deceptive allurement. The analogy between their words and ornaments is important. This analogy suggests how, by making signification ascribed to women's words suspect and ambiguous, their language is rendered enigmatic and secretive.[49]

In *'udhri* tradition there are many references to the act of conversation, which is considered a kind of *wisal* with the beloved. In many senses the *'udhri* lover is portrayed as incapable of withstanding the beauty or the lethal effect of his beloved's words. In one account given by Ibn Qutaybah, Jamil and a friend of his went to Buthaynah's campsite. Hearing of his arrival, she came out accompanied by other women to meet him. They all sat together to talk and after a while the women left the two lovers alone. They spent the whole night talking until the morning, when they had to bid farewell to each other. When Jamil was about to mount his camel, Buthaynah asked him to come close to her, which he did. She whispered something to him that caused him to faint and then she left. When he finally woke up he recited:

> Neither a storm cloud in a heavy
> millstone, Nor what bees keep in their stores
> Are sweeter than what you said
> After the saddle was placed on the breast of my camel[50] [22]

The loss of control by fainting can be seen as a metaphor for reaching the height of desire. Manzalaouni has pointed out that in the later collection of stories, *One Thousand and One Nights*, 'the mutuality of the simultaneous faint is the sentimental romance's surrogate for sexual intercourse'.[51] The pure water, 'a storm cloud in a heavy millstone', is a metaphor for the beloved's speech, it is 'a flow of clouds' in the aforementioned verse by Ibn al-'Arabi. And so the dual nature of thirst and the quenching of thirst arises again in the *'udhri ghazal*. It is not just kisses from the beloved's delicious mouth that quench the poet's thirst, but also her sweet words. In a similar context, al-Qutami, the Umayyad poet, declares:

> They kill us by a talk
> that is not known to whom they are scared of
> and what is hidden of this talk
> is not obvious to others.
> This is so because their talk
> is like water
> for a thirsty person[52]   [23]

When we return to Jamil's verse: 'not even whatever bees hid in their dwellings', we notice here how Jamil uses the image of the luscious honey produced by bees in reference to the sweet words that his beloved hides and tells only to him. This image directs us to a similar one related also to the beloved's mouth; it is the image of the luscious honey of her saliva. It is the honey that the poet receives or wishes to receive while kissing the beloved. Therefore, can we suggest that the mouth is presented in *'udhri* poetry as a desirable area, either in its physical form, as in kissing, or in immaterial form, as in speaking? The image of the beloved's 'honeyed speech' or her speech being even more luscious than honey is very popular in Arabic classical poetry. Abu Hayyah al-Numayri refers to the capacity of the beloved's speech in curing[53] not only sickness but even for saving one from the last inhalations of death.[54]

Another anecdote from the *'udhri* tradition shows how fond Majnun was of women's conversation. The anecdote also reveals his extreme reaction to Layla's words. Ibn Qutaybah provides the following anecdote about Majnun:

He would sit and talk to her among some of his people. Handsome and gracious, he was brilliant in conversation and poetic recitation. But she would shun him and converse with others, to the point where he was hurt. When she realized that, she turned to him and said: In front of other people, we both display hatred, While each of us is entrenched in the other's heart. Things worsened for him so much that his reason left him, and he wandered aimlessly with the wild beasts.[55]

In this anecdote, Majnun is portrayed as a man who takes pleasure both in listening to women's conversation and in reciting poetry to them. But what do the women's words in general, and Layla's in particular, signify? The narrative, as Khan notes, ascribed to this discourse a role in the genesis of male desire. Women's speech reflects poetic speech and mirrors it, which is why he is so fond of hearing their words.[56] So the male poet's listening is not so much an act of hearing the women's speech as one of hearing his own words reflected in her language. His attention to her words is thus ultimately a self-referential activity.[57] Nevertheless, Majnun's excessive reaction to Layla's verses is significant. It provokes an even more public display from him.[58]

In his treatise about love, *The Ring of the Dove,* Ibn Hazm considers conversation as the first device employed by those who seek union:

> The first device employed by those who seek union, being lovers, in order to disclose their feeling to the object of their passion, is allusion by means of words. Either they will quote a verse of poetry, or despatch an allegory, or rhyme a riddle, or propose an enigma, or use heightened language.[59]

Sometimes, it seems that the content of the beloved's speech does not matter to the poet. Just the mere fact that she actually spoke to him, even if only to curse him, is what matters because all the beloved's talk is beloved. Jamil illustrates this by saying:

> Buthaynah has said it,
> And all of her words to me are sweet even if she speaks ill[60]　　　　[24]

He also says:

> A false word from one whose speech I love,
> is more precious to me than one I hate speaking the truth[61]　　　　[25]

In some contexts, when the choice is made between actual physical touch and a woman's whisper, the poet confesses that whispers bring him the greatest pleasure. 'Umar b. Abi Rabi'ah claims: 'I was in between two women, one was whispering to me and the other was biting me, yet I could not feel the bite, for the enjoyment of the other's whisper overwhelmed it.'[62]

The enjoyment of talking to the beloved sometimes refers also to the purity of the relations between the *'udhri* poets and their beloveds. In numerous narratives, the lovers get together and talk until morning. A verse by Jamil describes a similar desire:

> I know nothing of what lies beneath her
> clothes, nor have I ever kissed her,
> I have never touched her.
> We just talked and were lost in each other's eyes[63] [26]

'Talking and looking' is presented in contrast to actual physical interaction, looking which does not exceed the edges of the outer dress, and speaking, from the mouth that he has not tasted. Nevertheless, Jamil composed other verses that could be seen as challenging this purported link between conversation and chastity. For example, in one verse, he links his beloved's words and her saliva:

> Ah me! Shall we ever spend another night like
> our night until we see the rising of the dawn;
> she showering her words upon me,
> and oft times showering her saliva upon me from her mouth?[64] [27]

The first verse recalls a similar one of Majnun, in which he also links the conversation with his beloved to the night:

> Ah me! Shall I ever spend the night whispering to you
> until I behold the rise of the dawn[65] [28]

Beyond their descriptions of their beloveds' speech as pure water and honey, *'udhri* poets also ascribe extraordinary effects to their words. Majnun claims:

> If I were blind, walking using a stick, and deaf
> when she calls me, I would respond to her[66] [29]

Jamil also expresses a peculiar wish:

> I wish I were blind and deaf while Buthaynah is guiding me,
> not a word from her speech is hidden from me![67] [30]

There is an insistence on Buthaynah's words not being hidden from him. Her words could act in place of his sight and hearing. Furthermore, love at a distance, as Bouhdiba demonstrates, is based almost exclusively on hearing or hearsay and is fed on fantasy.[68] The famous verse by Bashshar b. Burd reads: 'Sometimes the ear falls madly in love before the eye'.[69] In any case, these kinds of verses incite al-Washsha' to comment on them by saying:

> They [the poets] claim that women's speech is a cure for blindness, and it makes the deaf hear, and enlivens the dead, and raises people from graves before their due time. Some Bedouin said: Some of women's speech is like water that quenches thirst.[70]

Moreover, *'udhri* poets claim that the beloved's words could affect even the non-human world. Majnun, for instance, maintains:

> You kept me close until you put a spell on me
> with words that bring the mountain-goats down to the plains
> When I had no way out, you shunned me,
> But you left what you left within my breast[71] [31]

He also says:

> If she called to the doves they would answer her
> And were she to speak to the dead they would speak back to her[72] [32]

Kuthayyir depicts his beloved's speech in a similar image:

> And if Umm al-Walid were to talk to the mountain goats on mount Radwa,
> They would draw near to her and come down to her
> From the mountain passes of Da's and Aylah
> Even when the hunter is there with his dogs[73] [33]

In these verses the poets use the words *qawl*, *hadithaha* and *kallamat*, which indicate that it is not just the sound but that the beloved's words and speech are magical. Both poets use the image of *'usm*, the mountain-goat, which belongs to the pricket (*wa'l*) species that always stays in the mountains and never ventures down to the plains. So, the effect of the beloved's speech goes beyond the poet himself, to embrace other creatures. Her speech is powerful enough to make the wild mountain-goats relinquish their well-fortified location and descend to the plains. Here, these animals could even recklessly ignore the surrounding dangers like the intimidating hunting dogs. The pleasure these aloof animals find in her speech leads to their 'rapprochement' and make them 'descend', transforming any aloofness into a world of amiability.

Bodily Absence

The phantom presence of the beloved

The phantom of the beloved (*tayf al-khayal*) is a 'constantly mentioned convention of amatory preludes'[74] in the classical Arabic *qasidah*. It could be defined as a 'vision of the beloved appearing by night'.[75] *Tayf* is a verbal noun deriving from *tafa/yatifu*, 'to appear [in sleep, as a phantom]', while the second form of the verb, *tafa*, means 'to make a circuit', 'go around'. The verb *tafa* is used to describe the phantom's night visit. Khayal derives from *khala/yakhalu*, 'to think, suppose, fancy, imagine'.[76] So, *tayf al-khayal* is purely imaginary, an imaginative projection in a dream or dream-like state. In the classical Arabic *qasidah* the phantom of the beloved functions as an abandoned campsite that arouses the poet's emotions.[77] Some scholars have drawn a distinction between *tayf* and *khayal* based on their linguistic origins and their literary use.[78] However, it is remarkable that it is a traditional literary convention to use a combination of the two words in the term *tayf al-khayal*.[79] For example, Jamil uses both terms in different contexts while Majnun focuses on the word *khayal*, which will be highlighted in this section. Jacobi notes that:

> [*Tayf al-khayal*] was first conceived as an apparition or ghost, confronting the poet in the external world, not always welcome, and sometimes even terrifying him. Later, from the early seventh century onwards, it was referred to as a vision the poet sees in his dream, longed for and fulfilling his secret wishes, granting favours the beloved herself refused.[80]

Clearly *tayf al-khayal* acts as a symbol of the beloved's bodily presence, thereby indicating her absence. As soon as *tayf al-khayal* reaches the lover, it arouses his hidden yearning and sadness; Kuthayyir expresses the effect that 'Azzah's phantom had on him:

> *Khayal* from 'Azzah' has
> passed (*taf*) by in the dark and during
> still times and has stimulated my grief
> and her *khayal* has deranged all [the] way
> from *Buwayb* to [reach] *Thi'dawrani*[81] [34]

Tayf al-khayal only passes by night. Khuthayyir further explains it by using '*ba'd al-hudu*', which indicates times of tranquillity and stillness. That is because tranquillity and darkness allow for the revelation of the beloved's phantom, which evokes his grief and brings forth memories, along with the nostalgic wish to relive the past which can only be achieved through dreams and the imagination. It is also remarkable that the poet uses the verb '*tafa*' meaning 'passed' when describing the phantom's visit to him because this verb is itself derived from the noun *tayf*, which has often been used by poets to evoke feelings of fear, insecurity or even suspicion towards nature[82]. In addition, some poets link the noun *tayf* with *jinn* in their usage of terms such as '*tayf Jinnah*' or '*ta'if Jinnah*'. 'Urwah, for instance, says:

> I am not mad, I have no *jinn* inside me.
> It's this, my friend: my uncle has belied me[83] [35]

Qays says, addressing Lubna:

> Your *tayf* has visited me in the evening and caused me insomnia
> So I dropped endless tears[84] [36]

Here *tayf* is also linked to the night, causing sadness and continual tears and eventually preventing the poet from sleeping, as if this symbiosis of the beloved with the *tayf* indicates the absence of her physical body and the impossibility of her physical presence except through symbolism and the imagination. The poet's grief over her absence is reflected in flowing tears. The *tayf* visits the poet during his sleep only to fade away when he awakes; therefore, 'sleeplessness is a keyword, a prerequisite for the appearance of the phantom.'[85] A subsequent poet, Jarir, uses a similar image of a phantom of the beloved visiting at night, yet he links it with the motif of *talal*:

> Is it the phantom of Khalidah
> Coming through the night?
> No looming shape [campsite ruin] could I see dearer
> Than such a nightly vision[86] [37]

In other situations *tayf al-khayal* does not pay the poet a direct visit but rather makes a long journey that starts from the actual location of the physical presence of the beloved to reach the actual location of the poet. In other words, the beloved's body symbolically turns into the *khayal* that takes on the journey on her behalf, as Jamil says:

> *khayal* from Buthaynah has haunted me, Longing for me and agitating my longing
> It has penetrated through *Tila'al-hijr* and reached me
> Despite *al-Ash'arun and Ghafiq* in between[87] [38]

The power that his beloved lacks to take such a long journey and to cross *Tila'al-hijr* to reach the location of the poet is further hindered by *al-Ash'arun and Ghafiq*[88], her *tayf al-khayal* possesses this power instead.[89] The question of how her *khayal* was able to reach the poet in spite of the distance is hardly relevant within the context of dreams, but it gives the *khayal* more reality and even more substance.[90] Jamil here uses the verb 'haunted' and Salamah notes that the poet's use of this verb is quite normal to describe the *tayf* of the beloved as it is the same verb associated with the *jinn* and the *ta'if* of the *jinn*. It is also linked to other names of love such as *mass* and *lamam*. So, the lover goes insane because he falls in love with a human that resembles a *jinni*.[91] Regardless of the *jinni*-like power that characterise this *tayf*, it is described using the same terms as those used to describe the beloved, such as 'longing' and 'agitates longing'. In any case, the distance that the phantom covers is paradoxical; Seybold argues that:

> The lady is far away while her phantom is near. Distance is nearly always spatial, and the phantom's triumph is finding the right way over endless rough terrain. But distance also has a temporal dimension: the lady exists in

the past as a memory while the phantom appears in the present as a desire. Simultaneously far and near, past and present – again, two views of a single reality.[92]

Jamil expresses his surprise at the phantom's night visit while he was asleep:

> O Buthaynah, does your phantom *tayf* visit me gently in sleep? And my
> heart was inflamed with longing and it poured forth
> I was astonished that it would visit my bed in sleep,
> and were it to visit me awake it would be more astonishing[93]   [39]

Particularly fascinating in these verses is the key verb *sara*, 'to travel by night', which is used to describe the phantom's night visit. Contrary to Seybold's argument, I maintain that *tayf al-khayal* is portrayed as a visitor while the poet is asleep, not only when he is awake. As seen in Jamil's verses cited above, Jamil clearly says that Buthaynah's *tayf* visited him while he was asleep, though in the last verse he includes not only *tayf al-khayal* but also the actual figure of Buthaynah when he says: 'and were it to visit me awake it would be more astonishing'. The real meeting arouses his surprise because of the distance between himself and Buthaynah, so he is only hoping to meet her phantom by trying to sleep, even though he is not sleepy:

> Although I am not sleepy, I am trying to be drowsy,
> Hoping to meet her in my sleep[94]   [40]

A similar verse is attributed to Majnun:

> I cover my head with my garment, Although I am not sleepy,
> Perhaps a *khayal* from you will meet my *khayal*[95]   [41]

Al-Sharif al-Murtada (d. 1044), in his monograph *tayf al-khayal*, describes the second *khayal* in Majnun's verse as the poet's emaciated body.[96] However, *tayf al-khayal* becomes a means of realising dreams that are unachievable in reality because desires become real in dreams:

> Have I seen you Layla in my night dreams, or during my day where I have
> witnesses?
> I have held you close to me until I thought
> My fire was extinguished,
> But it wasn't; it was agitating instead [97]   [42]

So the appearance of *tayf al-khayl* is a result of longing and desire. The contrast between the gracious behaviour of the *khayal* and the disobliging attitude of the beloved is implied in this verse. That shows that *tayf al-Khayal* 'has not always been conceived as exactly the same thing'.[98]

Majnun links the hindrance created by the society that prevents him from contacting his beloved to the inability of this society to prevent contact with her through her phantom and his imagination:

> Since you deny me her words,
> why not forbid her image (*khayal*) from coming freely to me,
> despite the distance[99]   [43]

Unlike the beloved herself, her *khayal* is capable of challenging all social and natural obstacles that hinder their meeting. This allows the poet to make contact with the *khayal* that is almost equivalent to her own self. In *al-hawamil wa'l-shawamil* by Abu Hayyan al-Tawhidi (d. 1023), the author presents a conversation between himself and Miskawayh (a philosopher). This dialogue is an attempt to comprehend the poet's obsession with the phantom and its relation to the imagination, while the interlocutors try to understand the psychological role of the phantom in facing this longing.[100]

Hence, using the *tayf* as a means to reach impossible dreams is a topos of classical Arabic poetry. In a poem by Husayn b. al-Dahhak, he describes the visit of a gazelle's *tayf* in the darkness, as if the gazelle were perfumed by odours and longing for the poet. The poet achieves his desire with the gazelle after the creature held out and acted flirtatiously.[101] According to Abu Tammam, *tayf al-khayal* visited him because of the poet's own intention:

> A *khayal* from her visited (you),
> No, but a thought caused you to visit it
> When man sleeps, his mind does not sleep
> A gazelle whom I caught, after I had set up for it,
> Towards the end of the night, snares consisting of dreams[102]   [44]

Here, Jacobi observes, 'the initiative rests with the poet; his intellectual and imaginative faculties are envisaged as a hunter chasing the *khayal* and finally ensnaring it by dreams.'[103] Nevertheless, sometimes *tayf al-khayal* appears in classical poetry as a figure who is capable of anger. So it would act as the beloved herself would do. Abu Nuwas says:

> My *tayf* desired him in sleep, but he vanished,
> And one day I kissed his shadow, but he blamed me for it[104]   [45]

Moreover, the poet seems to be aware that *tayf al-khayal* partly symbolises the beloved, but is still just a dream that vanished in the morning:

> O you two lovers! You get reconciled in sleep, And in the morning you are
>   both angry again. Such are dreams, they deceive us,
> But it also happens that they come true[105]   [46]

The phantom form of the beloved symbolises the absence of her body, and at the same time, it is capable of travelling long distances to reach the poet. It is also able to fulfil the desires that the beloved herself is unable to achieve.

The residence of the beloved

Many of the dominant motifs in the *nasib*, the opening section of the classical Arabic poem, the *qasidah*, such as the ruined campsite, the beloved's *tayf* and her departure, create a sense of longing and sorrow. The poet may elaborate on any of these motifs; Kuthayyir, the *'udhri* poet, preserved these conventions to express his yearning not just for his beloved, but also for her belongings and any traces of her. We come across lines in his poetry that explicitly relate 'Azzah's departure to his sorrow.[106] As Stetkevych explains,

> There are equally unending insistences on motifs of arrivals at abandoned campsites, of departures from the tribal grounds, of sorrow at such arrivals and departures and over the emptiness that always lies before and after them, and of the glimpse of happiness in between – just enough happiness to reduce everything else to unceasing yearning.[107]

However, the *'udhri ghazal*, in general, divests itself of such motifs; visiting a place connected with the beloved replaces the scene of the poet halting at the ruined campsite, and this form of poetry does not generally have the motif of the departing woman. Moreover, the yearning for the place of the beloved is not limited to the opening section of the *qasidah* as, in a sense, the entire *'udhri qasidah* is a love *qasidah*. The representation of the place of the beloved in *'udhri* poetry indicates her absence, on the one hand, and the poet's endeavour to overcome this absence, on the other. Her place acts as a symbol of her actual body; 'Urwah says, conveying his longing to 'Afra':

> Do you every day aim for her country
> with eyes in which the pupils are drowning? O, carry me, may God bless you,
> to the settlement of *al-Rawhā'*, and then leave me[108]   [47]

Hence, the place of the beloved is portrayed in *'udhri* poetry as a symbol of her concrete presence. The body of the beloved is absent, and even its attributes such as gestures and speech are absent. The poet cannot surmount this absence, he cannot retrieve his beloved, her actual figure, gestures and voice, and hence he resorts to symbolising all these. Her absent body is represented by symbolic channels and in *'udhri* poetry it is her place or location that comes to replace the body. The place of the beloved becomes a substitute for her presence. Stones, walls and even traces in the sand are components that indicate her presence in the past despite her absence in the present. Pure absence can be observed in Majnun's verses:

> O house
> That I do not visit though this desertion is an offence (fault).
> I desert you though I am longing and visit you though I am scared
> And in your [house] observers watch me through time[109]   [48]

Majnun uses the lexicon of 'visit and desert', 'longing and observers' to reveal his being torn between absence and presence. The beloved's presence is not real, but it becomes real in the form of something material, such as her house. In Majnun's endeavour to surmount the total absence of his beloved and to attain her presence, he heads for her house, but he is unable to conquer this absence entirely as the observers 'watch him through time', so he is torn between visiting and deserting. In another verse, Kuthayyir reveals:

> I turn away from your home while I madly long for you,
> Just to show gossipy people that I have deserted your home[110]   [49]

Other *'udhri* poets express the struggle to conceal their desire to visit their beloved's residences. They maintain that they would visit the houses of the beloved's neighbours even if they do not like their inhabitants, while their hearts remain in the house that they are forced to abandon.[111] Because of a lack of social protection, the poet's journey to his beloved becomes full of dangers. 'The idea of the withdrawal of any social protection normally accorded to the individual is common to this restriction'[112] as one can observe in the stories of Qays and Jamil. In the following verses Majnun reproaches his friends for refusing to accompany him on his journey to see Layla:

> And should I leave Layla
> when there is nothing between me and her save one night journey; Indeed
>   I would then be patient
> Assume that I am a man from among you who has led his camel astray
> [Yet] he has a contract of protection, Indeed this right due is great
> But the friend who has been left behind is [surely] more of an obligation
> Than [the case of] a camel going astray
> May God forgive Layla today, indeed she has gone astray
> [she has acted] wrongfully,
> If she condemns me to die of love[113]   [50]

It seems that Majnun was aware of the grave dangers in visiting Layla, but still the path to her is preferable for him. In other verses, Majnun clearly maintains that he is not fond of the places themselves, but of her who lives in them:

> I pass by places (Layla's places) kissing this wall and that wall
> Longing for her who lived in these places
> Not the places themselves[114]   [51]

The phrase 'kissing this wall and that wall' acts as a clear symbol of kissing the beloved herself. She is absent, so cannot be held or kissed, but the walls that enclosed her symbolise her body and act as a metaphor of her actual presence. In a poetic moment, Majnun discovers that kissing the walls is in fact a questionable act, so he tries to defend himself by declaring that he longs for her who lived in the places and not for the places themselves. A similar idea may be found in the poetry of Qays; he declares that:

> I am not fond of your homeland,
> I am kissing the footprints of the one (his beloved)
> who stepped over its soil[115] [52]

Kissing the beloved's footprints indicates submission in love to the beloved to the extent of worship. Hence, the beloved is, as Majnun claims, a creature made of light who, when stepping on the soil of the earth, makes it more aromatic, even years later.[116] Qays explains his obsession as being with his beloved's footprints rather than being in love with the earth itself. Thus, anything that the beloved touches or steps on becomes sacred and it becomes almost an obligation for the poet to touch and kiss it. Furthermore, Kuthayyir asks his companions:

> My friends, this was the encampment of 'Azzah
> Stop and touch the earth which may have touched her skin
> and remain spending the night where she stayed and spent the night
> And do not doubt that God will forgive your sins,
> if you pray where she prayed[117] [53]

Therefore the *'udhri* poet goes to extreme lengths in searching for the traces of his absent beloved. He has no doubts that God will forgive people's sins if they follow his beloved and pray where she prayed. The place in which she once prayed becomes the channel between the poet and God. Hence, the poet has no doubts that God will forgive his sins because of his love. Here we notice that the concept of place has different meanings in *'udhri* love, and through this we find the common element that brings the two bodies – the body of place and that of woman – together is the place. For *'udhri* poets there are two kinds of places; the material one and the abstract one. Both are intertwined in the *'udhri* poem.

Majnun's poetry quoted below 'celebrates to an equal degree the beloved Layla and Najd':[118]

> As nights go by, even as I despair of ever returning, I yearn for Najd.
> Were there no Layla and no Najd, admit
> That you'd forsake all till Judgment Day[119] [54]

He also sang:

> O East wind of the highlands, When did you stir from Najd? Your journey through the night
> And passion upon passion add[120]   [55]

Considering these and similar verses, Stetkevych has noted:

> The Bedouin poet began possessing Tihama, Hijaz and above all, Najd, when he stepped out of them: and when he had lost these regions in the dispersion of the empire, these places, these names, then possessed him. Such possession implied the awareness of loss through the great paradox of nostalgic seizing of time – of time one once had and also of that much larger time to which one's soul feels a compelling affinity, to which it must return because it itself is possessed.[121]

Indeed, 'As landscape, Najd has been arrested and transformed in a poetic vision'.[122] But, especially for Majnun, Najd signifies the path to the beloved. Khan observes that the depiction of Majnun as lost in the space between two opposing geographical peripheries, without being able to find a way out, mirrors his spiritual and moral bewilderment. His geographic roaming from al-Sham to al-Yaman 'symbolises not just the fluctuations (lows and highs) in his myriad other states of being but also foregrounds his spiritual and moral liminality.'[123] The contours of a terrestrial topography, Khan continues, take on a linguistic and sexual significance. Linguistically, the wandering of the poet towards Najd symbolises the proclivity of *'udhri* verse for revelation since Najd also means 'the manifest or visible'. So Majnun's roaming between al-Sham and al-Yaman 'can symbolically be interpreted as evidence for the dialectic of secrecy and revelation that characterises *'udhri* romance'[124] since al-Sham is identified as the highland, whereas al-Yaman is described as the hidden lowland. Jamil's story, likewise, contains this dialectic of al-Sham and Najd. In one of his verses he declares:

> My heart sinks when she leaves
> And when she is in Najd my heart yearns for Najd[125]   [56]

There are many associations between land and the dialectic of revelation and secrecy in the Arabic language.[126] Majnun's roaming also represents the tragic wandering of his desire; Khan argues that:

Sexually, the lover-poet's wandering toward the Najd and away from al-Yaman also represents the romance lover's tendency to defer or postpone the consummation of his desire. The link between the female erotic and topography implicit in the etymology of the word 'al-Najd' is indicative of how even the poet's geographical wandering is occurs on a sexual terrain. Al-Najd also means the 'breasts of a woman' and if we extend this metaphor, then al-Yaman, as *al-ghur* meaning 'the belly, lowland, or hole', is the hidden female erogenous zone.[127]

Therefore, the body of a woman is a ground of adventure like the earth itself. The poet compensates for the absence of her body by aiming for her place. The land – of which her places are a part – acts symbolically as the beloved's body to imply her presence.

Presence through Absence: the Beloved's Presence in Nature

In addition to a presence found through the location of the beloved she is also present in the natural world. Although absent in body, signs of her can be discovered by the poet in every aspect of nature surrounding him. Jacobi argues that it is characteristic of a later age (after the pre-Islamic era) that the romantic attitude towards nature allows every object to be imbued with the poet's emotion.[128] Majnun's romance is a typical case in this regard. André Miquel demonstrates that no independent image of nature occurs in Majnun's poetry. However, certain elements of nature are described in referring to Majnun, to Layla and to their love. These depictions of nature are highlighted through the personal adventures of the lover that made him associate his love with nature.[129] Names of places from nature such as the mountain of Tubad, Nuʿman and Najd have become symbolic references to past memories of happy days:

> When *Tubad* saw me weeping he welcomed me
> I said: where are those who used to camp here
> and enjoy happiness and security?[130] [57]

Layla's image in Majnun's poetry is conjured up through various elements from the worlds of animals, plants and inanimate forms. Noteworthy here is the comparison he often makes between Layla and the gazelle.[131] However,

Layla is also referred to through other natural elements such as unstable sand dunes, so as to symbolise the passing of time that destroys everything:[132]

> Though unreachable, the single dune of sands,
> located in *al-Hima*, is still beloved to me[133] [58]

The *saba* (zephyr) is always described as a carrier of the beloved's memory. Its journey through the night, according to Majnun, adds passion to passion.[134] Another favoured image is of the shackled bird:

> The night they said: 'Come morning or come evening, Layla al-'Amiriyyah will have left,'
> My heart was like a sand-grouse
> Gulled into a snare
> She tugged at it all night,
> The wing already trapped[135] [59]

He continues, portraying himself in an image of trapped bird:

> O when will my tortured heart be cured (of your love) The arrows of death are between me and seeing you Despite the exile, the pain, the longing, the shivering You don't come closer but I don't go further
> I am like a bird within the swinging palms of a child The bird suffers death and the child enjoys the game The child is too young to feel for the bird
> And the bird has no feathers to fly away[136] [60]

Among the other images of birds in Majnun's poetry is the image of a sad singing dove, whose sadness is rendered as a metaphor of the poet's sorrow,[137] and he also compares his poetry and the dove's songs.[138] In his poetry, lovers are transformed into gazelles and Layla is transformed into the sun or a star. In an attempt to regain his dream of lost love, Majnun refers to nature and to the animate world in his poetry:

> If only we were two gazelles, grazing
> On meadows of *Huwazan*, in desolate land
> Oh, were we two doves amidst a wide waste,
> We'd fly and fly, and at evening time seek the sheltered nest

> Oh, were we two fishes swimming in the sea, Darting even farther into waters deep
> Oh, were we one now,
> And would that when death comes
> One grave were our bed[139]   [61]

Hence, a variety of natural elements serve to unite the lovers, even though their actual bodies cannot be united: 'Jamil looked at the sky in the hope that Buthaynah was looking at it at the same time, so that both their looks might meet.'[140] And when Qays lost the hope of his beloved's presence he consoled himself by saying:

> However, the breeze still keeps us in touch with each other
> We behold the sunset, every evening, at the same time;
> And our souls still meet in dreams[141]   [62]

In a later stage of his life, when Layla is lost to him forever, Majnun suffers from insanity and consequently escapes to live in the desert in the company of gazelles. Majnun goes to the same places where he used to find happiness, but this time to find certainty from Layla's presence. These places become his kingdom of the desert, insanity and poetry: this kingdom is like a secret garden that is removed from this world.[142] Another poetic image refers to the wild Majnun with whom the deer finds company and freedom. So this image of Majnun, who lives, eats and runs with the gazelles, suggests that he goes beyond comparing Layla with gazelles to suggesting that the image of the gazelle reflects his own self and his beloved, Layla. His beloved is portrayed through the magic of poetry and he is depicted through the life he has chosen for himself.[143] The gazelle, according to the poetic canon, is consecrated to freedom. In one anecdote among many Majnun would sacrifice almost anything to set a gazelle free:

> Majnun passed by two men that had hunted a gazelle. They had bound her with a rope and were taking her away. When Majnun saw her thrashing her feet in the rope, his eyes teared and he said to them: Replace her and take in her place a ewe from my sheep. (And Maymun in his narrative related: Take in place of her a young she-camel from my camels). So he gave the [ewe] to the two men and they freed [the gazelle]. She made her escape running

away (. . .). Majnun said gazing at her while she was running with great speed, fleeing fearfully:

O likeness of Layla, do not fear me for I today am a friend [to] the female wild beast O likeness of Layla, were you to tarry awhile, perhaps my heart would recover from its ravages

She flees, having been liberated from her bond by me. You – if only you knew –have been freed for Layla[144]

Therefore, as Dols notes, 'the portrayal of Qays [Majnun] among the animals – unique in Arabic poetry – is quite lovely . . . supernaturally, Qays is able to see the signs of love in nature and speak with the animals.'[145]

In any case, an initial superficial view of Layla's depiction indicates that her presence is scattered and fragmented among the natural elements of stones, wind and water. However, a more profound observation of the way that she is portrayed suggests that her existence includes all the natural elements of the universe that are written about her. As Khairallah notes, Majnun is depicted in the image of a person totally integrated into the natural animal world. His unity with nature is expressed positively through numerous points that portray him as completely at home in his desert environment. He is at peace on both a sub-rational and super-rational level of nature.[146] Khairallah also states that Majnun 'communes with super-human forces, a communion symbolised by his being possessed by Layla, but this communion is achieved through his sensitivity to the subhuman elements in nature'.[147] As one can observe in his *Diwan*, Majnun's poetry

> succeeds in conveying the impression of fundamental intimacy between Majnun and the world of symbols that surround him and always revive in him the memory of the beloved. Mountains, plains, and valleys, wells, trees, and the wind, gazelles, doves, and even locusts; all nature is a book replete with variations on Layla's name.[148]

Throughout this stage, Layla is at one with nature because of her frequent presence within the elements of nature, which in turn become reminders of Layla:

The rising of the guiding star and the sun,
agitate her memory[149] [63]

Therefore, 'Majnun's references to nature were not merely conventional'.[150] His frequent association of Layla with natural elements such as wind, gazelles and so on 'suggest the omnipresence of Layla in nature and in the mind of Majnun'.[151] He says:

> I am distracted from understanding any talk, Except what is about you,
>   for that is my concern
> I keep staring at those who talk to me so they may believe
> That I understand, but my mind is with you[152]   [64]

And every attempt to escape her overwhelming presence is in vain:

> I try to forget her remembrance, and yet
> It is as though Layla is typified for me everywhere[153]   [65]

Bearing in mind Stanbury's analysis of the romance of Troilus and Criseyde, I would likewise argue that in the romance of Majnun, his mind, mirroring Layla's image, becomes a reflecting surface, 'a passive screen on which her image is recorded'.[154] The image printed on Majnun's mirroring mind is his picture of Layla, created by his own imagination. In this light we can understand the anecdote told about Majnun, when he is roaming in the desert and suddenly sees Layla, but says to her: 'Go away, your love preoccupied me and distanced me from you!'[155] The famous Sufi Ibn 'Arabi reported this anecdote and commented enthusiastically on it. In fact, it is no wonder that the legend of Majnun became very popular among Sufis in later times.[156] 'The figure of Majnun was attractive to mystics because Majnun's rapture was analogous to their ecstatic states.'[157] Al-Shibli gives Majnun as a Sufi example:

> Whenever Majnun of the Banu 'Amir was asked about Layla, he would say, 'I am Layla'. Thus, by means of Layla, he would absent himself from Layla, until he remains present to his vision of Layla, and absent to every sense except Layla, and (thereby) sees everything present through Layla.[158]

Ibn 'Arabi conceived of Majnun as an ideal lover and considered his madness a symbol of the beatific vision, but he was not the only one; al-Ghazali interpreted his passionate love symbolically and al-Junayd considered him as one of God's saints.[159]

Conclusion

The duality of the present and absent bodies of the beloved in the *'udhri ghazal* has been the primary concern of this chapter. The *'udhri* poet depicts the physical body of his beloved by portraying her as the image of ideal beauty. Nevertheless, he also portrays her body symbolically or through symbolic channels. Symbolising the body of the beloved can be observed in many *'udhri* poetic themes such as the longing for the place of the beloved and the depiction of her in the form of a phantom. These themes reveal an attempt to regain the absent body of the beloved and to overcome this absence. On the other hand, the bodily presence of the beloved takes the forms of gestures and speech. Gestures act in the *'udhri* tradition as a means of communication between the lovers and speech is a potent factor in igniting love and in continuing to inflame passion. This presence-through-absence is also discussed in this chapter by examining the presence of the beloved in nature. An initial superficial view of the beloved's depiction indicates that her presence is scattered and fragmented among the natural elements of stones, wind and water. However, a more profound observation of such descriptions suggests that her existence actually absorbs the natural elements of the whole universe within which she is mentioned. Her remarkable omnipresence is illustrated in the *'udhri ghazal*. Hence, is it important for her physical body to be absent in this stage, so as to enable her to be omnipresent? In other words, does the absence of the beloved enhance poetry written about her? This is the question we shall examine in the next chapter.

Notes

1. The reader should note that I am examining gestures from the point of view of body language.
2. J. P. Hermann, 'Gesture and Seduction in Troilus and Criseyde', in Shoaf, *Chaucer's Troilus and Criseyde: Essays in Criticism*, p. 138.
3. Al-Jahiz, *Kitab al-qiyan [The Epistle on Singing-Girls of Jahiz]*, p. 19.
4. Ibid., p. 18.
5. Surat al-Nur (24:30–1).
6. Ibn Qayyim al-Jawziyyah, *Rawdat*, p. 35. Giffen (*Theory of Profane Love Among the Arabs*, pp. 126–7) notes that al-Jawziyyah, in chapters eight and nine of

Rawdat al-muhibbin, sets up the advocates of doctrines that allowed looking and easier standards of social and sexual conduct like so many straw men to be knocked down, reporting their teachings and citing evidence to prove them wrong. Ibn al-Jawzi, likewise, devoted almost ten chapters of his book, *Dhamm al-Hawa*, to this matter, emphasising the importance of the eyes as the gateway to dangerous sense impressions.

7. Giffen, *Love Theory*, p. 132.
8. Ibn Hazm, *Tawq*, p. 68.
9. Ibid., pp. 68–96. Interestingly, in medieval Western literature similar attention was paid to the gestures between the lovers. Boncompagno da Signa wrote a medieval taxonomy of lovers' gestures. He begins by listing the four lovers' signs: the nod, indication, signal and sigh. For more details see Hermann, 'Gesture and Seduction in Troilus and Criseyde', in Shoaf, *Chaucer's Troilus and Criseyde: Essays in Criticism*, p. 144.
10. Al-Isfahani, *Al-Aghani*, Vol. 2, p. 355, in Khan, *Sexuality and Secrecy*, p. 179.
11. Ibn al-Jawzi, in Giffen, *Love Theory*, p. 127.
12. Majnun, *Diwan*, p. 229.
13. Ibid., p. 75.
14. Lovers' union.
15. Majnun, *Diwan*, p. 55.
16. Ibid., p. 145.
17. Al-Isfahani, *Al-Aghani*, Vol. 2, p. 338, in Khan, *Sexuality and Secrecy*, p. 176. According to al-Isfahani, these verses caused Majnun to roam in the wildness of the desert.
18. Jamil, *Diwan*, p. 47.
19. Hermann, 'Gesture and Seduction', in Shoaf, *Chaucer's Troilus and Criseyde: Essays in Criticism*, pp. 154–5.
20. Jamil, *Diwan*, p. 42. In another context the poet-lover Waddah al-Yaman depicts the gestures between him and a married woman in a more scandalous image for the time, saying:

> I crept to her silently after her husband fell asleep and the night was cold
> And her hand was her husband's pillow
> She gave me a sigh out of the corner of her eye saying:
> Welcome, welcome, you will have what you desire despite all the calumniators

(cited in Kinany, *Development*, p. 206).

21. Khan, *Sexuality and Secrecy*, p. 161.

22. Kuthayyir, *Diwan*, p. 197.
23. Khan, *Sexuality and Secrecy*, p. 156.
24. Urwah, *Diwan*, pp. 22–3, unpublished translation, given in a private communication from Professor Van Gelder.
25. In an anecdote cited in *Rawdat al-muhibbin* the idea of the one being smitten by his own gaze is evident. Al-Asmaʿi was reported to have told the following anecdote: 'during the circumambulation of the Kaʿbah, I saw a girl who was like a wild cow and I began to watch her and to fill my eye with her beauty. Then she said to me: "Hey you! What is the trouble with you?" "What is it to you if I look at you?" I said. Then she recited: "And you, when you sent your eye scouting for your heart one day, Saw something over the whole of which you did not have power, Nor with part of which were you able to rest content".' See Ibn Qayyim al-Jawzyyiah, p. 95, in Giffen, *Love Theory*, pp. 123–4.
26. On the contrary, in medieval Western narratives, Stanbury argues, 'the sight lines of desire are most often projected by a male viewer'. A growing body of research has demonstrated that 'in Western culture this aggressive masculine eye dates from at least the classical era'. See Stanbury, 'The Lover's Gaze in Troilus and Criseyde', in Shoaf, *Chaucer's Troilus and Criseyde: Essays in Criticism*, p. 228.
27. It is noteworthy that in medieval Western literature a similar conceit of the gaze as an arrow is a familiar one. For example, in a roundel ascribed to Chaucer the beloved's gaze sends a dart that penetrates to wound the heart. Stanbury, 'Lover's Gaze', p. 226.
28. Al-Mutanabbi, *Diwan*, Vol. 3, p. 264.
29. Al-Safadi, *al-Ghayth al-musjam fi sharh lamiyyat al-ʿajam*, Vol. 2, p. 13.
30. Qays in Arberry, *The Seven Odes*, p. 62.
31. Al-Qurashi, *Jamharat ashʿar al-ʿArab*, Vol. 1, p. 140.
32. Qays, *Diwan*, p. 46.
33. Al-ʿAbbas b.al-Ahnaf, *Diwan*, p. 319, in Bürgel, 'The Lady Gazelle and Her Murderous Glances', p. 5.
34. Ibid., p. 102.
35. Ibid., p. 8.
36. Ibid., p. 9.
37. Ibid., p. 10.
38. See Chapter Four.
39. Kuthayyir, *Diwan*, p. 86.
40. Majnun, *Diwan*, p. 45.

41. Jamil, *Diwan*, p. 27, in Kinany, *Development*, p. 288. I have reversed the order of words since that makes better sense.
42. Jamil, *Diwan*, p. 45.
43. Khan, *Sexuality and Secrecy*, p. 154.
44. Al-Jahiz, *Kitab al-qiyan [The Epistle on Singing-Girls of Jahiz]*, p. 16.
45. Ibid., p.17.
46. Ibn Qutaybah, *'Uyun al-akhbar*, Vol. 4, p. 82.
47. Ibid., p. 83.
48. Ibid., pp. 82–3.
49. Khan, *Sexuality and Secrecy*, p. 154.
50. Ibn Qutaybah, *Al-Shi'r wa'l-shu'arā'*, p. 438. A similar version of the story is given in *Tazyin al-aswaq*, in which Jamil described Buthaynah's speech as more delicious than the pure rainwater in high mountains, p. 63.
51. Manzalaoui, 'Swooning Lovers: a Theme in Arab and European Romance', in *Comparative Criticism*, Vol. 8, p. 75.
52. Al-Qutami, *Diwan al-Qutami*, p. 80.
53. 'Then to eat of all the produce (of the earth), and find with skill the spacious paths of its Lord: there issues from within their bodies a drink of varying colours, wherein is healing for men: verily in this is a Sign for those who give thought': Surat al-Nahl (16: 69).
54. See al-Numayri's verses cited in Salamah, *al-'Ishq wa'l-kitabah*, p. 352.
55. Ibn Qutaybah, *al-Shi'r wa'l-shu'ara'*, p. 565, in Khairallah, *Love, Madness and Poetry*, p. 136. In the *Kitab al-Aghani* Majnun is described as 'addicted to the conversation of women and enamoured of them', Vol. 2, p. 356.
56. Khan, *Sexuality and Secrecy*, p. 152.
57. Ibid., p. 153.
58. Ibid., p. 157.
59. Ibn Hazm, *Tawq*, p. 65.
60. Jamil, *Diwan*, p. 113.
61. Ibid., p. 87.
62. Al-Abshihi, *Al-Mustatraf fi kull fanin mustadraf*, p. 219.
63. Jamil, *Diwan*, p. 49.
64. Ibid., p. 38.
65. Majnun, *Diwan*, p. 114.
66. Ibid., p. 234.
67. Al-Baghdadi, Khizanat al-adab wa-lubb lubab lisan al-'Arab, Vol. 6, p. 400.
68. Bouhdiba, *Sexuality in Islam*, p. 39.

69. Burd, *Diwan*, Vol. 3, p. 217.
70. Al-Washsha', *Kitab al-muwashsha*, p. 91.
71. Majnun, *Diwan*, p. 64.
72. Ibid., p. 200.
73. Kuthayyir, *Diwan*, p. 42.
74. Lyall, *The Mufaddaliyat: Vols 1–2. An Anthology of Ancient Arabian Odes*, p. 2.
75. Jacobi, 'Al-Khayalan – A Variation of the Khayal Motif', in *Journal of Arabic Literature*, No. 27, p. 2.
76. Seybold, 'The Earliest Demon Lover: The *Tayf al-Khayl* in *al-Mufaddaliyat*', p. 181.
77. Ibid., p. 182.
78. 'Izz al-Din, *Al-Tayf wa'l-khayal fi,l-shi'r al-'arabi al-qadim*, p. 69.
79. Ibid., p. 106.
80. Jacobi, 'Al-Khayalan', p.2.
81. Kuthayyir, *Diwan*, p. 235. Buwayb and Thi'dawrani are names of places.
82. A su'luk poet's mother says after his death: 'He traversed the land seeking safety from death but he died.' Al-Marzuqi, *Sharh Diwan al-hamasah li Abi Tammam*, Vol. 3, pp. 370–2.
83. Ibn Qutaybah, *al-Shi'r wa'l-shu'ara'*, p. 624.
84. Qays, *Diwan*, p. 109.
85. Seybold, 'The Earliest Demon Lover', p. 184.
86. Jarir b. 'Atiyah, *Diwan*, p. 314, in Stetkevych, *The Zephyrs of Najd*, pp. 85–6.
87. Jamil, *Diwan*, p. 68.
88. Tila'al-hijr, al-Ash'arun and Ghafiq are names of places.
89. Since pre-Islamic times, poets have expressed their surprise at the phantom's 'courage' and ability to travel so far in order to reach the poet. See Al-'Abd, *Diwan*, p. 76. The phantom is also connected with the idea of travel from afar; al-Muraqqish al-Akbar says:

> At night a phantom came from Sulayma
> And kept me awake while my companions slept
> I spent the night revolving the matter in my mind every which way
> Awaiting her people though they are far away
> Al-Akbar, 'Al-Mufaddaliyah no. 46', in Lyall, *The Mufaddaliyat*, Vol. 1, p. 460.

90. Jacobi, 'Al-Khayalan', p. 2.
91. Salamah, *Al-'Ishq wa'l-kitabah*, pp. 189–90.

92. Seybold, 'The Earliest Demon Lover', p. 185.
93. Jamil, *Diwan*, p. 19.
94. Ibid., p. 98. It is interesting that, among some other poets, there is a reference to more than one *khayal* as the poet is involved in a love affair with two women, who send their *khayal* at the same time. Al-'Ajjaj b. Ru'bah says:

    > Two khayal moved about and caused affliction,
    >
    > The khayal (of a woman) named, and that (of a woman) kept secret

    See Jacobi, 'Al-Khayalan', p. 3.
95. Majnun, *Diwan*, p. 233, in Jacobi, 'Al-Khayalan', p. 5.
96. Jacobi, 'Al-Khayalan', p. 5.
97. Majnun, *Diwan*, p. 76.
98. Jacobi, 'Al-Khayalan', p. 2.
99. Majnun, cited and translated by Khairallah, *Love*, p. 91.
100. Al-Tawhidi, *al-Hawamil wa'l-shawamil*, p. 140.
101. Al-Dahhak, *Diwan*, pp. 94–5.
102. Cited and translated by Jacobi, 'Al-Khayalan', p. 8. It is noteworthy, however, that 'the dream interpretations mentioned in al-Damiri's gazelle chapter all refer to various kinds of appropriation of a woman: acquiring a gazelle through hunting means to become the owner of a slave-girl by way of a ruse or a fraud, or to marry a wife. Killing a gazelle means to deflower a slave girl' and so on (Burgel, 'The Lady Gazelle and Her Murderous Glances', p. 10).
103. Ibid.
104. Abu Nuwas, *Diwan*, Vol. 4, No. 35, v. 1.
105. Ibid., No. 318.
106. See examples in Kuthayyir, *Diwan*, pp. 64, 67, 78, 137, 145, 164 and 183.
107. Stetkevych, *Zephyrs*, p. 103.
108. 'Urwah, *Diwan*, pp. 34–5.
109. Majnun, *Diwan*, p. 28.
110. Kuthayyir, *Diwan*, p. 99.
111. See, for instance, Kuthayyir, *Diwan*, pp. 36, 103 and Jamil, *Diwan*, p. 48.
112. Khan, *Sexuality and Secrecy*, p. 189.
113. Majnun, *Diwan*, p. 101, in Khan, *Sexuality and Secrecy*, p. 190.
114. Majnun, *Diwan*, pp. 127, 128.
115. Qays, *Diwan*, p. 19.
116. Majnun, *Diwan*, p. 40.
117. Kuthayyir, *Diwan*, p. 54, in Kinany, *Development*, p. 290.

118. Stetkevych, *Zephyrs*, p. 116.
119. Majnun, *Diwan*, p. 82, in Stetkevych, *Zephyrs*, p. 116.
120. Majnun, *Diwan*, p. 79, in Stetkevych, *Zephyrs*, p. 116. This verse is also ascribed to the poet Ibn al-Dumaynah.
121. Stetkevych, *Zephyrs*, p. 116.
122. Ibid., p. 117. He also argues that later poets will reduce the Najd motif to its purely abstract, symbolic value. It will be the aim and the road of all yearning (p. 118). See too his discussion of the symbolic crystallisation of Najd on pp. 119–21.
123. Khan, *Sexuality and Secrecy*, pp. 183–4.
124. Ibid., p. 184.
125. Jamil, *Diwan*, p. 31.
126. Khan observes that 'Majnun frequently seems to be either perched on a hill or roaming in a valley'. For more details see *Sexuality and Secrecy*, p. 184.
127. Ibid., p. 185.
128. Jacobi, 'Time and Reality in Nasib and Ghazal', p. 7.
129. Miquel, *Majnun Layla wa Tristan*, p. 71.
130. Majnun, *Diwan*, p. 212, in Kinany, *Development*, p. 238.
131. Ibid., pp. 212, 215, 221.
132. Miquel, *Majnun*, p. 73.
133. Majnun, *Diwan*, p. 26.
134. Ibid., p. 79. 'Of the Arabian East Wind, poetically associated so closely with Najd, the encyclopaedist al-Nuwayri (d. 733/1332) reports the tradition that 'never has God sent a prophet without sending with him the East Wind – *al-saba*'. The prophet Muhammad, too, was supported by the East Wind.' (Stetkevych, *Zephyrs*, p. 125). So this tradition may have something to do with the religious lexical language of Majnun about *al-saba* and its association with Layla, keeping in mind the sacred nature of Layla in his poetry.
135. Majnun, *Diwan*, pp. 61, in Stetkevych, *Zephyrs*, p. 162.
136. Ibid., p. 23.
137. Ibid., pp. 218–19.
138. Within medieval Western literature the dove is characterised as being true, faithful, honourable and trustworthy. Some authors connect doves with the written word and they allude to the organisational aspect of the dove's secretarial skills and to its devotion to its mate. From antiquity onwards the widowed turtle-dove was traditionally connected with mourning and weeping. The dove was also the bird of the goddess Venus whose chariot was drawn by

a flock of doves. For detailed discussion of these ideas see Regina Scheibe, 'The Major Professional Skills of the Dove in The Buke of The Howlat', in Houwen, *Animals and the Symbolic in Mediaeval Art and Literature*, pp. 107–37.
139. Majnun, *Diwan*, pp. 122–3, in Stetkevych, *Zephyrs*, p. 144.
140. Kinany, *Development*, p. 284.
141. Qays, *Diwan*, p. 102, in Kinany, *Development*, p. 284.
142. For more details on this see Miquel, *Majnun*, pp. 52–4.
143. Ibid., p. 66.
144. Al-Isfahani, *Kitab al-Aghani*, Vol. 2, p. 382, in Khan, *Sexuality and Secrecy*, pp. 248–9.
145. Dols, *Majnun*, p. 337.
146. Khairallah, *Love*, p. 87.
147. Ibid.
148. Ibid.
149. Majnun, *Diwan*, p. 227.
150. Khairallah, *Love*, p. 77.
151. Ibid., p. 78.
152. Majnun, *Diwan*, p. 179, in Khairallah, *Love*, p. 78.
153. Khairallah, *Love*, p. 77.
154. Stanbury, 'Lover's Gaze', p. 233.
155. Ibn 'Arabi, *al-Futuhat al-makkiyyah*, p. 1,467. www.alwaraq.net, 3 March 2007. See my full discussion of this anecdote in the following chapter.
156. For a discussion of *'udhri* love and its connection with Sufi love, see Adunis, *Al-thabit wa'l-mutahawwil*, Vol. 1, pp. 284–7.
157. Dols, *Majnun*, p. 322.
158. Al-Tusi, *Kitab al-luma'*, in Khairallah, *Love*, p. 102.
159. See Kahirallah, *Love,* pp. 101–2.

6

Textuality versus Reality

Introduction

The Umayyad poet Dhu al-Rummah was once asked: 'What would you do if your genius did not help you to compose poems (*inqafal dunak al-shi'r*)?' Dhu al-Rummah answered that it could never happen since he knew an ever effective way of arousing his genius. 'It is,' he said, 'just to remember your beloved while you are alone.'[1]

This anecdote about Dhu al-Rummah shows the complicated relationship between love and poetry, neither of which is shown to be simply a result of the other. The remembrance of the beloved inspires the poet to compose poetry, but that presupposes the beloved's absence in the first place. It is her memory, rather than her actual figure, the loss of her rather than the union with her, that inspires poetry. The poet here is aware that his intense emotion leads him to a place in the realm of the poets.

The earlier chapters of this book have discussed both the physical and symbolic depictions of the beloved's body in the *'udhri ghazal*. The duality of the presence and absence of the body was of primary focus in the previous chapter, which leads us to question the link between the absent body and poetry. Hence, in this chapter I will first look at the concept of 'one ideal beloved' in the *'udhri* tradition. The characteristic of having only one beloved is a core element of that tradition. Secondly, I will examine how *'udhri* poets address the idealisation of womanhood; specifically, the connection between this idealisation and the concept of the inaccessible woman and the very trope of inaccessibility. The trope of unfulfilled love – all-consuming only by nature of its being unfulfilled – and its being a goal in and of itself will be explored in detail. Next, I will discuss the paradox of the *'udhri* poet's complaint about love and his embracing of it. I then aim to offer an argument about the discourse of cultural value that developed around poetry, the reception of the poet as a hero and the representation of poetry as the ultimate goal.

One Ideal Beloved

As noted in a previous chapter, the *'udhri* poets transpose every aspect of the beloved's body into perfect and beautiful detail and personify her as the imaginary model of the ideal woman. This model is firmly engraved in both the collective consciousness and the literary tradition. In this chapter, I will argue that raising the beloved to the level of the ideal implies that she is the subject of imagination. Idealising the beloved in this way makes her into a fantasy. The question to be asked here is: does the idealisation of the beloved in the *'udhri* poem imply that she is inaccessible? Or, in other words, does the poet wish to present above all an image of his supposed virtue as inspired by the presence of such a unique beloved?

Sufyan b. Ziyad narrated:

> I asked a woman from the *'Udhrah* tribe, who was suffering so intensely from fatal love that I feared it would kill her: 'Out of all of the Arabian tribes, why is love killing the people of *'Udhrah*?' She replied: 'We are beautiful and chaste. Beauty leads us to chastity. Chastity brings softness to our hearts. Such love causes death. Yet we have eyes that see what you cannot see.'[2]

It is to be observed, from the woman's reply, that she first links beauty to chastity and then explains the connection by saying 'beauty leads us to chastity'. She declares that this is what ultimately leads her people to death. 'We have eyes that see what you cannot'. Thus, this woman provides an explanation of love unto death that emerged from her tribe, *'Udhrah*, by connecting extraordinary beauty, especially of the eyes, with chastity that is achieved by this presence of perfection. Therefore chastity, in her statement, is a result of a deep respect for ideal beauty.

When the beloved becomes an abstract idea she unavoidably becomes unattainable. This means, in all respects, that the poet evaluates her as being above or beyond all other women, whether a wife or even a mother. The beloved in *'udhri* poetry is the only one.[3] It is only Layla for Majnun, just Buthaynah for Jamil and solely Lubna for Qays . . . and so on.[4]

A part of idealising the beloved is to keep her as the only one. To avoid the idea of bearing children, this oneness must stay intact. Any reference to any aspect relating to the image of an attained woman will necessarily imply her ability to have children and thus will damage the image of her remote solitude. This suggests a parallel with monotheism. The beloved in the *'udhri* tradition is the only one, and she must remain so. Thus, she must be and remain removed from the act of reproduction.

As we have seen in Chapter Three, there is an insistent rejection of the notion of marriage between *'udhri* lovers. Thus, if any of them were previously married, as were Qays and Lubna, the love story must separate them again.[5] The explanation that is given here is that Lubna could not bear children. In this story, society insists that the consummated union between lovers must bear fruit, and life must continue into the new generation. In contrast, Qays believes in love itself, and nothing can change that love. He describes his love by saying:

> Your love is ingrained in my heart
> just as fingers are attached to the hands[6]   [1]

Before obeying his father, Qays suggested to him that he (his father) should marry again and have more children. Just as his father demands that his son take another wife, the son ironically requests that his father take another wife and refuses to divorce Lubna.[7] However, his poetry portrays his deep regret about obeying his father and divorcing Lubna:

> Do you weep on Lubna,   [sic]
> while you left her of your own accord? I see now that you were like a man,
> who goes to death of his own accord O, my heart, admit that you love
>   her, And then try to forget her; no, O love, Do whatever you will
> O my heart, tell me what you will do, when Lubna goes very far away
> You seem as if you have not been inured
> to separation and misfortunes[8]   [2]

Romance fans the flames of his love and, therefore, his poetic inspiration by isolating him from his beloved. Nevertheless, on the narrative level, this refusal to continue their physical union implies that the lovers should never have children. The only possible offspring for the *'udhri* lover is poetry. It is a linguistic creation, not a biological one. Therefore, poetry is the only outcome of *'udhri* love, as the lovers' involvement with each other results in poetry and not in offspring.

This is a crucial aspect of the *'udhri* tradition, as it contrasts with the Bedouin norms that *'udhri* poets largely respect. Reading Abu-Lughod's analysis of Bedouin society,[9] I would argue that *'udhri* poets present a different position regarding a woman's childlessness than does their society. Abu-Lughod observes that in Bedouin society women are associated with nature; 'as reproducers, women are responsible for giving birth to the children that are so desired and adored [. . .] fertile women are valued, admired, and envied. Barren women face a sad life.'[10] In contrast, in the *'udhri* tradition, the beloved woman is idealised and as such does not fulfill the role of women as 'reproducers' because she is unique and cannot have her image emulated or altered by her offspring.

The Desire for Possession

The structure of the *'udhri* romance reflects the dominant theme of longing, the strong desire to possess the dream/beloved, and the linguistic form within which this desire is shaped. There is not one single verse ascribed to Qays while he was with Lubna as her husband. His entire *diwan* exposes his torment and love for Lubna just after he lost her. Apparently she had to become unattainable for the poetry addressed to her to flower. I shall argue that the distance from and the idealisation and the solitude of the beloved enable her to play her decisive role, namely as a source of inspiration. The whole *'udhri* experience unconsciously distances the beloved in order to detonate the force of the poetry.

In Majnun's romance it is noticeable that it is his distance from Layla rather than his proximity to her that agitates his heart with love. In one account, al-Isfahani states that when news of Layla reached Majnun, he fell in love with her after she was described to him.[11] Thus, it was her absence, on the one hand, and the language that was used to 'describe' her, on the other hand, which engendered his desire for Layla. Bloch demonstrates that 'the object must be absent for desire to be fixed on it'.[12] It seems that Majnun recognises the conflict between 'attainment' and 'losing heart' as he says:

> Why, you madman, have you lost your heart
> for one for whose attainment you have no hope?[13] [3]

But soon after this censure to his heart he states that 'the most desirable thing to a man is what he is forbidden'.[14] So there is a permanent state of longing; 'the expression of male desire absents the female object of desire because this desire is anchored to the absence of the female in the first place',[15] as will be discussed in the following section.

This poetic flux among *'udhri* lovers and the frequent complaint about deprivation and distance could be a form of expressing their desire for the beloved and a reprise of it in a highly remarkable manner. One of Freud's students, Marie Bonaparte, has stated that works of art or literature 'govern the manner in which our strongest, though most carefully concealed, desires are elaborated. Desires which often are the most repugnant to consciousness, also govern the elaborations of a work of art.'[16] In many *'udhri* stories, the relationship between the lover and his beloved has grown since their childhood. So the longing for their sweet shared past shaped his experience as a lover and a poet. *'Udhri* poetry embodies the wish to become reunited with the childhood sweetheart. For instance, it is stated in the *Kitab al-Aghani* that:

> Majnun was in love with Layla… whose nickname was Umm Malik, when they were children. Each fell in love with the other while they were out tending the flocks of their families. They continued thus until they grew up and then she was veiled from him. And the following saying of his indicates this:
>
> > I fell in love with Layla when she
> > Was just a girl with forelock
> > When the swelling of her breasts had not yet
> > Been manifest to playmates
> > Two children tending the lambs
> > Would that we never had grown up, nor had
> > The lambs grown old![17]

The *Kitab al-Aghani* contains a similar story regarding Kuthayyir's love for 'Azzah, in which the poet saw his girl first when she was still a child.[18] The implicit desire for what he once knew, and then lost, is evident. Even the bizarre daydreams of the poet depict the excess of his emotion, and show how his repressed desires return in a poetic form. We might recall Freud's statement: 'the poet composes his verses as the dreamer creates his day dreams'.[19] Kuthayyir says:

> O, 'Azzah, I wish we were a couple of scabby camels – grazing away in an
>   empty place
> He who would see us would say:
> These are two scabby animals, whose disease is contagious, Even though
>   the female is beautiful
> If we should approach a watering place,
> Its people would shout out to us and beat us
> I wish that our owner were a man of great wealth, So he would neither
>   care for us
> nor miss us when we ran far away[20]   [4]

Kuthayyir was heavily criticised for these verses. One of the critics told him:

> You had wished for her and yourself the agony of being enslaved, humiliated and disfigured. What else have you left? What you had wished for her is rightly expressed by the saying: having animosity with a sane person is much better than befriending a fool.[21]

However, this kind of criticism neglects the excessive desire to be with the beloved under any condition or circumstances, even if repulsive. Khairallah observes that 'the desire to reconnect with the past can be satisfied only through symbolic channels. Hence, the archetypal character who achieves this kind of reconnection finds universal appeal, and is usually represented by a great variety of forms.'[22]

Poetry and the Absence of the Object of Desire

It is noteworthy that so many 'udhri lovers were poets.[23] This is essentially what earned these lovers a place in most Arabic collections of poetry. Yet I would argue that their deep consciousness of the fact that they are poets itself shapes their romances. If the beloved is the feminine ideal, or is depicted as such, she is unattainable and so her lover will suffer from his ardent love forever. Therefore, the lover will continually compose poetry to express the torture and repression caused by such love. Whether poetry is a sort of remedy, as several *'udhri* verses have suggested,[24] or is an object in itself, its presence in this tradition is essential.

When the beloved becomes a part of the dream world this necessarily implies her potential as a source of inspiration, as the poet-lover admits in the following anecdote. A woman denigrates the poet Kuthayyir by saying to him: 'God has demeaned you, since he made you known only by the name of a woman', meaning 'Azzah. Kuthayyir says: 'God has not demeaned me. By her, my reputation was enhanced, my life was enlightened, and my poetry became powerful.'[25] This anecdote shows that some people perceive Kuthayyir as having a lowly status, by associating his fame with a woman's name. Nevertheless, the poet himself views this association in a different light: 'my reputation was enhanced, my life was enlightened, and my poetry became powerful'. As Khan notes, the fact that 'Kuthayyir is shown mentioning the benefits accruing to him in the field of poetry perhaps suggests that *'udhri* poet-lovers risked being "enslaved" to a female beloved primarily in order to experience an "ennobling transformation" in their literary careers.'[26] In another story given in the *Kitab al-Aghani* some literary critics suggested that: 'living in the spirit of anticipation was more agreeable than the meeting of the beloved.' Commenting on two lines of poetry composed by the Umayyad poet al-Ahwas, in which he said that he knew two kinds of nights, a happy one spent with the beloved, and a restless one full of sorrow and cares, Ibn Jundab, a contemporary of al-Ahwas, said: 'I prefer the restless night to the other.' Al-Harami, the reporter of the story, added: 'That was because the sorrowful night gave him the opportunity of yearning, hoping and composing *ghazals*.'[27]

The assumption that this story implies, namely avoiding marriage or any sort of physical union between *'udhri* lovers, suggests several points that will be discussed in the following section. In fact, the narrators of stories were preoccupied with the idea of sensuality and its connection with love; therefore, they heightened it by dwelling so frequently on its absence. The absence of consummation between the *'udhri* lover and his beloved also continuously inflames his passion. This passionate love inspires beautiful poetry composed by the *'udhri* poet-lover. In addition, the poet or the narrators are aware that the unattainability of the beloved is in fact essential for composing poetry. Khan demonstrates:

> The more absent, occulted and elusive the female ideal, the more prominent and intense is the lover's desire for this ideal. If [a] male's expression results in the loss of the love object, this loss or absence of the beloved merely intensifies and perpetuates male desire and its revelation. When the object is concealed, when Layla's words or body are veiled, the revelation of Majnun's desire increases. The unavailability and inaccessibility of the love object merely increases its desirability in the eyes of the lover.[28]

Here we observe textuality verses reality; by creating obstacles between the lovers, the trope fans the flame of their love. Hence the questions that al-'Aqqad posed:

> Why did Jamil compose love poems for Buthaynah while he was aware that by doing so he would be prevented from marrying her? Was it because he was too aesthetic? Or was he too weak willed? Or was *al-ghazal* above everything else, and an end in itself?.[29]

These questions are worth considering. At the heart of these questions, I would argue, lie the seeds of their answers. However, al-'Aqqad's conclusion is less impressive than the questions he poses, as he claims: 'Whatever the reasons that caused Jamil to take this path, it is not a straight path, and, thus, Jamil deserves the dilemma in which he finds himself.' Clearly, Jamil's dilemma is not about possession. It is, I would rather suggest, about loss. Then again, loss inflames love and love inspires poetry.[30] A similar suggestion should apply to Majnun: 'It is the obsession itself which creates the distance here, Majnun's behavior – as a poet, one might add – that will drive them [Majnun and Layla] apart.'[31]

This parallel does not escape the notice of some scholars: al-'Azm maintains that *'udhri* love is in fact a sensual love, of which physical attraction is an integral part. However, no physical contact actually takes place[32] because the lover chooses to keep his love alive by creating more obstacles between himself and the object of his desire.[33] There are many narratives that illustrate this point: Jamil composes love poems for Buthaynah in spite of the fact that Bedouin convention would prevent a lover who has dishonoured his beloved, by flirting with her in public, from marrying her.[34] Moreover, she was proud of his poetry and swore to meet him whenever he came to see her, as al-Isfahani states: 'Then Buthaynah learned that he had paid court to her so she swore by God that whenever he came to her alone she would go out to him and not hide herself from him.'[35] Both of them, thus, were creating obstacles between their matrimonial union. As the sources suggest, Jamil was a noble, brave, rich, handsome gentleman[36] from a powerful tribe that protected him, even after the ruler had outlawed him.[37] On the other hand, Buthaynah's husband was an ugly, one-eyed man and, of course, not a poet. Thus, the opportunity for Jamil to take Buthaynah or elope with her was always there, but he did not take it.

In al-'Azm's opinion the *'udhri* lover enjoys the suppression of love. He avoids marriage or any possible union in order to keep his love at boiling point. To support his argument further, al-'Azm refers to the concept of love and the Don Juan character within Western literature.[38] There is a conflict between Don Juan and *'udhri* lovers on the one hand, and the established conventions of society on the other. They believe that married love is static and would utterly destroy the acute emotion they enjoy. However, the difference between them is that the *'udhri* lover keeps his destructive love intact not by jumping from one woman to another, as Don Juan does. Instead, he concentrates all his emotions on one unique beloved. He hopes to possess her, but, at the same time, he creates all kinds of possible obstacles to prevent himself from having her. Afterwards, passion leads the *'udhri* lover to madness and to roaming the desert, as the fire of love melts his body and mind. Hence, he achieves what Don Juan achieves not by moving from one woman to another, but by placing himself in a condition of repressed and unfulfilled desire. Naturally, al-'Azm continues, this condition leads the *'udhri* lover to experience suffering and torture. Nevertheless, he jealously guards his pain, because it is an essential part of the core of his experience.[39]

The theme of love that lasts forever is central to the *'udhri* tradition. *'Udhri* love is endless love, and nothing can detract from it, not even the mean reactions of the beloved; Jamil says:

> And it is not because she surrendered to me that I loved her;
> but she captured me by flirtation and withholding[40]   [5]

Thus, I am inclined to agree with Khan in her observation that

> [i]n fact, all the *'udhri* romances are about this endless deferral of desire's fulfillment. True love or desire in these romances is defined as that which ought not to be consumed [*sic* – for 'consummated'] . . . Union is ultimately not sought because it means the end of desire and pleasure . . . Ostensibly, the *'udhri* poet-lovers frame themselves as seeking fulfillment and marriage with the beloved, but then they thwart their chances to achieve these goals and portray themselves the victims of fate, social mores or the beloved's caprice.[41][

Moreover, I would argue that this passion grows separately from the beloved and it is in fact an obsession in itself. The object of love is not the real Layla or Buthaynah, who as human beings could change or get older; it is, rather, the desire itself. The ideal image of the beloved is meant to fan the flame of destructive emotion. One cannot help but examine the following striking anecdote. One day, while Majnun was roaming in the desert, stricken by madness, accompanied by beasts, and surrounded by deer, Layla, his beloved, appeared to him. Surprisingly enough, Majnun said to her: 'go away, your love has overcome me, and isolated me from you'.[42] Accordingly, it is not 'you' – not Layla – but 'your love' which had obsessed him.

In another anecdote, Majnun said, in responding to some woman's offer for him to fulfil his desire with them instead of with Layla: 'Were I able to divert desire from her [Layla] to you, I would turn it away from her and from each one after her and would live among people, harmoniously and with ease.'[43] In commenting on his response to the women, Khan argues that

> Majnun's reference to 'each one after her' can be interpreted as an indication of how it is upon an unrequited love, a fantasy beloved, that his desire is founded. Though the beloved image in this fantasy may change, it remains just that – a fantasy or an absent love object. Indeed, the object must be absent – it must not yield a presence or hold a promise of fulfillment – for desire to fixate upon it. Majnun portrays himself as unable to divert his desire to the women in the group only because they offer hope of requital and satisfaction in the love affair. His true love is a love that privileges the

deferral rather than the consummation of union. Ultimately, it is with the phantom or fantasy of his own desire that he is in love.[44]

Indeed, the 'fantasy of his own desire that he is in love' with is evident in the anecdote in which Majnun said to Layla: 'Go away, your love preoccupies and distances me from you'. The statement made by Krueger in her study of ancient French romances is relevant here: 'to take woman as metaphor and to make of her a pretext for literary discourse, is to appropriate and displace the subjectivity of the absent real woman.'[45] Thus, it is understandable that later on Ibn 'Arabi (d. 1240), the great Sufi figure, became interested in Majnun's statement and commented delightfully on it by saying:

> This is one of the rare instances, where domineering love is manifested as pleasant ... her presence came between his envisionment of her as a fathomed being, and her actual physical being. To him, her image is much nicer than her actual presence. Having lost that sense of pleasure of seeing her, he said, 'Just disappear'.[46]

It is worth noting, however, how *'udhri* love in general and Majnun's love in particular were eventually prized by Sufis as an expression of mystical love. As some Sufis saw in human love the entrance to the Way, Majnun's legend reaches the symbolic level. Hence, Majnun is presented as a Sufi example:

> Whenever Majnun of the Banu 'Amir was asked about Layla, he would say, 'I am Layla'. Thus, by means of Layla, he would absent himself from Layla, until he remains present to his vision of Layla, and absent to every sense except Layla, and (thereby) sees everything present through Layla.[47]

In any case, the transformation of Majnun's legend into an allegory of Sufi love is found particularly in Persian poetry. Starting from Nizami, the touch of mystical love is found in his adaptation of Majnun's love story. 'Preserving the outline of the romance, he retained the prominent episodes and added a number of his own invention. Inevitably, Nizami modified considerably the form and content of the legend.'[48] Nizami's poem was widely imitated wherever Persian culture spread and the poets borrowed heavily from his work. The most important feature of such works was the mystical rendering of the

Romance.[49] In Khairallah's view, Jami is the leading light in this respect in his 'Layla u Majnun'.[50]

Complaining and Embracing

It is remarkable to observe how often those lovers complain about their suffering in love. They usually portray it as a form of magic energy that captivates and enchants them. They 'proclaim that love was their fate and, using fatalistic arguments, declare that they could not help loving their damsels'.[51] Jamil, for example, says:

> He (the blamer) said: "Sober up!
> How long will you be mad about Buthaynah, without being able to do
>   anything about her?" I said: "Concerning her,
> God passed upon me the sentence that you see. Can God's decree be
>   controverted?
> Whether to love her means to be guided aright or to stray,
> I stumbled upon this love without intent[52]   [6]

In theses verses Jamil ascribes his love and its consequences, 'without being able to do anything about her', to fate. Therefore, it is understood that he is helpless in his love for Buthaynah, as what God has decreed cannot be altered. It does not matter, then, if love 'means to be guided aright or to stray', as the poet has to follow it anyway. Nevertheless, expressing the desire to escape from it, he says in exasperation:

> I wish I were rid of you, love,
> Will you leave me no rest?[53]   [7]

Moreover, Jamil reaches the point of cursing Buthaynah:

> May God cast motes into Buthayna's eyes!
> May he blacken her brilliant teeth![54]   [8]

This is the only time he uses a negatively charged poetic verse aimed at his beloved. Apparently this verse casts doubt on the (true love) that Jamil proclaims. Buthaynah herself is reported to have said to him: 'Oh Jamil, you claim that you love me, while you said: My God cast motes . . . ?' His reaction to her rebuke is crying and saying: 'I am the one who said:

> I wish I were blind and deaf while Buthaynah is guiding me,
> Not a word from her speech is hidden from me![55]   [9]

However, this strange verse, a prayer (*du'a*) against Buthaynah's beauty, has raised a debate among the classical literary authors as well as among contemporary scholars. Many Arab exegetes argue that this *du'a'* could bear a positive meaning. When a thing becomes so perfect, one might pray against it to provide a kind of protection for it. Some say that the actual meaning of the verse is: what stunning eyes and mouth she has! It is the same as saying: 'May God damn him, what a brave man he is!'[56] Some even interpret Buthaynah's eyes as her protectors, as in Arabic the word *'ayn* could be used to signify the visual organ, as well as referring to a spy. They argue also that her teeth represent her relatives who deny him the right to visit Buthaynah, as, again, the word *anyab* could bear two meanings: teeth, and people in high positions. Another interpretation suggests that Jamil is praying for her to have a long life, so the motes and black teeth are hints of getting old and living a long life.[57]

However, taking into account all the arguments, my position is that the basis of Jamil's *du'a'* is not hatred, but rather the violence of his love for Buthaynah. At some point, it became clear to him that her excessive beauty was the cause of his misery. That is why this verse lashes out at her beautiful eyes and delicious mouth – because they caused him so much pain. The beauty of the beloved is defined as the origin of the poet's suffering. This is what the classical exegetes have overlooked while trying to interpret this verse within the framework of praise for the beloved's beauty. I would rather argue that bodily beauty is not just portrayed in vivid depictions; it is also regarded as the source of fatal love. Likewise, the motif of wishing to get rid of love is frequently apparent in Qays b. Dharih's *diwan*; for instance, he says:

> I said to my heart when love tormented me
> and became unbearable:
> O heart that has been led by desires,
> awake, may God curse you for a heart[58]   [10]

and Jamil often uses the metaphor of bondage:

> O Buthaynah,
> your snares entrapped my heart the day of the hunt,
> but you escaped my snares[59] [11]

In fact, the theme of bondage and captivity runs right through the *'udhri* poems.[60] This can be observed in the common use of such terms as prisons, traps and chains. The image of the bond of love as a chain is prevalent in *'udhri* poetry. Hamori notes 'the cursing of Buthaynah and the complaint that love is a prison parallel the execrations, in the old poetry, of Time, in which the speaker is caught as in a current that pulls steadily towards the falls'.[61]

On the contrary, one should hear the undertone beneath this complaint and so-called fatalism: the latent desire for this love to continue and last. While Majnun is expressing his discontent with his fate by reciting:

> God who decreed that she would be for somebody else, Afflicted me with my love for her
> Why would he not afflict me with something else?[62] [12]

It is fundamental, though, to notice that some narratives associate Majnun with madness, according to this verse specifically. They claim that once he composed it, a voice in the darkness shouted at him: 'You who are discontented with Allah's fate! You are the one who interferes with his decisions', after which he lost his mind.[63]

Majnun preferred the mad love of Layla over sanity. As we read in the *Kitab al-Aghani*:

> When Majnun's parents tried to cure him by taking him on pilgrimage, they demanded that Majnun ask God to cure him from his passion for Layla. Interestingly, Majnun grabbed the Ka'bah and implored God to intensify and magnify his passion. He said: 'Oh God, increase my passionate love for Layla, and do not let me forget her forever'.[64]

In his poetry, Majnun clearly shows his devotion to his beloved by asking God to help him in his seeking for her:

> At Mecca, by night, the pilgrims prayed to God
> Beseeching forgiveness for their sins,

> While I called O God, the first thing I ask for myself is Layla, Then be my reckoner.
> If Layla is given to me in my lifetime,
> no worshipper's repentance will be greater than mine[65]   [13]

Moreover, the *'udhri* lover's persistence in his love goes so far as to make Majnun say:

> How excellent is the work of Satan,
> if my love for her is the work of Satan[66]   [14]

Kuthayyir confesses:

> They said that she departed
> And that I had to choose between forgetting her
> Or continuing to weep;
> I said that the latter would better soothe my pain[67]   [15]

Although he knows it is a dead end, Majnun's only solution to rid himself of this love is to have more of it:

> For Layla's love I treat my self with Layla,
> For wine a drunkard treats himself with wine[68]   [16]

Does the *'udhri* lover accept his fatal love and complain about it at the same time? Or is he in fact confining his love so as to avoid the excessive consequences of it, challenging the norms of society by claiming that his love is his fate decreed by God? It is not a choice. Nevertheless, it is a desirable fate, so much so that he asks his love to give him more of it every night:

> O love for Layla, each night double my grief
> O solace of love, we shall meet on the Last Day[69]   [17]

In other contexts also, describing the torment is a fundamental element in depicting love, as Bataille puts it: 'Only the beloved in this world can bring the continuity between two discontinuous creatures. Hence, love spells suffering in so far as it is a quest for the impossible … We suffer from our isolation in our individual separateness.'[70]

Ibn Hazm confirms: 'Love is a delightful malady, a most desirable sickness. Whoever is free of it likes not to be immune, and whoever is struck down by it yearns not to recover.'[71] In Ibn Hazm's statement one observes the link he has made between love and sickness. Love is a fate like 'sickness', but it is a 'desirable' one. In fact, the theme of love treated like sickness is particularly prominent in the *diwan* of 'Urwah and the *diwan* of Qays, a theme to be explored in the final chapter of this book, which deals with the lover's body.

Kinany correctly notes that *'udhri* lovers hid a remarkably free and powerful will behind their so-called fatalism. They did not want to get rid of their pain because pain is the only genuine criterion of true love. Nevertheless, he draws a parallel between the *'udhri* lovers' resignation and the resignation of the ascetic Muslim, as both hope for a better life in the world to come. He says, 'most of the *'udhri* lovers renounced the joys of life for the sake of their hopeless passion'.[72] He claims also that *'udhri* lovers were capable of resigning themselves to hard living in the hope of deserving a better one in the future, the hereafter. He compares *'udhri* lovers and pagan lovers, whose lives lack any idea of the afterlife, so they do not show any sign of resignation.[73]

However, one of the limitations of Kinany's explanation is that it does not explain the conflict between Islamic resignation and *'udhri* lovers' insistence on their burning passion, and it assumes that *'udhri* lovers are automatically ascetic Muslims and perfectly chaste. I would rather suggest that, much as the lover complains about his destiny, he also embraces it. Evidently Kinany's interpretation overlooks many of the *'udhri* verses which reveal the desire for the joy of love in this life. For instance, Jamil declares:

> I have given up all desire involving this world
> except the love of her
> Thus, I make no requests of the world,
> nor do I feel that I must have an ampler portion[74] [18]

Jamil has no request of the world, except his love for Buthaynah. He not only embraces it, he wishes for it. In fact, his love is the only wish that he has since Jamil has 'given up all desire involving this world', as he declares in the verse quoted above.

In this light we could understand the decisive role played by the motif of the blamer (*al-'adhil*) within *'udhri* poetry. Jamil's father summarised the argument of the blamers in these words: 'Women are replaceable'.[75] For Jamil, of course, they are not. He declares:

> Blamers took me to task [lit. excoriated me]
> because of my love for her.
> If only they suffered as I suffer!
> When they kept on reproaching me on account of you, I said to them:
> Do not exceed the proper bounds;
> Hold back some of this reproof and be moderate[76]   [19]

Love, for the *'udhri* poet, is fundamental in his life, but the blamer does not understand this because, according to Jamil, he does not suffer from love. Hamori notes that:

> The blamer has been a straw man of caution. His job was to try to prevent the protagonist from making the heroic gesture [. . .] the lines by Jamil are shot through with irony. The apostrophe to the blamers is in the old style. Unbridled speech is objectionable; the blamer should practice moderation . . . the blamers must be accusing Jamil of that very thing: lack of moderation.[77]

Interestingly, the figure of the blamer sometimes becomes a desirable figure in the romance, since he confirms the strength of love by blaming the lover. Ibn Hazm describes *al-'adhil* as a 'tough business, and a heavy burden to bear',[78] but he also indicates that:

> I have seen a lover so violent in his emotions, and so overwhelmingly infatuated, that he loved to be reproached more than anything in the world, in order that he might show his reproacher [blamer] how stubbornly he could rebel against his scoldings. He took a positive delight in opposing him, in provoking him to resistance and doubled reproof, and then in triumphs over his opponent.[79]

Thus, the *'udhri* poet jealously guards his love, and while he ostensibly complains about it in fact he recognises how fundamental it is to his life experience and, furthermore, to his poetry.

The Heroic Gesture

There is no doubt that a pre-Islamic poet like 'Antarah presents a defining symbol of the ambivalence in the 'poet/hero' image. 'Antarah was described as a hero, not only because he was a knight but also by virtue of his being a poet. His poetry allowed him to immortalise both his status as a knight and his great love for his cousin, 'Ablah. It is not surprising that 'Antarah became a legendary hero, immortalised through enduring folk tales that survive, both in written form and as oral traditions, even to the present day. Thus, in classical Arabic culture the poet was 'a cultural hero because his socio-political as well as spiritual status placed him in the leading position'.[80] In the pre-Islamic period, a poet was, as Hamori notes, 'the pride and ornament of his people, for he alone would perpetuate the fame of their noble deeds, dignify the memory of their dead, and trap their enemies in songs of mockery.'[81]

Nevertheless, with the emergence of Islam the 'poet/hero' image began to fade, giving way in the popular imagination to the 'devout hero', who would sacrifice all to strengthen and glorify the new religion.

The relationship between Islam and poetry has become a popular theme for academic debate. While some believe that the emergence of Islam weakened poetry, others argue that, on the contrary, it opened entirely new and interesting vistas for the medium.[82] The Umayyad period saw the emergence of a new group of poets: they too sought the status of folk heroes through their poetry, but through references more intimate than glorious: theirs was a return to love poetry (*ghazal*). Unlike their pre-Islamic forebears, however, the Umayyad poets benefitted from the advent of singing as entertainment and the plethora of composers and female singers available for inspiration. This phenomenon continued to grow and evolve through subsequent eras.

The heroic gesture of the *'udhri* lover is that of being a poet. 'If one is inclined to believe that Majnun's legend grew around, and in a way for the sake of, his poetry, then one could claim that his poetic daemon was also at the source of his love.'[83] Majnun lost everything but his poetry. He lost Layla, his health, his relatives, his status in the tribe and, eventually, his mind, but he never lost his ability to compose love verses. His story is 'the story of how hopeless love can make great poetry , even if so much else is destroyed along the way.'[84]

Is it really Layla that he longed for? We should bear in mind his words to Layla: 'go away, your love has overcome me, and isolated me from you'.[85] Nevertheless, his love does not isolate him from poetry. While he was roaming the desert, people would go to him just to listen to him reciting his poems. Khairallah has noted:

> Poetry as a crisis, a dilemma, is as much of a fatal possession as love or madness proved to be. Psychologically, the positive effects of language in general and of poetry in particular are manifold [. . .] Poetry could function as a charming power, or as a medium of psychological relief.[86]

Therefore, is it the search for poetry, the search for inspiration, that characterises the 'udhri lover? Is it for poetry that he creates the deferral of union within the 'udhri tradition? Khan conceives this essential link between language and the deferral of union:

> This wandering of desire or deferral of union is precisely what constitutes the pleasure of the lover. For the male lover, fulfillment of desire is equated with the end of pleasure for one very important reason. Fulfillment of desire would mean the end of his ability to luxuriate in the eloquence of language in the courtship ritual – whether the language be his own or that of/about the beloved. Certainly, the lover's literary prowess constitutes his desire so that desire's attainment would result in an end to the pleasure of his discursive identity and performance. Hence, a deferral rather than an achievement of union is sought.[87]

Thus, through language and poetry, poets achieve their poetic gesture. If the ability to recite old Arabic poetry was the quality that helped endear Majnun to Layla in the first place, his own poetry about her played a significant role in their love story later on. People around them focussed their attention on his poetry and acted accordingly. It was the fame of his poetry about Layla that caused her parents to refuse his marriage proposal. But, it seems that it does not matter if Majnun's love poetry proves to be a curse of sorts because of his self-consciousness as a poet.[88] Even the anecdotes that appear in the classical books about Majnun 'were invented for an explicative purpose, so it is normal that they focus on the poetic fragments, for which they are meant to provide a context.'[89] As we have already noted from Kuthayyir's reply to the woman who condemned him for composing poetry solely on a woman (his beloved 'Azzah), it is clear that Kuthayyir was aware of the heroic gesture he had achieved through poetry.

Conclusion

In this chapter I have offered a discussion of the notion of 'one ideal beloved' as a core element of the *'udhri* tradition. The lover is attached only to his unique beloved, to whom he devotes his love and poetry. Therefore, the concept of matrimonial union between the lovers is absent from these romances in order to maintain the beloved's uniqueness and to avoid replicating her in some way via offspring. On the one hand, the various images expressing desire in the poems indicate the beloved's depiction as an object of desire in the *'udhri ghazal*. On the other hand, the fulfilment of this desire can go no further than deferral at various levels. While framing themselves as seeking marriage, the *'udhri* poets thwart their chances to achieve their aim and then complain about their fate. However, the poets' complaint of their suffering in love is accompanied by a wish for their love to last forever. They frequently state that the blamers, in fact, intensify their love, rather than defeat it. Hence, passionate love, I would argue, is a means for the poet-lover to make a heroic gesture. Love poetry is inseparable from love, as *'udhri* lovers are poets themselves. In classical Arabic literature works on passionate love are, in fact, works on the *ghazal*. A poet is often considered as a lover; al-Washsha' says that 'endless is the number of poets who have loved'.[90] In the *'udhri* romances, the lover loses everything, including his beloved, except his ability to compose poetry. Being a poet seems to be his ultimate goal and heroic achievement. In fact it would not be too far off the mark to suggest that in classical Arabic literature the love story is an appendage to the poetry. To produce poetry is the act of heroism for which the experience of love is an enabler.

Notes

1. Al-Qayrawani, *Al-'Umdah fi sina'at al-shi'r wa naqduhu*, in Kinany, *Development*, p. 60.
2. Al-Jawzyyiah, *Rawdat al-muhibbin*, p. 337.
3. Jayyusi argues that the metamorphosis of the beloved as an ideal of womanhood was a rebellion against polygamous marriage and against the rejection of celibacy professed by Islam ('*Umayyad Poetry*', p. 423).
4. While 'Umar b. Abi Rabi'ah, for instance, says: 'Peace (*salam*) be upon her – if

she should accept it, And if she should dismiss it, then peace (*salam*) be upon another woman!' See 'Umar b. Abi Rabi'ah, *Diwan*, p. 162.
5. Qays ibn Dharih was forced by his parents to divorce his dear but barren wife and was not able to do without her afterwards. See *Al-Shi'r wa'l-Shu'ara'*, p. 628 and *Kitab al-Aghani*, Vol. 9, pp. 124–50.
6. Qays, *Diwan*, p. 65.
7. Al-Isfahani, *Kitab al-Aghani*, Vol. 9, p. 126.
8. Qays in al-Isfahani, *Kitab al-Aghani*, Vol. 9, p. 148, in Kinany, *Development*, p. 299.
9. Although Abu-Lughod's study is concerned with a contemporary community of Bedouin in the western desert of Egypt I argue that it may be partially useful to offer a wide-ranging framework to understand Bedouin society in general.
10. Abu-Lughod, *Veiled Sentiments: Honor and Poetry in a Bedouin Society*, p. 125.
11. Al-Isfahani, *Kitab al-Aghani*, Vol. 2, p. 365.
12. Bloch, *Medieval Misogyny and the Invention of Western Romantic Love*, p. 137.
13. Majnun, *Diwan*, p. 153, in Khan, *Sexuality and Secrecy*, p. 150.
14. Ibid., p. 154.
15. Khan, *Sexuality and Secrecy*, p. 150.
16. Wright, *Psychoanalytic Criticism: Theory in Practice*, p. 40. Referring to Freud here does not mean that I have necessarily applied his framework. Also, I am not going to treat the works as symptomatic. Nonetheless, the mere idea of the aesthetic of id-psychology ,which is grounded in the notion that the work of art is the secret embodiment of its creator's unconscious desire, is worth considering here. Richard Wollheim even argues that Freud was fully aware of the difference between treating art as biographical evidence and treating it as an aesthetic object (Wright, p. 29).
17. Al-Isfahani, *Kitab al-Aghani*, Vol. 2, p. 335, in Khan, *Sexuality and Secrecy*, p. 101.
18. Al-Isfahani, *Kitab al-Aghani*, Vol. 9, p. 19.
19. Freud, 'Creative Writers and Day Dreaming', in Lodge, *20th Century Literary Criticism*, p. 75.
20. Kuthayyir, p. 42, in Kinany, *Development*, p. 292.
21. Hamdun, *al-Tadhkirah al-hamduniyyah*, p. 880, www.alwaraq.net 1 August 2008.
22. Khairallah, *Love*, p. 22.
23. As I have mentioned in the introduction, my study concentrates on five *'udhri* lovers: Majnun, Qays, 'Urwah, Kuthayyir and Jamil. They are all poets whose

collections of poems (*diwans*) have been edited and published. Nevertheless, in some sources dealing with the theme of love one can find several narratives about other *'udhri* lovers, where few verses are ascribed to them. I am not sure if they are considered as poets or not, as we do not have evidence that they composed entire poems.

24. Majnun says: 'If you deny me Layla and the beauty of her conversation, you will not deny me rhymes and tears.' Majnun, *Diwan*, p. 228, in Khairallah, *Love*, p. 66.
25. Ibn Qutaybah, *Al-Shi'r wa'l-shu'ara'*, p. 415, in Khairallah, *Love*, p. 66.
26. Khan, *Sexuality and Secrecy*, p. 294.
27. Cited and translated by Kinany, *Development*, pp. 276–7.
28. Khan, *Sexuality and Secrecy*, p. 159.
29. Al-'Aqqad, *Jamil*, pp. 44–5.
30. It is worth noticing that some modern poets emphasise the absence of the beloved: 'Yeats even suggests that a male poet cannot possibly achieve both forms of "love": possession of the woman and of the poem are mutually exclusive, if the poet must lose the beloved to gain the desire that sustains his poetry – an economic trade-off that Yeats foregrounds in his work. He often implies that the beloved must be absent, incapable of reciprocation or receiving his desire, so that he may work up the poetry's desire in language . . . Although the poems often protest the loss of the beloved, they betray also an awareness that this loss creates the "space" of desire that engenders them.' www.questia.com\PM.qsta 21 September 2006.
31. Menocal, *Shards of Love. Exile and the Origins of the Lyric*, p. 146.
32. This idea is established according to some narratives and verses but we should keep in mind that such narratives and verses have always appeared with their contrary, as I have observed earlier.
33. Al-'Azm, *Fi'l-hubb*, p. 81.
34. However, this convention is questionable, as several statements suggest that poetry composed for a Bedouin woman should never prevent the poet, or any other man, from marrying her.
35. Al-Isfahani, *Kitab al-Aghani*, Vol. 8, p. 294.
36. Ibid., pp. 288–90
37. Ibid., p. 311.
38. Al-'Azm, *Fi al-hubb,* pp. 52–60.
39. Ibid., p. 89.
40. Jamil, *Diwan*, p. 74. Another *'udhri* poet, Kuthayyir 'Azzah, says: 'Do me good

or do me harm, I shall not blame you, not hate you, even when you make yourself hateful', Kuthayyir, *Diwan*, p. 57, in Kinany, *Development*, p. 291.
41. Khan, *Sexuality and Secrecy*, p. 198.
42. Ibn 'Arabi, *Al-Futuhat al-makkiyyah*, p. 1,467. www.alwaraq.net 3 March 2007. Khairallah notes that: 'This Sufi anecdote adds to Majnun's attitude a dimension hardly explicit in the *diwan*. Yet already Majnun's condition, supported by his inflamed imagination, was pointing in this direction [. . .] Even though the *diwan* does not formulate an anecdote like Ibn 'Arabi's one, such an anecdote is latent in the text.' (Khairallah, *Love*, p. 79).
43. Al-Isfahani, *Kitab al-Aghani*, Vol. 2, p. 383.
44. Khan, *Sexuality and Secrecy*, p. 197.
45. Krueger, 'Double Jeopardy. The Appropriation of Woman in Four Old French Romances of the "Cycle de la Gageure"', in Fisher and Halley, *Seeking the Woman in Late Medieval and Renaissance Writings: Essays in Feminist Contextual Criticism*, p. 23.
46. Ibn 'Arabi, *Al-Futuhat al-makkiyyah*, p. 1,467.
47. Al-Tusi, *Kitab al-Luma'*, cited in Khairallah, *Love*, p. 102.
48. Dols, *Majnun*, p. 322.
49. Ibid., p. 323.
50. For detailed discussion of Persian versions of Majnun's story and its connection with the Arabic version see Hilal, *al-Hayah al-'atifiyah bayna al-'udhriyah wa'l-sufiyah: dirasat naqd wa muqaranah hawla mawdu' Layla wa al-Majnun fi al-'adabayn al-'arabi wa'l-farisi*. Khairallah also offers a discussion on the Sufi elements in Majnun's legend in Persian, especially for Jamil's poetry: pp. 107–25.
51. Kinany, *Development*, p. 258.
52. Jamil, *Diwan*, pp. 30–1, in Hamori, *On the Art of Medieval Arabic Literature*, p. 42.
53. Ibid., p. 37.
54. Ibid., p. 23.
55. Al-Baghdadi, *Khizanat al-adab*, p. 400.
56. Ibid., p. 398.
57. Ibid.
58. Qays, *Diwan*, p. 28.
59. Jamil, *Diwan*, p. 88.
60. Jayyusi criticises the beloved in the *'udhri* tradition, as she never gives; 'the woman is hardly more than a recipient of love. She promises, but never fulfils. She loves, but in this literature she never gives' (Jayyusi, 'Umayyad Poetry',

p. 426). In fact, this quality is popularly considered as a positive feature of a beloved in the Arabic tradition in general. In spite of this convention, I would argue that the beloveds in the *'udhri* tradition offered great love and even composed verses to their lovers. The sources confirm to us that the beloveds were not as aloof and careless as some might think. As Jayyusi has noted, it is true that elopement is not a feature of these stories, but that does not mean that 'the code of honour in these stories proved itself stronger than love and life'. If that were the case, how can we explain the extensive anecdotes about the lovers meeting even after the beloved's marriage? In fact, there are many verses and narratives that portray the beloved as just as passionate as her lover. For instance, in a meeting between Layla and Majnun she revealed to him the she loves him more than he loves her and she promised him that she would never willingly be with another man. See al-Isfahani, *Kitab al-Aghani*, Vol. 2, pp. 355–6.

61. Hamori, *On the Art of Medieval Arabic Literature*, p. 45.
62. Majnun, *Diwan*, p. 18, in Kinany, *Development*, p. 259.
63. Al-Isfahani, *Kitab al-Aghani*, Vol. 2, p. 373.
64. Ibid., p. 342.
65. Majnun, *Diwan*, p. 41, in Khairallah, *Love*, p. 140.
66. Majnun, *Diwan*, p. 17, in Hamori, *On the Art of Medieval Arabic Literature*, p. 47. However, Ibn Qutaybah in *Al-shi'r wa'l-shu'ara'*, p. 566, states that this verse is falsely attributed to Majnun.
67. Kuthayyir, *Diwan*, p. 180, in Kinany, *Development*, p. 258.
68. Majnun, *Diwan*, p. 120, in Khairallah, *Love*, p. 76.
69. Majnun, *Diwan*, p. 94.
70. Bataille, *Eroticism, Death and Sensuality*, p. 20.
71. Ibn Hazm, *The Ring of the Dove*, pp. 100–1.
72. Kinany, *Development*, p. 259.
73. Ibid., p. 261.
74. Jamil, *Diwan*, p. 33, in Hamori, *On the Art of Medieval Arabic Literature*, p. 43.
75. Al-Isfahani, *Kitab al-Aghani*, p. 192.
76. Jamil, *Diwan*, p. 32, in Hamori, *On the Art of Medieval Arabic Literature*, p. 39. Similar themes occur in the *diwan* of Jamil, pp. 74, 98, 100.
77. Hamori, *On the Art of Medieval Arabic Literature*, p. 40.
78. Ibn Hazm, *The Ring of the Dove*, p. 96.
79. Ibid., pp. 96–7.
80. Khairallah, *Love*, p. 34.
81. Hamori, *On the Art of Medieval Arabic Literature*, p. 4.

82. For more elaborated discussions on this issue, see al-'Ani, *Al-Islam wa'l-shi'r*.
83. Khairallah, *Love*, p. 66.
84. Menocal, *Shards of Love*, p. 148.
85. Ibn 'Arabi, *Al-Futuhat al-makkiyyah*, p. 1,467.
86. Khairallah, *Love*, p. 66.
87. Khan, *Sexuality and Secrecy*, p. 201.
88. There are many anecdotes that suggest this poetic consciousness, for example Majnun's encounter with Qays b. Dharih in which Majnun had a competition with him even though he was isolated in the desert at the time. He said to Qays: 'I still am a better poet when I say …' See al-Walibi, *Diwan Majnun Layla*.
89. Khairallah, *Love*, p. 63.
90. Al-Washsha', *Al-Muwashsha*, p. 83.

7

The Representation of the Lover's Body in the *'Udhri* Tradition

Introduction

In *Lisan al-'Arab* the definition shown below is provided for the word *'ishq*:

> *'Ishq* is excessive love. The excessive lover is called *'Ashiq* because his intense feelings make him melt like the *'ishqah* tree. *'Ishqah* is a green tree that becomes yellow when crushed. It is, therefore, claimed that the noun *'Ishq* is derived from *'ishqah*.[1]

In Arabic it is noteworthy how many nouns refer to love. More interesting is the fact that perhaps half of them link love with sickness or mental diseases. 'A high proportion of the words express the woes of love – the longing, the pain, the grief, melancholy, confusion, and illness – rather than its pleasures.'[2] Thus, in a symposium that took place in the ninth century in the palace of Yahya al-Barmaki, love was defined as based on the like-mindedness of the partners and it was a major cause of suffering, capable of subjugating, intoxicating and humiliating the lover to the point of annihilation.[3]

Undoubtedly, the representation of the beloved's body is the main concern of the *'udhri* tradition. This does not, however, indicate the absence of the lover-poet's own body; the *'udhri* tradition rather puts great emphasis on it, considering it the greatest recipient of the effects of profound emotion. It is his body that is malnourished, sick, suffering from insomnia and prematurely aged. The *'udhri* lover sometimes even reaches the point of madness, but death alone seems to be the ultimate result of excessive passion. Hence, the vocabulary of sickness, healing, the doctor and magic – all of which affect the body – is frequently repeated in the *'udhri ghazal*. Some verses even confirm that the lover has become blind, mute and paralysed, simply owing to his passion.

Love as Malady in Classical Arabic Literature

In the Qur'an, *surat* Yusuf uses love to explain the somatic consequences of human emotions; to end their gossip 'Aziz's wife invites the women of the city to her house for a feast. Joseph comes in and all the women, who are traditionally thought to have been peeling oranges with sharp knives, 'slash their hands' because they are so entranced by him that they lose focus on what they are doing and so cut their hands instead of the fruit. They so lose their minds that they cannot distinguish between the fruit and their hands. Thus, the effect on them of seeing Joseph is expressed in a corporeal way. 'Indeed the emotion felt by the sight of Joseph was so great that the charming assembly was seized by a collective physiological pain.'[4]

In the classical Arabic tradition, when dealing with the theme of love, whether from medical or literary perspectives, it has been frequently stated that passionate love (*'ishq*) is a kind of sickness. This idea was not new at the time,[5] as Arab authors were influenced by Greek philosophy in this matter. In the fourth and seventh centuries CE, chapters on love were included in sections on mental illnesses by two Byzantine authors, where they reproduce traditional lists of symptoms and therapeutic suggestions.[6] Moreover, 'the difficulty of a medical diagnosis and treatment of an enervated and depressed young man or woman who suffered from lovesickness can even be found in ancient Egyptian literature.'[7] Arabic medical literature shows similar tendencies in the discussion of love as a malady. In the classical medical discourse of the Arabs, *'ishq* is included among the traditional mental sicknesses. For example, al-Majusi (d. 372/982) groups love with melancholy and provides a list of medicaments. Apart from Ibn al-Jazzar (d. c. 395/1004), who characterises lovesickness as a kind of critical intensification of the natural desire of the soul for all beautiful things, love stays within the traditional frame of reference.[8] In his medical book *Al-Qanun*, Ibn Sina (d. 1037) dedicates a chapter to love sickness, in which he portrays *'ishq* as a sort of illness similar to melancholia. He describes the characteristics of the illness as hollowness of the eyes and their dryness, the lack of moisture except when weeping, continuous movement of the eyelids, and laughing as if he sees something pleasant or hears happy news or jokes. His psyche is full of alienation and withdrawal, so that there is much deep sighing. His condition changes from exhilaration and laughter to sadness and weeping when he hears love poetry, especially when he remembers the separation and distance from his beloved [. . .] His behaviour is disordered, and his pulse is irregular, like those who are anxious.[9]

The link provided by Ibn Sina between the lover's sadness and love poetry is noteworthy. By establishing such a link, he suggests a bond between emotions and language. Language, especially in the form of poetry, revives passionate feeling. Therefore the role played by poetry in love is significant.

Ibn Sina goes on to give advice to doctors on how to cure the patient. He suggests, for instance, the uniting of the lover with his beloved, saying about one case, 'when he experienced union with his beloved, recovery occurred in a very short time'.[10] He also suggests several different treatments, depending on each individual condition such as: preoccupying the lover's mind so that he forgets what caused him to be seriously ill,[11] or joining the lover with someone other than the beloved in order that he forgets the latter, or giving the lover sincere advice or warning, or increasing sexual intercourse with slave-girls. Ibn Sina also states: 'Some people are consoled with entertainment and recitation, while for others it only increases their infatuation; it is possible to discover which is which.'[12] Ibn Sina's commentary on lovesickness shows that *'ishq* was a common topic in Islamic medical textbooks, alongside other mental disorders.[13]

In belles-lettres the malady of love was also a subject frequently treated. For example, al-Jahiz (c. 776–869) states that:

> I propose to describe *'ishq* for you, so that you may know how it is defined. It is a sickness that attacks the soul and spreads to the body by direct contagion, the soul being weakened by the violence done to the body and physical exhaustion being followed by moral weakness.[14]

In al-Jahiz's statement, cited above, he sharply distinguishes between the soul and the body, though he does observe the mutual effects between them.

Love, in his view, attacks the soul first and then spreads to the body, but once the body becomes weak, the soul is also affected by this weakness. Abu Bakr Muhammad b. Da'ud (255/868–297/910) devotes a full chapter, entitled 'The body's pining is a sign of agony (*kamad*)', to this question in his book *Kitab al-zahrah*. He explains the effect of emotion on the body from a medical perspective: 'the heat that is engendered by grief flows into the heart from all parts of the body and then ascends to the brain'.[15] He also mentions the particular role played by tears in this matter: 'vapours from which tears are produced when they are liquefied by the natural heat they possess'.[16] Abu Bakr al-Khara'iti (d. 327/938) was also tempted to write on the subject but adopted a rather more critical point of view; he entitles his treatise *I'tilal al-qulub (The Malady of Hearts)*. From the title it is apparent that the author views love as a malady and a chapter of his treatise is even entitled: 'On the condemnation of *hawa* (desire) and the following of it'. As Giffen notes, al-Khara'iti's influence was significant: 'Four centuries later, Ibn al-Jawzi, Ibn Qayyim al-Jawziyyah and al-Mughultai cite him as an authority on love theory.'[17] In *Kitab al-riyad* by Muhammad al-Marzubani (384/993 or 378/987) a definition of *'ishq* that again links it with malady is provided; 'Someone said to Zuhayr al-Madini: "What is *'ishq*?" He said: "Madness and submissiveness, and it is the malady of refined people".'[18] Abu Hayyan al-Tawhidi (d. 414/1023) in *Al-Muqabasat* suggests that love feeds the soul, but weakens the body.[19]

In any case, the literary production on this subject is too abundant to be documented in detail here. However, I will concentrate on one text, anonymously authored, quoting it at length because it provides a comprehensive view on the subject under discussion and has been frequently quoted by many authors:

> Love is a desire which is born in the heart and in which gather elements of avidity. Whenever it gains in strength the lover becomes more agitated and persistent, his disquiet intensifies and his insomnia increases. When this happens his blood burns and changes into black bile, and his yellow bile is inflamed and transformed into black bile. The excess of black bile impairs thinking, and impaired thinking is accompanied by blunted wits, diminished reasoning, hoping for the impossible, and wishing for the unfeasible,

to the point that it all leads to madness. Then, the lover sometimes kills himself and sometimes dies of grief, or he goes to his beloved and dies of joy or perishes of distress. Sometimes he moans heavily, causing his spirit to remain concealed for twenty-four hours. He continues [in his state] until he is taken for dead, and he is then buried while still alive. Sometimes he heaves a deep sigh and his soul is stifled in his pericardium. The heart then closes in on the soul and does not release it until he dies. Sometimes during moments of relaxation he raises his eyes to look around and he suddenly sees the person he loves, his blood drains and his colour changes. The person who is in such a state can be relieved through the grace of the Lord of the Worlds, not through the ministrations of any human. This is because a malignant state which occurs from an isolated cause arising by itself is susceptible to thorough elimination by the elimination by its cause, But when two causes occur in such a manner that each one of them occasions the other, there is no way in which either one of them can be eliminated. And since black bile causes continuous thinking and continuous thinking causes the burning of the blood and the yellow bile and their transformation into black bile, then whenever the black bile predominates it intensifies thinking, and whenever thinking becomes intense it reinforces the black bile. This is an incurable disease which doctors are unable to treat.[20]

This text has had a long and influential life in the literary tradition. It appears at different lengths and in several different versions, and is reproduced in many works beginning in the third century AH, such as *Nawadir al-falasifah* by Hunayn b. Ishaq (d. 260/877), *Kitab al-zahrah* by Abu Bakr Muhammad b. Da'ud al-Isfahani (d. 297/910), *Muruj al-dhahab* by al-Mas'udi (d. 354/956), *Dhamm al-hawa* by Ibn al-Jawzi (d. 597/1200) and *'Uyun al-anba'* by Ibn Abi Usaybi'ah (d. 668/1270). It is said to be copied from the Greek,[21] though the Greek original is lost.[22] In any case, this text presents well-structured aspects and it shows great awareness of the putative emotional effects of love on one's own body. I would argue that it proves that the lover's body was a theme of interest on a theoretical level according to the popular subject of love in classical Arabic belles-lettres. The text suggests a mutual relationship between the lover's excessive emotions and his body. Once love 'is born in the heart', it attacks the lover's body; his insomnia increases and 'his blood burns'. At this point the effect will return to 'thinking' that causes 'blunted wits, diminished reasoning and hoping for the impossible', which will eventually lead the lover to madness or death. The concept of death is a crucial aspect of passionate love ('*ishq*) and it is clearly emphasised here. Death, the text suggests, will undoubtedly reach the lover, either as a result of his grief or of his joy if he suddenly beholds his beloved. Biesterfeldt and Gutas provide the following commentary on the text:

> [this text] ascribes to the lover a number of symptoms [. . .]. It has a medical framework. It analyses love by means of humoral etiology; and it makes use of popular and literary commonplaces about love much as the *problemata* as a genre deal with everyday concerns.[23]

If that is the case, it is no wonder that the lover is treated as a patient in some medical texts, such as the aforementioned *Treatise on Love* by Ibn Sina, in which he provides a discussion of the symptoms and suggested treatments for the lover. Moreover, it seems that particular practices were employed when dealing with suffering lovers; their love would be treated either as a sickness or as a kind of magic. Therefore, the lover would be taken to both physicians and diviners, as we shall see in the stories about 'Urwah and Majnun. In some cases, the lover has to drink '*sulwanah*', which is believed to be a cure for '*ishq*. *Sulwanah* is an amulet in a crushed bead whose liquid is drunk by an afflicted lover to cure him of this love.[24] Seeing love from this angle explains the motif of dedicating prayers to the lover, as one would pray for a sick man. Interestingly, al-Washsha' considers praying for lovers as a duty of *udaba'*; he provides many narratives about people who offer *du'a'* for lovers while they circumambulate the Ka'bah.[25] He even states that 'It is claimed that no sins will be inflicted on lovers and that the pains they endure compensate for their sins.'[26] Answering a question about lovers, the judge Shurayk b. 'Abdullah said: 'whoever possesses the most intense feelings of love will receive the biggest share of rewards.'[27]

The Effect of Love on the Lover's Body in the *'Udhri* Tradition

I have sketched above the classical Arabic theoretical perspective on the effects of the emotion of love on the body.[28] Yet the physical presence of the lover's own body can also be traced in poetry. In fact, most of those authors who deal with the theme of love in their writing rely on Arabic poetry as a primary source for their theoretical formulations. 'The best discussion of love turns frequently to verse to illustrate aptly the ideas under discussion, to reinforce the author's statements, or to express his thought more subtly.'[29] Several aspects of the effect that love has on the *'udhri* lover's own body are depicted in the *'udhri ghazal*. These aspects are intertwined, but for the sake of this analysis I have separated them into several categories, each of which is discussed below.

Crying

The theme of weeping is one of the oldest themes in classical Arabic poetry.[30] In *'udhri* poets' *diwan*s there are numerous allusions to weeping. It seems that shedding tears – according to *'udhri* poets – functions in several ways: divulgence, resistance, evidence and healing. Tears are a divulgence and a disclosure of the poet's feelings and of what his heart is incapable of bearing. His feelings are expressed in the form of tears, revealing a hidden pain and a concealed love. No matter how this lover struggles to conceal his love, tears remain the most vivid traces and indicators of love; Jamil says:

> Oh my friends, what I conceal of this love,
> tears will soon reveal[31] [1]

Weeping is evidence and proof of the poet's sincere feelings. Majnun explicitly refers to this:

> The representation of the passion of youth is made through tears and these
> tears are the fairest evidence[32] [2]

Kuthayyir not only indulges in tears; he also invites his eyes to drop tears to prove his love and concealed passion:

> I ask the water of the eye to continue
> hoping that it will be a witness to that concealed passion[33] [3]

Moreover, according to *'udhri* poetry, weeping is a cure and a comfort. It is a means of healing the acute pains of love:

> I was told of her abandonment,
> and asked to choose between patience and weeping
> And I chose to weep for its immediate effect to heal my burns[34] [4]

However, weeping does not always indicate weakness and disclosure; it sometimes serves as a weapon for the lover, used to resist his society's oppression. Therefore, even if this oppressive society stops Buthaynah from meeting Jamil and Lubna from meeting Qays, it cannot stop them from expressing their emotions and weeping in agony.[35] Majnun provides us with a poetic image that endows tears with a significant psychological dimension:

> What runs down from the eye is not its water
> But a soul which melts and drips[36]   [5]

The *'udhri* poem presents tears as the destined and inevitable fate of lovers. Tears represent disclosure, resistance, witness, or a means of healing from the agonies of love; they are present on a permanent basis. The *'udhri* poet asserts the continuity of his tears through a range of figural possibilities, as tears are like a river that does not stop flowing and a well that does not dry up.[37] The simile that relates tears and clouds depends on the related imagery of flows.[38]

In the case of the absence of his beloved, the poet never lacks reminders of her that stimulate his tears and the ardour of his love. These reminders may be natural elements like fire,[39] air[40] and water.[41] These reminders may also be avian creatures like doves[42] and crows – as Majnun's eyes, for instance, drop tears when hearing the sound of crows.[43] The blowing of the breeze, the cooing of the dove, the cawing of crows, the lightning that accompanies thunder: all these are also reminders that stimulate the poet's nostalgia and passionate feelings. It is enough for Majnun to hear the name Layla to make him wet his shawl with tears.[44]

However, the stimulation of tears is not confined to the absence of the beloved; it is also attributed to her presence:

> As soon as the eyes behold her,
> they drop tears while keeping a still look towards her[45]   [6]

The lover does not see any conflict in this as long as weeping forms a genuine element of his overall perception of love and self-expression. Whether his beloved is present or absent, he is always in agony and facing tears and sadness. He cries in fear of her alienation or abandonment.[46] He cries when she approaches and when she departs, as there is no limit to his sadness and no hindrance to his tears. He cries until the tears turn into blood:

My eyes would still drop running tears or blood –
if my eyes accede to my wishes[47] [7]

We should bear in mind that such poetic images contain violence where passion is linked to blood. Blood carries indications of killing and bloodshed. Love causes blood to drop from the eyes and the body of the lover when targeted by the arrows of lovesickness and deprivation. This idea is also linked to the idea of passion itself as a power that is closer to hatred than to affection in its violence and intensity.[48] Within the same context Bataille wonders: 'What does physical eroticism signify if not a violation of the very being of its practitioners? – a violation bordering on death, bordering on murder?'[49]

It is impossible in this context to avoid thinking of tears as a liquid that extinguishes fires. It means that the connotation of tears contradicts that of fire. Fire is used in this poetry as the primary signifier for the power of love. In this particular poetic imagination fire has different qualities, such as purifying fire or lustful fire. In Majnun Layla, fires inside the lover reach the extent of being capable of melting iron with the lover's frenzied breaths.[50] The trope of passionate fire recalls the trope of thirst and the need for cooling water. Hence, *'udhri* poets describe themselves as thirsty in expression of their yearning for the beloved. Qays explicitly describes himself as thirsty when referring to his yearning for Lubna.[51] Majnun links the image of water with that of fire in a contradictory poetic depiction:

If my sighs are to reach the sea;
the sea will dry up due to its burning flame[52] [8]

Jamil links Buthaynah's fire to the water of his eyes:

Your tears become plentiful
as Buthaynah's tent fire loomed up ahead of you[53] [9]

It is important to note that the fire attributed to Buthaynah refers to two different things: one is that the fire that is lit for warming or guiding – and that is the apparent meaning. The second and deeper meaning is the metaphoric fire that inflames the poet's feelings, which he tries to confront by plentiful tears. Through the tears of lovers, we can attribute love, passion and thirst to a power generated by fire. Tears are seen not only as expressions of love; they rather represent the overall power of love, for tears are the water that quenches fire. But tears are also the result of this burning power of love.[54]

It is noteworthy that the theme of fire is prominent in some of the anecdotes ascribed to *'udhri* poets. For example, the *Kitab al-Aghani* presents a scene in which fire and the nudity of the lover's body are connected. Majnun – as the anecdote shows – was seeking fire while wrapped in a cloak, Layla brought out the fire in a rag for him and they stood conversing. When the rag burned out, Majnun tore a piece from his cloak and lit it instead. Then he tore another and another until nothing remained of the cloak.[55] Khan observes that:

> The exchange of words (language) between the lovers is made simultaneous with the burning of fire as well as the denuding of the male's lover's body. Burning of fire and baring of body here act as metaphors for linguistic expression [. . .]. Layla is both the spark that ignites his desire and the night that is unveiled by his passion.[56]

The theoretical paradigm of later classical Arabic literature enhances the theme of the crying lover; one of the chapters in Ibn Da'ud's book *Kitab al-zahrah* is entitled: 'He who cannot find solace, his weeping increases'. In this chapter he explains that the only true tears are those of a genuine lover; an artificial lover could claim love but without any explicit evidence of tears from his eyes.

Malady and wasting away

The language that contains references to sickness, wasting away, paleness, malady, the damaged liver (*kabid maqruhah*) and physicians is very conventional in Arabic love discourse. Salamah refers to two central aspects in the relationship between love and malady, where love is either linked to other known diseases or is seen in itself as an illness.[57] The other manifestation of love's link to diseases is in the vocabulary that is commonly used to refer to both love and disease: *shagaf, jawa, 'amad, khabal, kalaf* and *wala'*.[58] The word *huyam*, for example, means passion but is also used to refer to a type of fever that affects camels and causes them to experience a burning thirst. 'Urwah begins by describing his *huyam* as a disease:

> I am attacked by either despair or the disease of passion (*huyam*)
> So, you ought to refrain from approaching me lest the disease affects
>   you[59]   [10]

Love also seems to be linked to tuberculosis; Muhammad b. al-Zubayr said: 'while with 'Urwah b. al-Zubayr, I heard him saying to a fellow from *'Udhrah*'s tribe: You people have the most tender hearts. The fellow replied: Yes, I have left over thirty there with tuberculosis and they have no disease but love.'[60]

The story of the *'udhri* poet 'Urwah is typical in this respect. He was promised his beloved cousin 'Afra' if he became wealthy; so he went away to seek wealth, but during his absence 'Afra' was married off to another man who took her to Syria. Her father went to an old grave, restored it and put it in order and asked the tribe to keep the matter secret. When 'Urwah arrived, 'Afra's father told him that she had died and took him to the grave. 'Urwah remained there for several days, wasting away and slowly perishing, until a girl from the tribe came to him and told him what had happened.[61] There are several accounts of what followed, but it is significant that all the accounts insist on 'Urwah's sickness and death. In these verses, addressing his friends, he reveals the desperate physical condition of his body:

> If you would take off my shirt from me you would clearly see how much I
>   have suffered on account of 'Afrā', my friends! Then you would see little
>   flesh, decaying bones,
> and a heart perpetually palpitating [62]   [11]

His relatives tried to cure him as they would any sick person. In one version of his story in the *Kitab al-Aghani* it is stated that

> he left 'Afra' and returned to his people, wasted and thin. He had sisters, a maternal aunt and a grandmother, who began to admonish him, but it did not have any effect. They took him to Abu Kuhaylah Rabah b. Shaddad, the client of the Banu Thu'aylah, who was the diviner of Hijr, so that he could treat him. But his treatment did not have any effect on him.[63]

In another account, he

> would go to the water cisterns where the camels of 'Afrā' would come to drink, and then would press his breast against them. People would say to

him, 'Take it easy, for you'll kill yourself! Fear God!' But he would not accept their advice, until finally he was nearly done for and felt death approaching. Then he said, I despair: I have been given to drink the sickness of passionate love. Be warned by me, lest you will have what I suffer.[64]

It has often been said of 'Urwah that 'nothing but his shadow (ghost, phantom) was left'. The attention that the narrator (*rawi*) focuses on 'Urwah's bad health as a result of passionate love is significant in these accounts. In the last account quoted above his relatives seek the medical advice of an expert, but the latter is useless in curing such a great sickness. We might recall here what Ibn Da'ud said about those who are lovesick: 'This is an incurable disease which doctors are unable to treat'.[65] 'Urwah puts his story, detailing the attempt to cure him, in poetic form:

> I left it to the diviner of al-Yamamah to name his fee, and the diviner of
>   Hijr, if only they could cure me. They have left no trick they knew
>   untried,
> no potion but they gave it me to drink.
> They sprinkled water on my face for a while
> and were quick to visit me, with those who visit the sick. They said: May
>   God cure you! By God, we have no power
> over what your ribs contain[66] [12]

Furthermore, the word illness (*marad*) is frequently associated with the word physician (*tabib*) in the '*udhri ghazal*. Apparently, as 'Urwah declared in the verses above, the suffering lover is seeking a cure from the physicians or the diviners. But the lover-poet then states that both physicians and diviners are hopeless in his case. On one hand, he has no choice but death or patience; Majnun says:

> Two physicians!
> Were you to treat me I would reward you both, so why do you forgo the
>   fee?
> They said sadly:
> 'Nothing can help you so either die of grief,
> or strengthen yourself with patience.'[67] [13]

On the other hand, the lover-poet implies that he knows his cure; it is not medical treatment but his beloved:

> Layla's family have made me long for her
> and today I have no cure except in Layla[68] [14]

Jamil also declares:

> O Buthaynah, show some generosity
> and requite your suffering lover and salve his maladies and pains![69] [15]

If the beloved blessed the lover just once with a visit while he was sick, because of his love for her, then there would be nothing left for him to desire in this life and he would therefore be happy to die. Qays says:

> Qays was treated for the love of Lubna,
> which was his sickness, and love is a terrible sickness. When the women
>   came to visit me one day my eye said:
> 'I see not the one I desire.'
> If only Lubna would visit me, then I would gladly die
> but she comes not amongst those who visit[70] [16]

Qays believes love to be a terrible malady (*da' shadid*). According to *'udhri* poetry, all the malady's symptoms are obvious in the lover: paleness, thinness, fever and thirst. As for paleness and wasting away, Qays illustrates this point:

> Love has signs that are patent in a youth
> He becomes pale and his knuckles stick out from his hands[71] [17]

His usage of the word 'signs' is noteworthy in this context; it gives evidence to the claim that the idea of proving love by using bodily symptoms was already circulating in Arabic culture in Qays' time. One should bear in mind that this idea became very conventional in Arabic love theory. Both Ibn Da'ud and al-Washsha', for instance, consider the emaciated body to be evidence of true love: in his book *Kitab al-zahrah,* Ibn Da'ud devotes a whole chapter to this, entitled: 'The body's pining is a sign of agony (*kamad*)'. He explains the effect of emotion on the body, utilising medical concepts: 'the heat that is engendered by grief flows into the heart from all parts of the body and then ascends to the brain'.[72]

There are many tales in *Masariʿ al-ʿushshaq* that enhance the theme of the sick lover. In one account, al-Sarraj narrates that a slave girl who is loved by a pious youth sends him a red rose, which he straps to his upper arm as he lies on his deathbed.[73] In the *ʿudhri* tradition, there are frequent references to the theme of wasting away in Majnun's story and his poetry alike. For example, he claims:

> I have had so much hardship with her
> that I melted with passion and my bones turned to dust[74]   [18]

Here he ascribes extraordinary effects to love. Love is like death in which the bones become feeble. Sura 36 in the Qur'an reads:

> And he makes comparisons for Us, and forgets his own (origin and) Creation: He says, 'Who can give life to (dry) bones and decomposed ones (at that)?' Say, 'He will give them life Who created them for the first time! for He is Well-versed in every kind of creation.[75]

Majnun's use of a religious lexicon is also evident when he enquires about whether it is lawful for Layla to hurt his body or not.[76] Jamil, likewise, pleads Buthaynah to fear God and not to kill her lover.[77]

Jamil clearly associates *ʿudhri* love with physical wasting, as is exemplified in an episode when he criticises a man called Jaʿfar who ate food while claiming that he was in love:

> Jaʿfar surprises me! He avidly eats my loaf of bread, while shedding tears
>   because of Juml [a girl's name]
> If your attachment were ʿudhrite you would not eat your belly full: love
>   would have made you forget gorging yourself[78]   [19]

In any case, it is significant how the theme of emaciation of the lover becomes essential in classical Arabic *ghazal* poetry. There are endless examples that confirm the importance of this theme.[79]

Fainting

In 'Urwah's story, as illustrated in the *Kitab al-Aghani,* there is a scene where the lover suffered from fainting and only the smell of ʿAfra's veil could awake him:

> When he departed from them his condition deteriorated, after having been healthy and on the way to recovery. He suffered from fainting fits and palpitations. Whenever he lost consciousness they would throw on his face a veil that had belonged to 'Afra' and which she had given to him; then he would come to his senses.[80]

Fainting represents a desire not to communicate with the outside world or even feel it. However, when the outside world is represented by the beloved or anything that relates to her, the lover is revived as if fainting were a death in miniature and the smell of the beloved alone would enable one to gain life after death. The Qur'anic scene of the prophet Jacob who regains his sight after his son's shirt is thrown over his face[81] is clearly present in the narrator's imagination when it comes to the stories of *'udhri* lovers.

Thus, fainting is another example of the physical effects of love[82] and it is particularly common in the story of Majnun. There are several scenes in his romance where he faints – for example, after Layla recites these verses to him:

> Both of us appear in front of people
> To hate each other
> And yet each is entrenched with his friend
> The secrets of the glancer are not hidden
> If the eyes disclose what he conceals

Hearing this, he falls into a swoon and rises having lost his senses.[83] The frequency of the scenes of fainting in Majnun's romance led Taha Husayn to treat Majnun's character somewhat sarcastically:

> It was not enough that you would talk to him about Layla, for him to faint and fall on his face [. . .] He spent all his life either falling on his face, or wandering at large. He never, or almost never, knew a calm, reasonable life; all his life was full of anxiety, divided between fainting and madness.[84]

Husayn's criticism is based on his disdain for what he sees as the irrational details of *'udhri* narratives, as he fails to see the literary complexity of these stories as well as their rich symbolic aspects. In Majnun's romance there is always 'a connection between a fainting spell and the sight or mention of Layla, and between the fainting spell and the poetry uttered immediately before or after these spells.'[85] Majnun's poetry often dwells upon this point:

> The wind from her has brought a cool breath, of her perfume upon my heart
> I swooned, for my patience was long gone
> and I had had neither answer nor reply[86]   [20]

In these verses, Majnun is not only completely besotted by the presence or the vision of his beloved, he also faints merely as a result of the moving wind, which acts as a signifier of his beloved.[87] In one account, Majnun faints out of rage and jealousy when he meets Layla's husband and asks him if he has ever touched Layla. Her husband replies: 'By God, if you put me under oath, yes'. Majnun then grasps two handfuls of hot embers and holds them until he falls unconscious while the embers and the burnt flesh of his palms scatter on the ground.[88] Here, an extreme bodily reaction is attributed to the lover, where he burnt his hands and fainted. The reaction of fainting is not just associated with 'udhri poets, for their beloveds are also associated with it at some points, often amusingly so. Thus Ibn Qutaybah narrates an anecdote about a man from the Murrah tribe who while on business passed close to Najd, where he was taken care of by a woman. She asked him about Majnun and he replied saying that Majnun was wandering in the desert with wild animals, possessing neither sense nor understanding except when Layla was mentioned to him; then he would weep and recite poetry for her. The man from Murrah then said: 'She wailed and wept until, by God, I thought that her heart would break.' Then the woman recited some verses and she cried until she fainted, and when she regained consciousness she told him that she was Layla.[89]

In his comparative study, Manzalaoui shows that the phenomenon of the tearful and fainting lover is also common in Chaucer; the hero of *Troilus and Criseyde* is of this nature and Troilus's fainting does successfully win him Criseyde. Moreover, the trope of the fainting lover is not confined to Chaucer; swoons are attributed to the two manliest of all heroes, Tristan and Lancelot.[90] Manzalaoui declares that 'the weeping and fainting lover represents, for the figure of the hero in medieval romance, the furthest development from resolute warrior and voyager-hero of epic.'[91] In any case, among the striking similarities between Arabic tales of *The Arabian Nights* and Chaucer's Troilus, as Manzalaoui points out, are the similarity in tone and attitude, love at first sight, the topos of the bow and arrow of love that inflicts a wound upon the lover's heart, the sense that love is a fated disaster and the double faint of the lovers.[92]

Madness

Among the synonyms of love in the Arabic language, about twenty relate love, in varying degrees, to insanity. This list contains words such as *huyam, tabul, taym, khabal, lamam* and *mass*.[93] Madness also has its various forms, and one of them is expressed as '*ishq*',[94] as noted by the early philologist and lexicographer al-Asma'i, who travelled among the Bedouin Arabs. In this light, one can understand the significant emphasis placed on madness in classical Arabic love stories.[95] This may explain why Ibn al-Jawzi and Ibn Qayyim suggested that the first line of defence against falling into *hawa* is to let oneself be guided by reason (*'aql*), or by the rational soul. And so they stand in these respects in direct conflict with the central thrust of the *adab* tradition.[96]

Manzalaoui notes that, in comparison with Western literature, 'madness is frequently the terminal fate in Arabic tales, while in the Occidental ones it occurs (whether in a true or feigned form) as an episode in the life of a lover, rather than as his end'.[97] This idea is reiterated in the following lines by Shakespeare:

> Lovers and madmen have such seething brains,
> Such shaping fantasies that apprehend
> More than cool reason ever comprehends[98]

In Majnun's romance, after Layla marries another man, Majnun completely loses his reason despite all attempts to cure him. This is the basis of the legend and, of course, also explains the legendary appellation attributed to him of Majnun the madman. Ibn Qutaybah, in one of the early Arabic accounts about Majnun, states that 'He was nicknamed al-Majnun (the madman), since his reason had left him because of the intensity of his passion.'[99] In this account, Ibn Qutaybah offers a detailed description of Majnun's madness:

[Layla] would shun him and converse with others, to the point where he was hurt. When she realized that, she turned to him and said: In front of other people, we both display hatred, While each of us is entrenched in the other's heart. Things worsened for him so much that his reason left him, and he wandered aimlessly with the wild beasts. He would not put on any garment without tearing it to pieces, nor he would understand anything unless Layla was mentioned to him. Once she was mentioned, he would recover his reason and talk about her without dropping a letter.[100]

Dols observes that 'the freedom of the harmless madman and familial care are conspicuous features in the early Arabic accounts'.[101] However, the version of this particular account in the *Kitab al-Aghani* includes some additional details. For example, when Majnun failed to perform the ritual prayer and his father asked him for an explanation, he would not respond with [even] a word. His father, the narrator, continues: '... used to confine and chain him, and then he [resorted to] biting his tongue and lips until fearing for him, we let him go his way. And so, he madly wanders.'[102] Listening to Layla's verses led Majnun to wander in the desert. Khan notes that, in this account, Majnun is portrayed as being unerringly voluble in language that is highly erring (poetry) and his fluency in poetic speech is compared to his muteness when asked to utter prayers.[103]

In any case, Majnun's madness, as expressed in several accounts, appears to be a 'break with the commonly accepted norms of behaviour, whether on a personal or on a social level'.[104] He wandered in the desert and made friends with beasts, speaking to no one and completely neglecting his physical appearance.[105] So, 'however Majnun's madness is interpreted, it cannot completely conceal the discernible stigma that has commonly been attached to insanity in Arab society'.[106] The narrators of Majnun's story bring to our attention his physical appearance in particular, though they also provide some stereotyped elements of mad behaviour in general. His physical condition 'becomes his distinguishing mark as an incarnation of the love-mad poet, and in contrast to other heroes of the same type of romance'.[107] One might recall, for instance, the images used to describe Jamil; the narratives portray him as a handsome, noble knight, who wears fine clothes and acts appropriately.[108] However Jamil says:

When I said: give me back my reason (caught by you) I want to live like
   other people (without passion)
She said: you are asking an impossible thing[109]   [21]

Majnun, on the other hand, is portrayed as the archetypal madman and as having become childlike. Although Dols claims that 'Majnun's withdrawal was an expression of his rejection of society and his own humanity',[110] it could also be argued that pity was aroused by his act. For example, after tying him up, his family freed him, fearing that he would hurt himself when biting his lips and tearing his garments; furthermore, all those who visited him in the desert seemed to show him compassion. Nevertheless, Majnun's madness appears to be in conflict with society, as Khairallah points out:

> Majnun seems to be the farthest expression of the glamorized rebellion against social, religious, and intellectual conventions. These alienating conventions seem to have generated a counter-alienation, an outcry for total freedom, and a desire to return to unity with nature, where life is imagined to be beyond good and evil [. . .] Totally naked, Majnun lets his hair grow all over his body. He grazes with animals and runs with them, mainly with gazelles, who resemble his God: Layla. This behaviour marks his irremediable madness. Thus, several anecdotes identify his appearance with that of the jinn themselves. The insistence on this characteristic of Majnun's appearance could be interpreted both as an expression of the popular imagination behind the legend, and as a crystallization of Majnun's identification with the irrational forces of nature.[111]

Majnun's unkempt physical appearance, as revealed by his long nails, his long and dishevelled hair, his nudity and the growth of his body hair, all portray an image that is unacceptable for Muslim men. Many critics such as André Miquel, Asad Khairallah, Michael Dols and Ruqayya Khan have noted the anti-Islamic tendencies illustrated in Majnun's characterisation as a wild man. Dols declares that: 'the savage would appear as the negator of Muslim social values'.[112] Alternately, Khan demonstrates that 'Majnun is both negated against and the negator: he is both the sinful wild man and the romanticized, rebellious wild man.'[113] She sees his bestiality and nudity as bodily signs of a moral decay caused by his disregard for familial and religious conventions.[114] However, both Khan and Khairallah see in Majnun a romanticised picture of the poet who returns to natural perfection, living outside society's boundaries, and instead living in harmony with the animals who have become accustomed to him.[115] The use of the image of the 'Bedouin wild man as a means of rebellion against established society itself' is, Khan argues, tragic:

> Majnun represents the image of the wild man – the madman in the desert, without a name, a genealogy, a home or a history – employed as an icon of rebellion against the 'civilizing mission of Islam'. His geographical errancy or mad wanderings in search of the Najd are sentimentalized as a nostalgic gravitation toward the pristine Bedouin homeland.[116]

However, the emphasis Khan puts on Majnun being Bedouin, and thus a representation of Bedouin rebellion against the civilising mission of Islam, is a questionable one. I would rather see Majnun's depiction as an individual whose behaviour contrasts with both Islamic and Bedouin norms, establishing his own conduct as an outcast of society.

In his poetry, Majnun tries to deny his madness, linking his ability to compose poetry to his obsession with Layla:

> They speak of a madman crazed with her memory
> By God, I have no madness, nor am I bewitched
> If I try to compose poetry not in her remembrance
> I swear by your fathers, my verse will not obey[117]   [22]

It is worth noting that while condemning Majnun for being a madman out of his love, the 'wise' men also chase after him in order to hear to his poetry.[118] If he is bewitched by magic, Layla is his magic, and for her sake he composes his poetry that those 'wise' men are longing to hear. In short, Majnun's mad outpourings are received, to some extent, as a source of knowledge.[119]

Death

Masari' al-'ushshaq, a work by al-Sarraj (d. 500/1106), greatly popularised the theme that the consequences of passionate love were tragic. The word *masari'* comes from a root that has a connection with 'throwing down to the ground'. From this the meanings 'to fall down in an epileptic fit', 'to go mad' or 'to be killed in battle' are derived. The word is appropriate in the title of this book, for it embraces almost all the afflictions described in its pages: fainting, madness and death.[120] *Masariʿ al-ʿushshaq* is just one example and, in fact, most love stories in classical Arabic literature place an atypical poignancy on the tragedy associated with love, but needless to say, this manner is typical of the *ʿudhri* tradition. In Arabic treatises that deal with the theme of love, one can find endless examples of the tragic end of a lover[121] including insanity, wasting away, sudden death or the double death of the pair, as in this tale:

> Ibn al-Ashdaq says: I was making my ritual circumambulation of the Kaʿba at Mecca, when I remarked a young man standing under the eaves-trough, his head held down beneath his robe, moaning like a man in fever. I greeted him: he returned my salutation and then said, 'From where do you come?' 'From Basra' I replied. 'Are you returning there?' he asked. 'Yes', I said. 'When you reach al-Nibaj, go forth to the villagers and cry out, "Hilal, o Hilal!" A young girl will come forth to you. Recite this verse to her:
> I craved for a doom hurled out of your eyes
> That you might see in me a man killed by love.'
> He died on the spot. When I reached al-Nibaj, I went forth to the villagers and called out, 'Hilal, o Hilal!' A girl came forth to me, more beautiful than I had ever seen. 'What have you to say?' she asked. 'A young man at Mecca recited this verse to me…' 'What did he do next?' she asked. 'He died'. She fell down dead upon the spot.[122]

In this tale, death is almost a choice as the poet identifies the moment of his death in accordance with the intensity of both his love and his poetry. It is implied that the heart of the narrator (*rawi*) is moved by the plight of the frustrated lovers, who ultimately die because of their ardent passion. He acts as the go-between, making sure to deliver the lover's message to his beloved, and then to relate the story in the most sympathetic tone. However, much of the contents of *Masariʿ al-ʿushshaq* appear in numerous later works, which use *ʿudhri* love stories as examples of how love affects its victims, often killing them in one way or another. One of those works, *Kitab al-wadih al-mubin fi dhikr man istushhida min al-muhbin,* is devoted entirely to the martyrs of love. It provides a clear link between the lovers who died because of their passionate love, and the concept of martyrdom, explicitly labelling all victims of love as martyrs. In fact, the author of *Kitab al-wadih*, Mughultay (d. 762/1361), is relying upon a well-established tradition, which is ascribed to the Prophet himself: 'He who loves, yet remains chaste, conceals his secret and dies, dies a martyr'.[123] The first mention of this hadith about the martyrs of love, as Giffen notes, is in the *Kitab al-zahrah* of Ibn Da'ud, although it became more widely known later.[124] Even though the genuineness or spuriousness of its origin is questionable,[125] this idea enjoyed a measure of success. Several variant versions of this tradition are quoted sympathetically in some of the Arabic love treatises. Two centuries after Ibn Da'ud, Ibn al-Jawzi included ten versions of the hadith in his book *Dhamm al-hawa*.[126] If the great *jihad* is the battle against one's *hawa*,[127] then it is understood that 'one who falls violently in love, restrains his passions, remains upright and chaste, and consequently dies of love, would seem to be one who had battled against the lusts of the flesh.'[128] Thus this hadith, Manzalaoui maintains, 'denotes a desire to lend religious cachet to the interest in sentimental and passionate love. It arises from a genuine recognition within Islam of the moral psychomachia as the truest of holy wars: applied to the temptation of a sexual situation'.[129] However, in his verses, Jamil adds a different meaning to the concept of a martyr:

> They say: 'Take part in the Holy War, Jamil. Go on the raid.'
> But what *jihad* do I want
> Besides the one that has to do with women? Conversation in their
>   company
> Brings joy;
> But each man who dies in their midst
> Is a martyr[130]   [23]

Hence, the martyr, according to Jamil, is not the one who dies in a holy war, nor is he the one who has concealed his love and avoided his beloved. On the contrary, he is the one who is to die among the women whose conversation he enjoys and ultimately whose beauty kills him. Thus,

> Jamil bids for martyrdom by asserting that since he suffers on a battle-ground where he too is slain – albeit slain by his love for women – he also qualifies as a martyr-hero [. . .] The poet-lover claims that he suffers and dies while defending himself against the fatal attraction of women.[131]

Consequently, the concept of death or the 'mortality of the body' is closely related to 'ultimate love'. *'Udhri* love and suffering are inseparable, and the suffering eventually leads to death. The poet usually resorts to this concept when he feels incapable of possessing his beloved. Qays declares:

> O love for Lubna,
> you have tortured me so let me either die or live
> Death is easier than a life of separation and distance[132]   [24]

Hence, death is preferable to a life of separation. Death is seen as a desirable objective or simply as a relief for the ardent lover. The concept of the death wish is evident in the *'udhri* ghazal; death is seen as the calm end to suffering. Jamil wishes:

> O if only I could meet my death suddenly,
> if it is not ordained that we meet[133]   [25]

On the other hand, the death wish has another element besides the calm end to suffering. It is the way to seek closeness to the beloved after death, if this is not possible in life. For example, 'Urwah looks forward to being with 'Afra' even though it could not happen in this life:

> I love the day of Judgment since I have been told
> That I shall meet her there[134]   [26]

The explanation here is simply that love for *'udhri* poets is immortal. Love, as they illustrate, has no end; it is the ultimate truth of their being. Qays demonstrates the immortality of his love:

> Our love will survive every event,
> And will visit us in the darkness of the grave[135]   [27]

So the wish for the lovers to be buried in graves close to each other, if not in the same grave, appears in *'udhri* poetry:

> God I seek your refuge
> not to part between Buthaynah and me neither in my lifetime nor after
>   my death. And let her be my neighbour if I die,
> how nice my death would be if she was near to my grave[136]   [28]

Majnun also declares:

> O if only we could live together
> and if we die my bones lie beside her bones[137]   [29]

'Urwah, likewise, says:

> I long for the day of resurrection
> since it is said that 'Afra' and I will meet there[138]   [30]

In the story of 'Urwah, after leaving his beloved and her husband, 'Urwah went on his way, expressing his passion by reciting poetry. He continued doing so until his death, which came three days before he would have joined his tribe, indicating that death for him was, to some extent, a choice. When 'Afra' heard the news of his death she was greatly distressed and lamented him in verses until she died, only a few days after him.[139] In another account, the narrator al-Nu'man relates his meeting with 'Urwah, who is wasting away, and his mother. In this account 'Urwah seems to be waiting for his death and can sense it coming closer. When al-Nu'man asked the mother about her son, she replied: 'By God, a whole year long I haven't heard him utter a word or a groan until today. Then he came to me and said,

> If ever my mothers have been crying, well, today I think I shall be taken away.
> They will want to let me hear them but I shall not hear it
> when I lie exposed on the necks of the people.   [31]

And so [said al-Nu'man], 'before I left the tribe I had washed his corpse, wrapped him in a shroud, performed the ritual prayer for him, and buried him.'[140] From this anecdote, one can elicit how death resulting from love is a choice, as the poet shows his willingness to die by reciting poems that trigger passion. Seeking consolation in these poems is like attempting to treat one illness with another. Reciting these poems prior to death is like a licence that entitles the poet to join the company of love victims. When Ibn 'Abbas heard the story of 'Urwah, he said: 'this one is killed by love: no blood money is due, nor retaliation'.[141]

It is no wonder, then, that the story of 'Urwah became an archetype of the lover who died from his passion. He became, like some lover-poets before him, a model that other *'udhri* poets followed. Death for the sake of love was not new; it was the path that the true lovers of the past had taken, as Jamil says:

> Before me Hind's lover and his friend Muraqqish died and 'Urwah was
>   cured of his heartache
> Each of them died of love and my passion for her is greater.
> I think, nay, I know that she will send me the way they went[142]   [32]

Any love, Majnun declares, is worthless if it does not kill the lover, as it did with the old lovers.[143] Furthermore, Majnun, Qays and Jamil themselves became models for the martyrs of love and as such, subsequent poets referred to them as the true representations of that malady. Al-'Abbas b. Al-Ahnaf, for instance, says:

> Jamil did not love like myself
> Verily, neither did 'Urwah, the martyr of love[144]   [33]

The image of the beloved as a killer is a striking one in the *udhri ghazal*. She is depicted as the one who is responsible for the poet's death. As he dies for her love, Jamil says:

> My bosom friend, in your whole life, Have you ever seen a slain man
> Weep for love of his slayer as I do?[145]   [34]

She is described as being capable of controlling both the poet's life and his death,[146] however no ransom is demanded from her and she will not be punished for her 'crime'.[147] Even though the beloved is shown as capable of bringing agony and death, she is depicted as a source of life at the same time; and even if the poet were already dead, she could bring him to life again; Jamil says:

> Were a herald from you to announce my funeral
> and I was on the arms of men I would come alive again[148]   [35]

Majnun also demonstrates:

> Had she been with me when dying,
> her words would have stopped my death throes[149]   [36]

In one account, Majnun's relatives fear that he might throw himself down from the mountain.[150] Even though committing suicide did not constitute an honourable death or a sign of courage among Arabs either before or after Islam,[151] and in fact the idea is forbidden in the latter, *'udhri* poets transformed suicide into a positive act:

> Qays wanted to throw himself from the pinnacle of the mountain
> It is no surprise that love can kill a man –
> it turns him as it wills from side to side[152]   [37]

This view of suicide contrasts with Jacobi's claim that 'Death proves and shows the intensity of love, and may be wished for, but there is no mention of self-sacrifice and suicide.'[153] In a verse by Abu Mishar Al-'Udhri, who followed the *'udhri* path, he clearly states that an *'udhri* lover should not die in his bed.[154]

Furthermore, in the classical Arabic tales influenced by the *'udhri* tradition, suicide was sometimes considered to be the real proof of love. An example that confirms this supposition is a story cited in many sources, including *Tazyin al-Aswaq* and *Tawq al-Hamamah*. It is about an Andalusian man who sold his beloved slave when facing financial difficulties. When she reached the home of her new master, who was a Berber, her former owner almost expired, so he offered the man who had bought her all his possessions if he would restore her to him, but the Berber refused. The former owner appealed to the king. The king, most touched by his plight, commanded the Berber man to be summoned to court and asked him to free the girl. But the buyer refused, saying that he was even more deeply in love with her than the Andalusian man, so the king could do nothing about it. The Andalusian, in despair, threw himself down from the top of a building to the ground, but he did not suffer any great injuries. When the king asked him why he had done that, he replied that he could live no longer after losing his beloved. Thus, the king decided that the solution was to ask the Berber man to prove that his love was true by casting himself down from the roof of the pavilion, as the Andalusian had done already. But the Berber man was unable to throw himself and so he allowed the 'true' lover to have the girl.[155] The king's phrase is attributed to an inherited cultural and spiritual tradition that provides a link between love and death. It views death as a continuation of love for and on the part of the beloved. Even though love is perceived as a disorder that affects the balance of the mind, the deprivation of it does not mean the return of equilibrium.[156]

The highly influential myth of deadly 'udhri love, therefore, has seen a long tradition of fascination and transfiguration.[157] The subsequent poets continue to link their love with death; al-'Abbas b. al-Ahnaf, for instance, says:

> Oh Zalum! It is time for me to go to my grave
> I have wasted away before my death in my own clothes You have made me taste the bitter morsel of death by love Can you not by your life have mercy on my youth?[158] [38]

As previously mentioned, the Arabic treatises on love are full of such stories and of discussions such as whether the dead lover is to be considered a martyr and whether his death is lawful. Furthermore, why does a lover face such a tragic end? One attempt to answer the last question parodies such lovers by describing their malady as a medical case. Ibn Da'ud explains:

> The first attack of despair is the worst, because the heart is not yet used to it and is not prepared to resist it. He who survives this first attack will manage to bear the other attacks as well. The reason why the first attack can in other cases be lethal is that the heart becomes hot, since it is affected by such horrible things. In such cases, the function of the rest of the body is to supply the heart with an equal amount of cold. But when the heat is too much the septum cordis get torn, which causes death.[159]

Raven states that Ibn Da'ud's view is certainly inspired by Greek science.[160] However, I have already provided a discussion about lovesickness in the Arab discourse in the first section of this chapter.

Conclusion

The changes that occur in the lover's body as he descends into lovesickness become signs of moral values related to the manners of love and to the literary values of criticism. Thus, some of the changes are seen in the emanations of love and consequently become qualities that are much sought after, as they make it possible to distinguish between true lovers and those who only claim to be so. Al-Washsha' states that:

Signs of love that primarily denote the lover include emaciation, constant illness, shortage of sleep, pale face, addiction to isolation, continuing tears, meditating status, moans, nostalgia and consecutive sighs. No matter how the lover tries to conceal and endure his love, sooner or later it will be revealed.[161]

To enhance his point, al-Washsha' quotes a poet who said:

> No-one but those who have loved know sorrow, and not all those who say
>   'I love' speak the truth The true lovers are known by their gauntness
> from their long pact with sorrows and sleeplessness[162]   [39]

The *ghazal* poetry of the Abbasid poet al-'Abbas b. al-Ahnaf is full of similar themes, such as the tearful, sleepless lover and wasting away. He says:

> Separation has not healed the wound of the heart and my head has
>   become white before its time
> The burning heat of separation from my love has wasted away my body
>   and my heart, from the fires of its love,
> has a terrible sickness for which there is no physician[163]   [40]

On the basis of the discussions in this chapter, one may conclude that the values attached to this sort of excessive love contradict all moral, social and religious values, values that are firmly based on moderation. I have discussed the tragic outcomes lovers face, through examining the physical symptoms ascribed to love-madness as they appear in *'udhri* tradition. The extreme reactions of the lover's body reflect his excessive passion; which, on the one hand, proves to be his true emotion, and on the other hand, gains him a place in literary collections and anthologies on love in classical Arabic literature. These extreme bodily responses to love opened the door to a wide discourse of the lover's circumstances (*ahwal al-'ashiq*) and what caused them and to what extent he accepted responsibility for his acts.[164] This discourse involved medical, religious, philosophical and literary perspectives, though the theory of love among Arabs was not formulated by philosophers or physicians, but rather by religious men (*fuqaha*) and literary men (*'udaba'*). Hence, the use of the poetry of love as a resource for articulating broader theories of love became a well-established tradition in Arabic literature. In fact, most of the writing on this subject was done by literary men, who were well versed in Arabic poetry, both old and new, and so were positively disposed toward it.¹⁶⁵ The *'udhri* poets afterwards became the models of true lovers who suffered tremendously, so much so that the signs of their suffering became evident in their bodies.

Notes

1. Ibn Manzur, (ع ش ق), p. 252.
2. Giffen, *Theory of Profane Love*, p. 93.
3. Behrens-Abouseif, *Beauty in Arabic Culture*, p. 66.
4. Bouhdiba, *Sexuality in Islam*, p. 25.
5. Traditional classical and medieval concepts of medicine linked lovemaking, lust and ecstasy with moderation (or temperance or reasonability). But excess held serious medical dangers. For more on this, see Foucault, *The History of Sexuality*.
6. Biesterfeldt and Gutas, 'The Malady of Love', in *Journal of the American Oriental Society*, Vol. 104, No. 1, p. 22.
7. Dols, *Majnun*, p. 316.
8. Biesterfeldt and Gutas, '*The Malady of Love*', p. 23.
9. Ibn Sina, *Al-Qanun fi'l-Tibb*, www.alwaraq.net, 15 October 2011, p. 484.
10. Ibid.
11. The physician al-Razi (d. 313/925) suggests similar treatments for melancholia, which include active endeavours such as hunting, chess, drinking, singing, competitive sports, travel and other activities. See Dols, *Majnun*, p. 55.
12. Ibid., p. 485. Interestingly, the practice of pulse-diagnosis, which is suggested by Ibn Sina as a means to identify the beloved, was employed with considerable effect by the great mystical poet Jalal al-Din Rumi in one of his allegorical stories. See Dols, *Majnun*, p. 317.
13. The medical interpretation of *'ishq* was especially welcomed by those writers who wished to discourage passionate love. See Giffen, *Theory of Profane Love*, p. 64.
14. Al-Jahiz in Pellat, *The Life and Works of Jahiz*, p. 263.
15. Ibn Da'ud, *Kitab al-zahrah*, p. 400.
16. Ibid., p. 401.
17. Giffen, *Theory of Profane Love*, p. 16.
18. Al-Marzubani in Giffen, *Theory of Profane Love*, p. 19.
19. Al-Tawhidi, *Al-Muqabasat*, p. 364.

20. Anonymous text cited and translated by Biesterfeldt and Gutas, 'The Malady of Love', pp. 40–5.
21. Some of the Arab authors ascribe the text to Hippocrates.
22. Biesterfeldt and Gutas, 'The Malady of Love', p. 45, and see the detailed discussion on the origin of the text on pp. 51–3, in which the authors tend to believe that it is derived from a late Alexandrian text.
23. Ibid., p. 53.
24. Salamah, Al-'Ishq wa'l-kitabah, p. 456.
25. Washsha', Al-Muwashsha, pp. 106–7.
26. Ibid., p. 107.
27. Ibid., p. 108.
28. It should be borne in mind that an awareness of the bodily effect of love as shown in literature is not unique to the Arabs. In the introduction of *The Art of Courtly Love* by John Jay Parry some of the relevant ideas within Western culture are presented. The poet Ovid, who lived in Rome in the time of Emperor Augustus and among whose poems are *The Art of Love* and *The Cure of Love*, states that for love of a woman the lover must become pale and thin and sleepless. See Capellanus, *The Art of Courtly Love*, p. 5.
29. Giffen, *Theory of Profane Love*, p. 57–8. Giffen points out that some authors such as Ibn Da'ud began to collect verses on a subject or idea comparing different ways of expressing the same idea. This critical activity lent itself to refined awareness of the whole spectrum of emotions, situations and experiences of love.
30. It is considered an essential motif in the opening section of the *qasidah*; the poet stops at the ruined campsite, which evokes his memories and leads him to weep over his now departed beloved.
31. Jamil, *Diwan*, p. 25
32. Majnun, *Diwan*, p. 77. Note how he uses the word *dalil* (proof) and the link he makes between this word and the word 'tears', p. 170.
33. Kuthayyir, *Diwan*, p. 78.
34. Ibid., p. 180.
35. Jamil, *Diwan*, p. 46; Qays, *Diwan*, p. 51.
36. Majnun, *Diwan*, p. 96, in Khairallah, *Love*, p. 92.
37. Kuthayyir, *Diwan*, pp. 112, 114.
38. Kuthayyir, *Diwan*, p. 180; Jamil, *Diwan*, p. 97 and Majnun, *Diwan*, p. 159.
39. Jamil, *Diwan*, p. 48.
40. Majnun, *Diwan*, p. 37.

41. The flowing stream moves Majnun to tears. See Majnun, *Diwan*, p. 28.
42. Jamil, *Diwan*, p. 37; Majnun, *Diwan*, p. 39.
43. Majnun, *Diwan*, p. 62. For their indication of the black omen of separation, Salamah explains that crows in Arab culture refer to two different indications: 1.) the Qur'anic crow that is seen as a post bird, delegated by God to Qabil to teach him funeral rituals and that delegated to Noah to obtain news of the flood; 2.) the literary crow that brings the bad omen of separation and loss when it makes sounds and that is often signified in Arabic poetry (Salamah, *Al-'Ishq wa'l-kitabah,* pp. 297–8).
44. Majnun, *Diwan*, p. 227.
45. Kuthayyir, *Diwan*, p. 64.
46. Majnun, *Diwan*, p. 133.
47. Majnun, *Diwan*, p. 24. The theme of tears turning into blood became a popular one in love poetry. See, for instance, Abu Tammam, *Diwan Abi Tammam bi sharh al-Khatib al-Tabrizi.*
48. The lover might reach levels of hatred towards his beloved, as described in *'udhri* poetry: for the *'udhri* poet who wished death to his beloved see al-Isfahani, *Kitab al-Aghani*, Vol. 1, p. 155.
49. Bataille, *Eroticism*, p. 17. This is understandable even when the passion fulfills itself as it 'provokes such violent agitation that the happiness involved, before being the happiness to be enjoyed . . . it is so great as to be more like its opposite, suffering' (Bataille, p. 19).
50. Majnun, *Diwan*, p.30.
51. He says:

    > See the parched birds which circle round the water night and day, but for fear
    >   of being beaten never drink their fill
    > or come close to the cool ponds
    > They see the froth of the water and death together and are attentive to the
    >   voices of the water bearers
    > They are no more afflicted than I am with the heat of longing and ardour but
    >   the enemy has hindered me
    > (Qays, *Diwan*, p. 155).

52. Majnun, *Diwan*, p. 30.
53. Jamil, *Diwan*, p. 48.
54. Salamah, *Al-'Ishq wa'l-kitabah*, p. 58.
55. Al-Isfahani, *Kitab al-Aghani*, Vol. 2, p. 348.

56. Khan, *Sexuality and Secrecy*, p. 159.
57. Salamah, *Al-'Ishq wa'l-kitabah*, p. 130.
58. See Salamah's diagram for these terms and their links to other diseases, pp.133–4.
59. 'Urwah, p. 53. This verse is also ascribed to Majnun, p. 229. Note his use of the adjective *ha'im* (passionate) in association with the noun *'atab* (wreck) that leaves his body in latters, p. 25.
60. Al-Antaki, *Tazyin al-aswaq*, p. 19.
61. See the full story in al-Isfahani, *Kitab al-Aghani*, Vol. 24, pp. 283–98.
62. 'Urwah, p. 36, given in a private communication from Professor Van Gelder.
63. Al-Isfahani, *Kitab al-Aghani*, Vol. 24, p. 293.
64. Ibid.
65. Ibn Da'ud, in Biesterfeldt and Gutas, '*The Malady of Love*', p. 45.
66. 'Urwah, *Diwan*, pp. 39–40.
67. Majnun, *Diwan*, p.123. See also Qays, *Diwan*, p. 23.
68. Majnun, *Diwan*, p. 29.
69. Jamil, *Diwan*, p. 53.
70. Qays, *Diwan*, p. 41.
71. Qays, *Diwan*, p. 66. Kuthayyir also says: 'That Dumri's daughter is asking me: why are you pale?'. See Kuthayyir, *Diwan*, p. 223.
72. Ibn Da'ud, *Kitab al-zahrah*, Vol. 2, p. 400.
73. Al-Sarraj, *Masari' al-'ushshaq*, Vol. 1, p. 16.
74. Majnun, *Diwan*, p. 201.
75. Ya Sin (36:77–8).
76. Majnun, *Diwan*, p. 137.
77. Jamil, *Diwan*, p. 52, 82.
78. Jamil, *Diwan*, p. 82, in Van Gelder, *Of Dishes and Discourse. Classical Arabic Literary Representations of Food*, p. 112. However, in other reports active love and a good appetite are deemed perfectly compatible. The famous 'Ayshah b. Talhah is impressed by one of her several husbands and says to him admiringly the morning after their wedding night: 'I have never seen anyone like you; you have eaten as much as seven men, prayed as much as seven men, and fucked as much as seven men.'
79. Al-Ahnaf, for instance, declares: 'All that love for her has left of me is a last gasp in a gaunt body' (*Diwan*, p. 130, trans. Hamori, p. 213). Mutanabbi is not only wasting away because of love but he is also proud of this thinness and

indeed of anyone who is thin: 'For love of you I truly love my emaciation, and every emaciated man' (Al-Mutanabbi, *Diwan*, Vol. 3, p. 24).
80. Al-Isfahani, *Kitab al-Aghani*, Vol. 24, p. 289.
81. Surat Yusuf (12:96).
82. Fainting lovers are a well-established theme in the tales of *The Arabian Nights*. See, for instance, Manzalaoui's discussion of the tale of 'Ali b. Bakkar and Shams, in which the two lovers embraced each other and fell down fainting at the door (Manzalaoui, 'Swooning Lovers', pp. 74–6).
83. Al-Isfahani, *Kitab al-Aghani*, Vol. 2, p. 338, in Khan, *Sexuality and Secrecy*, p. 167. For more examples see pp. 341, 370.
84. Husayn, *Hadith al-arbi'a'*, p. 198, in Khairallah, *Love*, p. 93.
85. Khairallah, *Love*, p. 93.
86. Majnun, *Diwan*, p. 67.
87. Khairallah points out that the motif of fainting is popular with the Sufis, who pass from perplexity to fainting on the way to the vision of, and unity with, the beloved. The highest degree of this experience is expressed by the term *sar'* (epileptic fit or death). Khairallah, *Love*, p. 94.
88. Khairallah, *Love*, p. 87.
89. Ibn Qutaybah, *Al-Shi'r wa'l-shu'ara'*, pp. 566–7, in Khairallah, *Love*, p. 138.
90. Manzalaoui, '*Swooning Lovers*', p. 71.
91. Ibid., p. 73.
92. Ibid., pp. 76–82.
93. The last word *mass* has multiple meanings including madness, intercourse and passionate love. The link between the *jinn* and madness is also implicated in the word *mass*. For a detailed discussion of the words that link love with madness see Salamah, *Al-'Ishq wa'l-kitabah*, pp. 163–78. For the motif of Majnun being touched by *jinn*, see Khairallah, *Love*, p. 89.
94. Giffen, *Theory of Profane Love*, p. 64.
95. For example in *One Thousand and One Nights* the tale of Qamar al-Zaman and Budur is a tale of mutual love-madness. Qamar suffers from madness and pines for his beloved, while Budur is afflicted by violent madness and has to be physically restrained; finally the reunion of the two lovers was the ideal cure for both of them. See Burton, *The Book of The Thousand and One Nights*, Vol. 3, pp. 1,062–251.
96. Giffen, 'Love Poetry and Love Theory in Medieval Arabic Literature', in Grunebaum, *Arabic Poetry Theory and Development*, p. 114.
97. Manzalaoui, '*Swooning Lovers*', p. 44.

98. Shakespeare, *A Midsummer Night's Dream* (V, i, 4–22).
99. Ibn Qutaybah, *Al-Shi'r wa'l-shu'ara'*, p. 563, in Khairallah, *Love*, p. 135.
100. Ibn Qutaybah, *Al-Shi'r wa'l-shu'ara'*, p. 565, in Khairallah, *Love*, p. 136.
101. Dols, *Majnun*, p. 313.
102. Al-Isfahani, *Kitab al-Aghani*, Vol. 2, p. 338, in Khan, *Sexuality and Secrecy*, p. 176.
103. Khan, *Sexuality and Secrecy*, p. 180.
104. Khairallah, *Love*, p. 82.
105. In his attempt to define Majnun's legend within a mystical framework, Khairallah claims that these manifestations have the further significance of being parallel to some mystical states (*ahwal*) and stations (*maqamat*). Nevertheless, he admits that the mystical interpretation of these manifestations of madness, and the relating of them to the presence of a possessing spirit, is only one way of understanding the legend (Khairallah, *Love*, p. 94).
106. Dols, *Majnun*, p. 332.
107. Khairallah, *Love*, p. 83.
108. Al-Isfahani, *Kitab al-Aghani*, Vol. 8, p. 290. See also al-'Aqqad's discussion on Jamil's fine appearance, pp. 25–6.
109. Jamil, *Diwan*, p. 25, in Kinany, *Development*, p. 288.
110. Dols, *Majnun*, p. 333.
111. Khairallah, *Love*, p. 85.
112. Dols, *Majnun*, p. 335.
113. Khan, *Sexuality and Secrecy*, p. 93.
114. Ibid., pp. 99–100.
115. Khairallah, *Love*, p. 87; Khan, *Sexuality and Secrecy*, p.93. Khan emphasises the symbol of gazelles in Majnun's wilderness, but she neglects the other animals, which are not peace-loving animals, such as wild beasts (*wahsh*), which are associated with Majnun as well as gazelles in the narratives.
116. Khan, *Sexuality and Secrecy*, p. 99.
117. Majnun, *Diwan*, p. 118, in Khairallah, *Love*, p. 95.
118. See, for example, al-Isfahani, *Kitab al-Aghani*, Vol. 2, pp. 371, 386.
119. From the title of Abu'l-Qasim al-Hasan al-Naysaburi's book *'Uqala' al-majanin'* [*The Wise Fool*] one could observe the ambiguity surrounding the reception of the madman in Arabic culture. The narratives ascribed in this book to mad people imply a great sense of wisdom, and show how 'normal' people seek that kind of wisdom. Moreover, many people who have been associated with madness are depicted as lovers, whether of human beloveds or

of God, and they always seem to be aware of their condition and sometimes even happy about it. (See Al-Naysaburi, *'Uqala' al-majanin*).
120. Giffen, *Theory of Profane Love*, p. 108. Interestingly the tragic effects of love have been used by Muslim authors who have a strong interest in morality to condemn [love]. In their discourse, the passionate lover is always tragically driven to fornication, incest, murder, suicide or madness. See, for instance, al-Jawzi, *Dhamm al-hawā*, [In Blame of Love]. However, a book like *Masari' al-'ushshaq* is written with sympathy for the sorrows of love.
121. See, for instance, al-Washsha', *Al-Muwashsha,* pp. 94–8; al-Nuwayri, Vol. 2, pp. 160, 184; Ibn Qutaybah, *'Uyun al-Akhbar*, Vol. 4, pp. 128–34, in which one can find many stories of the tragic ends of lovers. Ibn Hazm, in his *Tawq*, devotes a chapter entitled 'Of Death' to the martyrs of love. He says (p.220): 'Sometimes the affair becomes so aggravated, the lover's nature is so sensitive, and his anxiety is so extreme, that the combined circumstances result in his departure out of this transient world.'
122. Al-Sarraj, *Masari' al-'ushshaq,* Vol. 1, pp. 308–9, in Manzalaoui, 'Tragic Ends of Lovers: Medieval Islam and the Latin West', *Comparative Criticism 1*, pp. 43–4.
123. Ibn Da'ud, *Kitab al-zahrah*, p. 117, in Giffen, *Theory of Profane Love*, p. 99.
124. Giffen, *Theory of Profane Love*, p. 99.
125. Ibn Qayyim al-Jawziyah delivered an attack upon the tradition in his *Rawdat al-muhibbin wa nuzhat al-mushtaqin*, pp. 180–2.
126. Giffen, *Theory of Profane Love*, p. 100. Nowhere does Ibn al-Jawzi give any indication of his own attitude toward the tradition of the martyrs.
127. It appears in *Al-Bayhaqi's Sunan* as a statement ascribed to the Prophet; see the discussion about its authenticity in www.islamonline.net/servlet/satellite?cid=1122528606158&pagename=islamonline-arabic-Ask_Scholar/FatwaA/FatwaAAskTheScholar, 10 October 2009.
128. Giffen, *Theory of Profane Love*, p. 103. See her full discussion of the concept of the martyr in Islam and its connection with this tradition, the association between the ideal of chaste conduct and martyrdom in Islam, on pp. 100–5.
129. Manzalaoui, '*Tragic Ends of Lovers*', p. 38.
130. Jamil, p. 27, in Hamori, *Art*, p. 46.
131. Khan, *Sexuality and Secrecy*, p. 116.
132. Qays, *Diwan*, p. 34. See also Kuthayyir, *Diwan*, p. 20.
133. Jamil, *Diwan*, p. 39.
134. 'Urwah, *Diwan*, p. 41, in Kinany, *Development*, p. 300.

135. Qays, *Diwan*, p. 123, in Kinany, *Development*, p. 262.
136. Jamil, *Diwan*, p.36. See also for similar wishes: Jamil, *Diwan*, p. 22, Majnun, *Diwan*, pp. 24, 123 and 'Urwah, *Diwan*, p. 44.
137. Majnun, *Diwan*, p. 191.
138. 'Urwah, *Diwan*, p. 41.
139. Al-Isfahani, *Kitab al-Aghani*, Vol. 24, pp. 295–6.
140. Ibid. See also Ibn Qutaybah's similar versions of the story of 'Urwah's death (*Al-Shi'r wa'l-shu'ara'*, pp. 625–6).
141. Al-Isfahani, *Kitab al-Aghani*, Vol. 24, p. 297.
142. Jamil, *Diwan*, p. 32. See also Majnun, *Diwan*, p. 197 and Qays, *Diwan*, p. 43.
143. Majnun, p. 124. Many poets apologised for being alive while they were in love; see al-Sarraj's discussion on the *majlis* of al-Mubarrad in *Masari' al-'ushshq*, Vol. 2, p. 260. In fact, no poet could claim to be the first to die of love, as each one has become part of the lover-poet circle where all lover-poets, even pre-Islamic ones such as al-Muraqqash and Ibn 'Ajlan al-Nahdi, face the same destiny. See Salamah, *Al-'Ishq wa'l-kitabah*, p. 405.
144. Al-Ahnaf, *Diwan*, p. 15, in Bürgel, p. 95. See also al-Sarraj, *Masari' al-'ushshaq*, Vol. 1, p. 282, Vol. 2, pp. 36 and 73.
145. Jamil, *Diwan*, p. 73.
146. Kuthayyir, *Diwan*, p. 110.
147. Ibid., pp. 84, 87.
148. Jamil, *Diwan*, p. 20.
149. Majnun, *Diwan*, p. 191.
150. See a similar story about a Bedouin lover who threw himself from a mountain in al-Sarraj, *Masari' al-'ushshaq*, Vol. 2, pp. 106–7.
151. Al-Jahiz maintains that any Arab who killed himself was blameworthy. See *Kitab al-Hayawan*, Vol. 2, p. 279.
152. Majnun, *Diwan*, p. 48.
153. Jacobi, *Die Udhra: Liebe und Tod in der Umayyadenzeit*, www.wiko-berlin.de/index.php.
154. Al-Sarraj, *Masari' al-'ushshaq*, Vol. 1, p. 94.
155. Ibn Hazm, *Tawq*, pp. 227–9 and al-Antaki, *Tazyin*, p. 268.
156. 'Abdallah, *al-Hubb*, p. 119.
157. Jacobi, *Die Udhra*.
158. Al-Ahnaf, *Diwan*, p. 35.
159. Ibn Da'ud, in Raven, 'Ibn Da'ud al-Isbahani and Greek Wisdom', *Proceedings*, p. 68.

160. Ibid.
161. Al-Washsha', *Al-Muwashsha*, p. 76.
162. Ibid., pp. 76–7.
163. Al-Ahnaf, *Diwan*, p. 33. Similar themes in his *Diwan* occur frequently. See, for instance, his verses on pp. 45, 62, 137, 232, 251 and 269.
164. Studying the Andalusian love story *Bayad wa Riyad*, Robinson argues that the characters 'conform in large measure to literary and/or social types which would have been clearly identifiable to members of the 13th century audience, and the plot centers around the potentially didactic dilemma of how to maintain socially accepted courtly norms when confronted with lovesickness.' See Robinson, 'The Lover, His Lady, Her Lady, and a Thirteenth-Century Celestina: A Recipe for Love Sickness from al-Andalus", in Grabar and Robinson, *Islamic Art and Literature*, p. 90.
165. Giffen, '*Love Poetry*', p. 111.

Conclusion

The primary objective of this book has been to trace how the body is represented in the ninth and tenth centuries CE literary tradition of *'udhri* love. To a great extent, this goal has been achieved by analysing poetry and narratives ascribed to *'udhri* poets that have appeared in several literary collections of classical Arabic literature. In particular, the study relies on the *Kitab al-Aghani* ('The Book of Songs'), the monumental tenth-century collection of biographies of Arab poets and their poetry. It also relies on the collections of poetry (*diwans*) of *'udhri* poets, which have been edited by several scholars. The book focuses on the difference between what the poetry itself says and what later sources such as the *Kitab al-Aghani* say about the *'udhri* poets and poetry by discussing the development of the tradition and its overlapping historical layers. This book discusses and reappraises a number of scholarly approaches to the subject and attempts to chart a new approach through a new reading of the primary sources.

The methodology used in this study is, in its essence, a close literary analysis of classical literary texts. Despite certain pitfalls, this method can effectively demonstrate how the body is represented in the *'udhri* tradition. In addition, this approach allows the researcher to consider different interpretations of a text. As a result, this book demonstrates that the body lies at the heart of the *'udhri* tradition. The lack of possession and absence of physicality serve only to heighten the lovers' desire since these features merely draw more attention to that which is being denied. This shows the privileged position of the body through the prominent duality of its presence and absence. The very concept of chastity involves a conscious denial of physical contact, and this consciousness often implies a strong awareness of physicality.

CONCLUSION | 227

This book explains how the past is reconstructed in the *'udhri* tradition by discussing the way in which stories and narratives about poets and events over the course of the ninth and tenth centuries gave rise to certain narrative compositions that in effect invented a tradition. The study sheds light on the possible explanations of what sparked a fresh interest in *'udhri* love in the ninth and tenth centuries, providing a discussion of the period of documentation, criticism and authorship. It also examines the influence of Sufism and the Persian interest in the *'udhri ghazal*, as it is well known that the Persians had shown particular interest in the story of Majnun and Layla. Moreover, love is used as a narrative trope to address moral and ethical issues, so the study raises questions about the possibility that the spread of libertinism in the Abbasid era helped to create a desire to return to the *'udhri ghazal*, which is considered to be the complete opposite of libertinism.

This study also provides a discussion of texuality verses reality. It has asserted that the classical Arabic texts simultaneously provide contradictory anecdotes, as if trying to leave open the possible interpretations one may derive from a given work. There are fascinating contradictions found within the *'udhri* tradition regarding physical contact between the lovers; if certain narrators have related stories about *'udhri* lovers making a particular claim about them, others relate different stories that give the opposite impression. The role played by *ruwah* (popular storytellers) is important to note, for they paid special attention to love stories and recited them to different audiences that naturally would have held a variety of notions about chastity and love. It is probable that this often resulted in the promotion of two or more contradictory interpretations of one single story or body of poems. However, the contradictions in *'udhri* poetry regarding physicality may also possibly be resolved in light of the many different contexts within which the poet composed his verses. He might have composed them in different phases of his relationship with his beloved, which might have taken various forms. Besides, human emotions within love are complex and cannot be simply classified into the categories of virtuous and sensuous, and these themselves may not necessarily be opposing concepts. This fact gives many traditions of love poetry a conflicted nature, as the poet's emotions fluctuate between representing the unattainable glorified image of his beloved and expressing his own instinctive desire to unite with her.

In poetry, the desire to obtain the object of love is expressed constantly in the *'udhri* tradition. Certain repetitions of terminology strike the reader of *'udhri* poetry: thirstiness, touching, saliva, beds, longing, kissing, embrace, appointments and so on. It is irrelevant whether this desire was in fact satisfied or not; that is a matter for students of the historical context, which is not my concern here. Rather, I am interested in the literary imagination. In any case, neither marital nor sexual union is ever a feature of *'udhri* narratives, which therefore provide a direct contrast with the standard Islamic discourse around marriage. The *'udhri* tradition challenges the ideal of marital bonds between *'udhri* lovers. Furthermore, while Islamic discourse emphasises the goal of reproduction as a result of sexual enjoyment, the *'udhri* tradition contains no trace of children. The only possible offspring for the *'udhri* lover is poetry. It is a linguistic product, not a biological one. Therefore, language is the only result of *'udhri* love. In fact, it is part of idealising the beloved to keep her unique, inimitable and childless.

The idealisation and solitude of the beloved, and the fact that she is far off, enable her to play her decisive role for the poet, that of inspiration. The entire *'udhri* experience unconsciously distances the beloved in order to heighten the poetry's emotional energy. The narrators are preoccupied by the concept of sensuality and its connection with love, and enhance it by frequently dwelling upon its absence. The so-called lack of consummation between the *'udhri* lover and his beloved also itself inflames his passion continuously. This passionate love inspires beautiful poetry within the *'udhri* poet-lover. In addition, the poets or the narrators are clearly aware that the unattainability of the beloved is in fact an essential precondition for composing poetry. In the *'udhri* romances, the lover loses everything, including his beloved, but retains his ability to compose poetry. Therefore, for an *'udhri* poet, being a poet appears to be his preferred, ultimate and chosen goal over the possession of his beloved.

This study has endeavoured to show that the representation of the beloved in the *'udhri ghazal* has been influenced by pre-Islamic poetry, which offers to *'udhri* poets an authoritative image of the beautiful woman. This image suggests, for example, that whiteness of the skin, softness of the body, slenderness of the waist and a general resemblance to the gazelle and the sun are all stock indices of feminine beauty. So the pre-Islamic tradition provides the stereotype of female beauty, and establishes a poetic figurative language for describing the beloved. However, the *'udhri* poet's reliance upon this established repertoire raises questions about the authenticity of the poet's experience as well as the development of his audience's expectations.

The *'udhri ghazal* provides detailed descriptions of the beloved's desirable body. It also depicts an image of the beloved as being synonymous with the softer elements of the world, such as water and light. This book suggests a link between the image of the beloved as gazelle, sun or rain, and ancient Arab mythology. It also suggests a link between this mythology and the preferable image of a desirable woman as a corpulent one. The comparison of the beloved with a gazelle is one of the major topoi of classical Arabic love poetry. Thus, in this study I have explored the metaphorical image of the beloved as gazelle along with its mythic associations. The gazelle was considered sacred and Arabs would allow these animals to go free instead of killing them.

In addition, the emphasis on the image of a deer with its fawn could be understood as a representation of the woman who has become sacred through motherhood. The ancient Arabs portrayed her as a mother-deer and a mother-oryx. The resemblance between the sun and woman in classical Arabic poetry also has its roots in ancient Arab mythology. The sun was one of the gods that used to be worshipped by the ancient Arabs. They ascribed characteristics of motherhood to the sun, conceiving it as the Mother God, which is why the sun is referred to as being female. Moreover, the description of the beloved's saliva as raindrops and wine suggests a link between her and sacred objects, since wine also carries certain religious meanings.

The image of the corpulent woman, which is a dominant image for a desirable woman in the *'udhri ghazal*, is also inherited from ancient religious belief. The Mother Goddess was one of the deities that were worshipped by the ancient Arabs. Her corpulent body symbolises fertility and motherhood. Motherhood is a principal function of the Mother Goddess, who gives life and enriches tribes of warriors and preserves the human race. It is essential that a deity is depicted with all the characteristics for which he or she is being worshipped. However, the later poets may have preserved the image of the female corpulent body but removed the ancient pagan religious associations from it. Therefore, this image became a model of desirable female beauty, whilst moving away from its possible ancient roots.

The *'udhri* poet was expected to work within the framework of the established literary tradition. Alternatively, the genre is governed by the poet-lover's obsession with idealising every aspect of his beloved into tropes relating to beauty. Therefore, it may be argued that the *'udhri* imitation of the older norms does not mean that the poet does not see his beloved with his own eyes. Rather, it suggests that he sees and describes his beloved in terms shaped by his cultural and aesthetic inheritance. She becomes, through his loving eyes, the very archetype of ideal beauty. No one can replace her, even the literary model of beauty. She becomes the model, the archetype, illuminated and illustrated with all the necessary and desirable colours and contours of beauty.

A comparative approach shows that other appropriations of *'udhri* love stories replicate this reliance upon stock features of beauty. For example, this study has provided a comparison between Layla's portrayal in Majnun's poetry and her portrayal in later Persian miniature paintings, which are based on the Majnun legend. As has been shown, her depiction in Arabic poetry, which finds striking parallels in a series of Umayyad and later Arab paintings and sculptures, varies greatly from her depiction in medieval Persian painting. Nonetheless, although it is almost a contrasting image, Layla's portrayal is always enacted through a stereotype, in both Arabic poetry and medieval Persian painting.

Although sensual feeling runs through many images in *'udhri* poetry and influences its descriptive language, especially while imitating the older norms and patterns, it also often sublimates beauty to worlds that transcend human ones. In many cases in *'udhri* poetry the beloved's beauty surpasses human beauty and is marked by supernatural attributes. The beloved's beauty is beyond nature and is associated with many extraordinary effects, since the poet's admiration for beauty resembles religious belief. This beauty goes beyond time itself. It is timeless beauty and eternally youthful. When the beloved's body surmounts time this implies its perfection and immortality. It is an immortal body that achieves the status of worshipped statues and images. Therefore, this study has highlighted themes such as the beloved's eternal youth, her omnipotence and the devotion for her that goes beyond reason.

The bodily presence in the *'udhri ghazal* does not always take the form of a physical body. Sometimes it emerges through symbolic channels, where symbolising the body appears alongside its physical depiction, and this is closely linked with the ideas of the present and absent bodies of the beloved. Symbolising the body of the beloved can be observed in many 'udhri poetic themes such as the longing for the beloved's place and the depiction of her in the form of a phantom. These themes reveal an attempt to regain the absent body of the beloved and to rise above this absence.

Certainly, the representation of the beloved's place in 'udhri poetry indicates her absence on the one hand, and the poet's endeavour to overcome this absence on the other. Her location acts as a symbol of her actual body. Furthermore, the bodily presence of the beloved also takes the form of glances and speech. Glances and other signals act in the 'udhri tradition as a means of communicating between the two lovers, while speech enjoys a privileged position as a factor in causing love and inflaming passion.

This presence-through-absence is also discussed by examining the presence of the beloved in nature. An initial superficial view of the beloved's depiction indicates that her presence is scattered and fragmented among natural elements such as stones, wind and water. However, a more profound analysis of her depiction suggests that her existence actually absorbs these, the natural elements of the universe within which she is situated. Her remarkable omnipresence is a key feature of the 'udhri ghazal.

One of the major contributions of this study is its examination of the representation of the lover-poet's body. The changes in the body of the lover become signs of moral values relevant to the manners of love and the literary values of criticism. Thus many changes are seen as direct emanations of love and consequently become values that are sought after and that distinguish between true lovers and those who only claim to be so. I have discussed the tragic fates of lovers in examining the phenomena of fainting, madness and death as they appear in the 'udhri ghazal. The lover's body manifests extreme reactions as a result of his excessive passion; that is what, on the one hand, proves his true emotion, and on the other hand, wins him a place in literary collections and anthologies on love in classical Arabic literature. By examining the depiction of the lover's own body, I suggest that the image of the beloved forms a complete contrast to that of her lover. She is depicted as the most beautiful object and the one who possesses eternal youth, while he is presented as a man who is sick, thin, old and mad, one who is obsessed by his passionate love.

In addressing the aforementioned areas, this study sheds new light on the body including its representations and associations in the *'udhri* tradition. In addition, this work opens the door to new discussions on the relationship between love poetry and Arab society in the classical age. Indeed, it leaves that door open for further discussion, for it would be impossible to address comprehensively all of the questions this study has raised. For example, issues such as the variety of Islamic discourse around chastity and marriage in the period under discussion could be investigated in greater detail. This is a rich area for research, especially if linked with classical Arabic literature of love in both poetry and prose. Moreover, the tragic fate of lovers in classical Arabic literature might be studied through further engagement with recent theorisations of representations of love and violence. It is hoped that this study will encourage further literary studies of representations of the body, which unfortunately remain rare in the case of scholarship on Arabic literature compared with the state of such scholarship on Western literatures. Yet the Arabic sources are immensely rich and varied. In this way, this book is only a beginning for what may be hoped will be an entirely new approach to classical Arabic literature.

Appendix

Chapter 1

[1]
كأن فجاج الأرض حلقة خاتم علي فما تزداد طولا ولا عرضا

[2]
كلانا بكى أو كاد يبكي صبابة لصاحبه واستعجلت عبرة قبلي

[3]
أبيت مع الهلاك ضيفا لأهلها وأهلي قريب موسعون ذوو فضل

Chapter 2

[1]
فلرب عارضة علينا وصلها بالجد تخلطه بقول الهازل
فأجبتها بالرفق بعد تستر حبي بثينة عن وصالك شاغلي
لو أن في قلبي كقدر قلامة فضلا وصلتك أو أتتك رسائلي

[2]
قالت جُننتَ على رأسي فقلت لها الحب أعظم مما بالمجانين
الحب ليس يفيق الدهر صاحبه وإنما يُصرع المجنون في الحين
لو تعلمين إذا ما غبتِ ما سقمي وكيف تسهر عيني لم تلوميني

[3]
وإني لأرضى من بثينة بالذي لو أبصره الواشي لقرت بلابله
بلا، وبألا أستطيع، وبالمنى، وبالوعد حتى يسأم الوعد آمله
وبالنظرة العجلى وبالحول تنقضي أواخره لا نلتقي وأوائله

[4]
(لا والذي تسجد الجباه له) مالي بما دون ثوبها خبر
ولا بفيها ولا هممت بها ما كان إلا الحديث والنظر

[5]
فإن كان فيكم بعل ليلى فإنني وذي العرش قد قبلت فاها ثمانيا
وأشهد عند الله إني رأيتها وعشرون منها إصبعا من ورائيا
[6]
إذا سمتها التقبيل صدت وأعرضت صدود شموس الخيل صل لجامها
وعضت على إبهامها ثم أومأت أخاف عيونا أن تهب نيامها

Chapter 3

[1]
فيا ليت شعري هل أبيتن ليلة كليلتنا حتى نرى ساطع الفجر
تجود علينا بالحديث وتارة تجود علينا بالرضاب من الثغر
[2]
ولست بناس أهلها حين أقبلوا وجالوا علينا بالسيوف وطوفوا
وقالوا جميل بات في الحي عندها وقد جردوا أسيافهم ثم وقفوا
وفي البيت ليث الغاب لولا مخافة على نفس جمل والإله لأرعفوا
[3]
ألم تعلمي يا عذبة الريق أنني أظل إذا لم أسق ريقك صاديا
[4]
ولو أن جلدا غير جلدك مسني وباشرني دون الشعار شريت
[5]
يا ليتنا والمنى ليست مقربة أنا لقيناك والأحراس قد رقدوا
نعم لحاف الفتى المقرور يجعلها شعاره حين يخشى القر والصرد
[6]
أرى الإزار على ليلى فأحسده إن الإزار على ما ضم محسود
[7]
تمنيت من وجدي بعفراء أنني إزار لها تحت القميص يمان
[8]
وإني لمشتاق إلى ريح جيبها كما اشتاق ادريس إلى جنة الخلد
[9]
وما حائمات حمن يوما وليلة على الماء يخشين العصي حوانِ
عوافي لا يصدرن عنه لوجهة ولا هن من برد الحياض دوانِ
يرين حباب الماء والموت دونه فهن لأصوات السقاة روانِ
بأجهد مني حر شوق ولوعة عليك ولكن العدو عداني

[10]
يا أكمل الناس من قرن إلى قدم وأحسن الناس ذا ثوب وعريانا
نعم الضجيع بعيد النوم تجذبه إليك ممتلئا نوما ويقظانا
[11]
فيا ليت شعري هل أبيتن ليلة بحيث اطمأنت بالحبيب المضاجع

Chapter 4

[1]
" رأيت جبهةً كالمرآة الصقيلة، يزينها شعر حالك كأذناب الخيل المضفورة، إن أرسلته خلته السلاسل، وإن مشطته قلت عناقيد عنبرة كرم جلاه الوابل، ومع ذلك حاجبان كأنهما خطا بقلم، أو سودا بحمم، قد تقوسا على مثل عين العبهرة التي لم يرعها قانص ولم يذعرها قسورة، بينهما أنف كحد السيف المصقول، لم يخنس به قصر، ولم يمعن به طول، حفت به وجنتان كالأرجوان، في بياض محض كالجمان، شق فيه فم كالخاتم، لذيذ المبتسم، فيه ثنايا غر، ذوات أشر، وأسنان تعد كالدر، وريق تنم إليك منه ريح الخمر، أم نشر الروض بالسحر، يتقلب فيه لسان ذو فصاحة وبيان، يقلبه عقل وافر، وجواب حاضر، يلتقي دونه شفتان حمراوان كالورد، يحلبان ريقاً كالشهد، تحت ذاك عنق كإبريق الفضة، ركب به صدر تمثال دمية، يتصل به عضدان ممتلئان لحماً مكتنزان شحماً، وذراعان ليس فيهما عظم يحس، ولا عرق يحبس، ركبت فيهما كفان رقيق قصبهما لين عصبهما، تعقد إن شئت منها الأنامل، وتركب الفصوص في حفر المفاصل، وقد تربع في صدرها حقان كأنهما رمانتان. من تحت ذلك بطن طوي كطي القباطي المدمجة، كسي عكنا كالقراطيس المدرجة. تحيط تلك العكن بسرة كمدهن العاج المجلو، خلف ظهر كالجدول ينتهي إلى خصر لولا رحمة الله لانخزل، تحته كفل يقعدها إذا نهضت، وينهضها إذا قعدت، كأنه دعص رمل، لبده سقوط الطل، يحمله فخذان لفاوان كأنهما نضيد الجمار، تحملهما ساقان خدلجتان كالبردي وشيا بشعر أسود، كأنه حلق الزرد، ويحمل ذلك قدمان كحد السنان تبارك الله في صغرهما كيف تطيقان حمل ما فوقهما، فأما سوى ذلك فتركت أن أصفه، غير أنه أحسن ما وصفه واصف بنظم أو نثر ".

[2]
تريك إذا دخلت على خلاء وقد أمنت عيون الكاشحينا (...)
وثديا مثل حق العاج رخصا حصانا من أكف اللامسينا
ومتنى لدنة طالت ولانت روادفها تنوء بما يلينا

[3]
هصرت بفودي رأسها فتمايلت علي هضيم الكشح ريا المخلخل
مهفهفة بيضاء غير مفاضة ترائبها مصقولة كالسجنجل
تصد وتبدي عن أسيل وتتقي بناظرة من وحش وجرة مطفل
وجيد كجيد الريم ليس بفاحش إذا هي نصته ولا بمعطل

[4]
وما سعاد غداة البين إذ رحلوا إلا أغن غضيض الطرف مكحول
تجلو عوارض ذي ظلم إذا ابتسمت كأنه منهل بالراح معلول
شجت بذي شبم من ماء محنية صاف بأبطح أضحى وهو مشمول
[5]
سقتني شمس يخجل البدر نورها ويكسف ضوء البرق وهو بروق
[6]
تضيء الظلام بالعشاء كأنها منارة ممسى راهب متبتل
[7]
أنيري مكان البدر إن أفل البدر وقومي مقام الشمس ما استأخر الفجر
ففيك من الشمس المنيرة ضوؤها وليس لها منك التبسم والثغر
لك الشرفة اللألاء والبدر طالع وليس لها منك الترائب والنحر
ومن أين للشمس المنيرة بالضحى بمكحولة العينين في طرفها فتر
وأنى لها من دل ليلى إذا انثنت بعيني مهاة الرمل قد مسها الذعر
[8]
فقالوا: أين مسكنها ومن هي فقلت: الشمس مسكنها السماء
[9]
أقول لأصحابي هي الشمس ضوؤها قريب ولكن في تناولها بعد
[10]
خذوا بدمي إن مت كل خريدة مريضة جفن العين والطرف فاتر
[11]
فما ظبية أدماء واضحة القَرا تنص إلى برد الظلال غزالها
تحت بقرنيها برير أراكة وتعطو بظلفيها إذا الغصن طالها
بأحسن منها مقلة ومقلدا وجيدا إذا دانت تنوط شِكالها
[12]
سبتني بعيني ظبية يستنيمها أغن البغام أعيس اللون راشح
إلى أرك بالجزع من بطن بيشة عليهن صيفن الحمام النوائح
كأن القماري الهواتف بالضحى إذا أظهرت قينات شرب صوادح
[13]
كأن قرنفلا وسحيق مسك وصوب الغاديات شملن فاها
[14]
كأن المدام وصوب الغمام وريح الخزامى وذوب العسل
يعل به برد أنيابها إذا النجم وسط السماء استقل

[15]
سبتك بمصقول ترف أشوره إذا ابتسمت في طيب ريح وفي برد
كأن عتيق الراح خالط ريقها وصفو غريض المزن صفق بالشهد
[16]
وما قهوة صهباء في متمنع بحوران يعلو حين قضُّت شَرارها
لها محصنات حولها هن مثلها عواتق أرجاها لبيع تجارها
بأطيب من فيها إذا المسك بله من الليل أروى ديمة وقطارها
[17]
وذي أشر عذب الرضاب كأنه إذا غار أرداف الثريا السوابح
مجاجة نحل في أباريق صفققت بصفق الغوادي شعشعته المجادح
تروق عيون اللائي لا يطعمونها ويروى برياها الضجيع المكافح
وغر يغادي ظلمه ببنانها مع الفجر من نعمان أخضر مائح
قضى كل ذي دين وعزة خلة له لم تنله فهو عطشان قامح
[18]
كأن فتيت المسك خالص نشرها تغل به أردانها والمرافق
تقوم إذا قامت به من فراشها ويغدو به من حضنها من تعانق
[19]
إذا نحن أدلجنا وأنت أمامنا كفى لمطايانا بريحك هاديا
[20]
أبت الروادف والثدي لقمصها مس البطون وأن تمس ظهورا
[21]
وتحتهما حققان قد ضربتهما قطار من الجوزاء ملتبدان
[22]
إذا ما مشت شبرا من الأرض أزحفت من البهر حتى ما تزيد على شبر
لها كفل يرتج منها إذا مشت ومتن كغصن البان مضطمر الخصر
[23]
يا أكمل الناس من قرن إلى قدم وأحسن الناس ذا ثوب وعريانا
[24]
هي البدر حسنا والنساء كواكب وشتان ما بين الكواكب والبدر
[25]
كأني أرى الناس المحبين بعدها عصارة مصل الحنظل المتفلق
فتكره عيني بعدها كل منظر ويكره سمعي بعدها كل منطق
[26]
رهبان مدين والذين عهدتهم يبكون من حذر العذاب قعودا

لو يسمعون كما سمعت حديثها خروا لعزة ركعا وسجودا
والميت ينشر أن تمس عظامه مسا ويخلد أن يراك خلودا
[27]
أراني إذا صليت يممت نحوها بوجهي وإن كان المصلى ورائيا
وما بي إشراك ولكن حبها وعظم الجوى أعيا الطبيب المداويا
[28]
وأنت التي إن شئت أشقيت عيشتي وأنت التي إن شئت أنعمت باليا
[29]
وما هو إلا أن أراها فجاءة فأبهت حتى ما أكاد أجيب
[30]
تقول بثينة إذ أبصرت قنوا من الشعر الأحمر
برأسي كبرت وأودى الشباب فقلت مجيبا لها أقصري
أتنسين أيامنا باللوى وأيامنا بذوي الأجفر
أما كنت أبصرتني مرة ليالي نحن بذي جهور
ليالي أنتم لنا جيرة ألا تذكرين بلى فاذكري
وإذ أنا أغيد غض الشباب أجر الرداء مع المئزر
وإذ لمتي كجناح الغراب ترجل بالمسك والعنبر
فغير ذلك ما تعلمين تغير ذا الزمن المنكر
وأنت كلؤلؤة المرزبان بماء شبابك لم تعصري
قريبان مربعنا واحدا فكيف كبرت ولم تكبري
[31]
كأني أنادي صخرة حين أعرضت من الصم لو تمشي بها العصم زلت
صفوح فما تلقاك إلا بخيلة فمن مل منها ذلك الوصل ملت
[32]
ألم تعلمي يا أم ذي الودع أنني أضاحك ذكراكم وأنت صلود
[33]
إني إليك بما وعدت لناظر نظر الفقير إلى الغني المكثر
يعد الديون وليس ينجز موعدا هذا الغريم لنا وليس بمعسر
ما أنت والوعد الذي تعدينني إلا كبرق سحابة لم تمطر
[34]
ووالله ما قاربت إلا تباعدت بصرم ولا أكثرت إلا أقلت
[35]
متى يشتفي منك الفؤاد المعذب وسهم المنايا من وصالك أقرب
فبعد ووجد واشتياق ورجفة فلا أنت تدنيني ولا أنا أبعد

كعصفورة في كف طفل يزمها تذوق حياض الموت والطفل يلعب
فلا الطفل ذو عقل يرق لما بها ولا الطير ذو ريش يطير فيذهب

[36]
إني عشية رحت وهي حزينة تشكو إلي صبابة لصبور
وتقول بت عندي فديتك ليلة أشكو إليك فإن ذاك يسير

[37]
وما أنصفت أما النساء فبغضت إلي وأما بالنوال فضنت

[38]
أسيئي بنا أو أحسني لا ملومة لدينا ولا مقلية إذ تقلت

[39]
يهواك ما عشت الفؤاد وإن أمت يتبع صداي صداك بين الأقبر

[40]
وإني لأهوى الحشر إن قيل أنني وعفراء يوم الحشر ملتقيان

Chapter 5

[1]
إذا اكتحلت عيني بعينك لم تزل بخير وجلت غمرة عن فواديا

[2]
نظرت إليها نظرة ما يسرني بها حمر أنعام البلاد وسودها

[3]
إذا نظرت نحوي تكلم طرفها وجاوبها طرفي ونحن سكوت
فواحدة منها تبشر باللقا وأخرى لها نفسي تكاد تموت

[4]
مُنعتُ من التسليم يوم وداعها فودعتها بالطرف والعين تدمع
وأخرست عن رد الجواب فمن رأى محبا بدمع العين قلبا يودع

[5]
كلانا مظهر للناس بغضا وكل عند صاحبه مكين
وأسرار الملاحظ ليس تخفي إذا نطقت بما تخفي العيون

[6]
ولكن جعلت اللحظ بيني وبينها رسولا فأدى ما تجن الضمائر

[7]
وطرفك إما جئتنا فاحفظنه فذيع الهوى باد لمن يتبصر
وأعرض إذا لاقيت عينا تخافها وظاهر ببغض إن ذلك أستر..
فمازلت في إعمال طرفك نحونا إذا جئت حتى كاد حبك يظهر

[8]
فأقسمت لا أنسى لعزة نظرة لها كدت أبدي الوجد مني المجمجما
عشية أومت والعيون حواضر إلي برجع الكف ألا تكلما

[9]
وما هو إلا أن أراها فجاءة فأبهت حتى ما أكاد أجيب
وأصرف عن رأيي الذي كنت أرتئي وأنسى الذي أعددت حين تغيب
ويظهر قلبي عذرها ويعينها علي فما لي في الفؤاد نصيب

[10]
وأنا الذي اجتلب المنية طرفه فمن المطالب والقتيل القاتل

[11]
وما ذرفت عيناك إلا لتضربي بسهميك في أعشار قلب مقتل

[12]
إن العيون التي في طرفها حور قتلتنا ثم لم يحيين قتلانا
يصرعن ذا اللب حتى لا حراك به و هن أضعف خلق الله أركانا

[13]
خذوا بدمي – إن مت- كل خريدة مريضة جفن العين والطرف فاتر

[14]
ريم رمى قاصدا قلبي بمقلته أفديه من قاصد قلبي وأحميه

[15]
إني أصيد وما لمثلي قوة ظبيا يموت إذا رآه الصائد

[16]
يجيء برياها الصبا كل ليلة وتجمعنا الأحلام في كل مرقد

[17]
إذا ما أتاه الركب من نحو أرضه تنفس يستشفي برائحة الركب

[18]
لكل حديث عندهن بشاشة وكل قتيل عندهن شهيد

[19]
غراء مبسام كأن حديثها در تحدر نظمه منثور

[20]
وحديثها كالغيث يسمعه راعي سنين تتابعت جدبا
فأصاخ يرجو أن يكون حيا ويقول من فرح هيا ربا

[21]
وكأن تحت لسانها هاروت ينفث فيه سحرا
وكأن رجع حديثها قطع الرياض كسين زهرا

[22]
فما مكفهر في رحى مرجحنة ولا ما أسرت في معادنها النحل
بأحلى من القول الذي قلت بعدما تمكن في حيزوم ناقتي الرجل
[23]
يقتلننا بحديث ليس يعلمه من يتقين ولا مكتومه بادي
فهن يبدين من قول يصبن به مواقع الماء من ذي الغلة الصادي
[24]
وبثنة قد قالت وكل حديثها إلينا ولو قالت بسوء مملح
[25]
ولباطل ممن أحب حديثه أشهى إلي من البغيض البازل
[26]
(لا والذي تسجد الجباه له) مالي بما دون ثوبها خبر
ولا بفيها ولا هممت بها ما كان إلا الحديث والنظر
[27]
ألا ليت شعري هل نبيتن ليلة كليلتنا حتى نرى ساطع الفجر
تجود علينا بالحديث وتارة تجود علينا بالرضاب من الثغر
[28]
ألا ليت شعري هل أبيتن ليلة أناجيكم حتى أرى غرة الفجر
[29]
ولو كنت أعمى أخبط الأرض بالعصا أصم فنادتني أجبت المناديا
[30]
ألا ليتني أعمى أصم تقودني بثينة لا يخفى علي كلامها
[31]
وأدنيتني حتى إذا ما فتنتني بقول يحل العصم سهل الأباطح
تجافيت عني حين لا لي حيلة وغادرت ما غادرت بين الجوانح
[32]
فلو أنها تدعو الحمام أجابها ولو كلمت ميتا إذا لتكلما
[33]
ولو بذلت أم الوليد حديثها لعصم برضوى أصبحت تتقرب
تهبطن من أكناف ضأس وأيلة إليها ولو أغرى بهن المكلب
[34]
طاف الخيال لأهل عزة موهنا بعد الهدو فهاج لي أحزاني
فألم من أهل البويب خيالها بمعرس من أهل ذي ذروان
[35]
فما بي من سقم ولا طيف جنة ولكن عبد الأعرجي كذوب

[36]

قد زارني طيفكم ليلا فأرقني فبت للشوق أذري الدمع تهتانا

[37]

أسرى لخالدة الخيال ولا أرى طللا أحب من الخيال الطارق

[38]

ألم خيال من بثينة طارق على النأي مشتاق إلي وشائق
سرت من تلاع الحجر حتى تخلصت إلي ودوني الأشعرون وغافق

[39]

أمنك سرى يا بثن طيف تأوبا هدوا فهاج القلب شوقا وأنصبا
عجبت له أن زار في النوم مضجعي ولو زارني مستيقظا كان أعجبا

[40]

وإني لأستغشي وما بي نعسة لعل لقاء في المنام يكون

[41]

وإني لأستغشي وما بي نعسة لعل خيالا منك يلقى خياليا

[42]

أفي النوم يا ليلى رأيتك أم أنا رأيتك يقظانا فعندي شهودها
ضممتك حتى قلت ناري قد انطفت فلم تطف نيراني وزاد وقودها

[43]

فهلا منعتم- إذ منعتم حديثها- خيالا يوافيني على النأي هاديا

[44]

زار الخيال لها لا بل ازاركه فكر إذا نام فكر الخلق لم ينم
ظبي تقنصته لما نصبت له في آخر الليل أشراكا من الحلم

[45]

تمناه طيفي في الكرى فتغيبا وقبلت يوما ظله فتعتبا

[46]

يا عاشقين اصطلحا في الكرى فأصبحا غضبى وغضبانا
كذلك الأحلام غرارة وربما تصدق أحيانا

[47]

أفي كل يوم أنت رام بلادها بعينين إنساناهما غرقان
ألا فاحملاني -بارك الله فيكما- إلى حاضر الروحاء ثم دعاني

[48]

ألا أيها البيت الذي لا أزوره وهجرانه مني إليه ذنوب
هجرتك مشتاقا وزرتك خائفا وفيك علي الدهر منك رقيب

[49]

أصد وبي مثل الجنون لكي يرى رواة الخنا أني لبيتك هاجر

[50]
أأترك ليلى ليس بيني وبينها سوى ليلة إني إذا لصبور
هبوني امرءا منكم أضل بعيره له ذمة إن الذمام كبير
وللصاحب المتروك أعظم حرمة على صاحب من أن يضل بعير
عفا الله عن ليلى الغداة فإنها إذا وليت حكما علي تجور
[51]
أمر على الديار ديار ليلى أقبل ذا الجدار وذا الجدارا
وما حب الديار شغفن قلبي ولكن حب من سكن الديارا
[52]
وما أحببت أرضكم ولكن أقبل إثر من وطئ الترابا
[53]
خليلي هذا ربع عزة فاعقلا قلوصيكما ثم ابكيا حيث حلت
ومسا ترابا كان قد مس جلدها وبيتا وظلا حيث باتت وظلت
ولا تيأسا أن يمحو الله عنكما ذنوبا إذا صليتما حيث صلت
[54]
أحن إلى نجد وإني لآيس طوال الليالي من قفول إلى نجد
وإن يك لا ليلى ولا نجد فاعترف بهجر إلى يوم القيامة والوعد
[55]
ألا يا صبا نجد متى هجت من نجد لقد زادني مسراك وجدا على وجد
[56]
يغور إذا غارت فؤادي وإن تكن بنجد يهم مني الفؤاد إلى نجد
[57]
وأجهشت للتوباد حين رأيته وهلل للرحمن حين رآني
فقلت له أين الذين عهدتهم حواليك في خصب وطيب زمان
[58]
وإن الكثيب الفرد من جانب الحمى إلي – وإن لم آته – لحبيب
[59]
كأن القلب ليلة قيل يغدى بليلى العامرية أو يراح
قطاة غرها شرك فباتت تجاذبه وقد علق الجناح
[60]
متى يشتفي منك الفؤاد المعذب وسهم المنايا من وصالك أقرب
فبعد ووجد واشتياق ورجفة فلا أنت تدنيني ولا أنا أبعد
كعصفورة في كف طفل يزمها تذوق حياض الموت والطفل يلعب
فلا الطفل ذو عقل يرق لما بها ولا الطير ذو ريش يطير فيذهب

[61]
ألا ليتنا كنا غزالين نرتعي رياضا من الحوذان في بلد قفر
ألا ليتنا كنا حمامي مفازة نطير ونأوي بالعشي إلى وكر
ألا ليتنا حوتان في البحر نرتمي إذا نحن أمسينا نلجج في البحر
وياليتنا نحيا جميعا وليتنا نصير إذا متنا ضجيعين في قبر

[62]
فإن نسيم الجو يجمع بيننا ونبصر قرن الشمس حين تزول
وأرواحنا بالليل في الحي تلتقي (ونعلم انا بالنهار نقيل)

[63]
فما طلع النجم الذي يهتدى به ولا الصبح إلا هيجا ذكرها ليا

[64]
وشغلت عن فهم الحديث سوى ما كان منك وحبكم شغلي
وأديم نحو محدثي ليرى أن قد فهمت وعندكم عقلي

[65]
أريد لأنسى ذكرها فكأنما تمثل لي ليلى بكل سبيل

Chapter 6

[1]
لقد ثبتت في القلب منكم مودة كما ثبتت في الراحتين الأصابع

[2]
أتبكي على لبنى وأنت تركتها وكنت كآت حتفه وهو طائع
فيا قلب صبرا واعترافا لما ترى ويا حبها قع بالذي أنت واقع
ويا قلب خبرني إذا شطت النوى بلبنى وبانت عنك ما أنت صانع
كأنك بدع لم تر الناس قبلها ولم يطلعك الدهر فيمن يطالع

[3]
ما بال قلبك يا مجنون قد خلعا في حب من لا ترى في نيله طمعا

[4]
ألا ليتنا يا عز كنا لذي غنى بعيرين نرعى في الخلاء ونعزب
كلانا به عر فمن يرنا يقل على حسنها جرباء تعدي وأجرب
إذا ما وردنا منهلا صاح أهله علينا فما ننفك نرمى ونضرب
نكون بعيري ذي غنى فيضيعنا فلا هو يرعانا ولا نحن نطلب

[5]
ولست على بذل الصفاء هويتها ولكن سبتني بالدلال وبالبخل

[6]
وقال أفق حتى متى أنت هائم ببثنة فيها قد تعيد وقد تبدي؟

فقلت له: فيها قضى الله ما ترى علي، وهل فيما قضى الله من رد
فإن كان رشدا حبها أو غواية فقد جنته ما كان مني على عمد
[7]
عدمتك من حب أما منك راحة وما بك عني من توان ولا فتر
[8]
رمى الله في عيني بثنة بالقذى وفي الغر من أنيابها بالقوادح
[9]
ألا ليتني أعمى أصم تقودني بثينة لا يخفى علي كلامها
[10]
وقلت لقلبي حين لج بي الهوى وكلفني ما لا يطيق من الحب
ألا أيها القلب الذي قاده الهوى أفق لا أقر الله عينك من قلب
[11]
صادت فؤادي يا بثين حبالكم يوم الحجون وأخطأتك حبائلي
[12]
قضاها لغيري وابتلاني بحبها فهلا بشيء غير ليلى ابتلانيا
[13]
دعا المحرمون الله يستغفرونه بمكة شعثا كي تمحى ذنوبها
وناديت يا رحمن، أول سؤلتي لنفسي ليلى ثم أنت حسيبها
وإن أعط ليلى في حياتي لم يتب إلى الله عبد توبة لا أتوبها
[14]
يا حبذا عمل الشيطان من عمل إن كان من عمل الشيطان حبيها
[15]
وقالوا نأت فاختر من الصبر والبكا فقلت البكا أشفى إذن لغليلي
[16]
تداويت من ليلى بليلى عن الهوى كما يتداوى شارب الخمر بالخمر
[17]
فيا حبها زدني جوى كل ليلة ويا سلوة الأيام موعدك الحشر
[18]
رفعت عن الدنيا المنى غير ودها فما أسأل الدنيا ولا أستزيدها
[19]
وعاذلين ألحوا في محبتها يا ليتهم وجدوا مثل الذي أجد
لما أطالوا عتابي فيك قلت لهم: لا تكثروا بعض هذا اللوم واقتصدوا

Chapter 7

[1]
خليلي ما ألقى من الوجد باطن ودمعي بما أخفي الغداة شهيد

[2]
وآية وجد الصب تهطال دمعه ودمع الشجي الصب أعدل شاهد

[3]
أقول لماء العين أمعن لعله بما لا يرى من غائب الوجد يشهد

[4]
وقالوا نأت فاختر من الصبر والبكا فقلت البكا أشفى إذن لغليلي

[5]
وليس الذي يجري من العين ماؤها ولكنها نفس تذوب وتقطر

[6]
إذا بصرت بها العينان لجت بدمعهما مع النظر اللجوج

[7]
ولو أن عينا طاوعتني لم تزل ترقرق دمعا أو دما حين تسكب

[8]
وكم زفرة لي لو على البحر أشرقت لأنشفه حر لها ولهيب

[9]
لاحت لعينك من بثينة نار فدموع عينك درة وغزار

[10]
بي اليأس او داء الهيام أصابني فاياك عني لا يصيبك ما بيا

[11]
متى تكشفا عني القميص تبينا بي الضر من عفراء يا فتيان
وتعترفا لحما قليلا وأعظما دقاقا وقلبا دائم الخفقان

[12]
جعلت لعراف اليمامة حكمه وعراف نجد إن هما شفياني
فما تركا من رقية يعلمانها ولا شربة إلا وقد سقياني
فقالا شفاك الله والله مالنا بما حملت منك الضلوع يدان

[13]
طبيبان لو داويتماني أجرتما فما لكما تستغنيان عن الأجر
فقالا بحزن مالك اليوم حيلة فمت كمدا أو عز نفسك بالصبر

[14]
أرى أهل ليلى أورثوني صبابة وما لي سوى ليلى الغداة طبيب

[15]
يا بثن جودي وكافي عاشقا دنفا واشفي بذلك أسقامي وأوجاعي

[16]
عيد قيس من حب لبنى ولبنى داء قيس والحب داء شديد
وإذا عادني العوائد يوما قالت العين لا أرى من أريد
ليت لبنى تعودني ثم أقضى إنها لا تعود فيمن يعود

[17]
وللحب آيات تبين بالفتى شحوب وتعرى من يديه الأشاجع

[18]
كلفت بها حتى أذابني الهوى وصير عظمي بالعظام رميما

[19]
ويعجبني من جعفر أن جعفرا ملح على قرص ويبكي على جمل
فلو كنت عذري العلاقة لم تكن بطينا وأنساك الهوى كثرة الأكل

[20]
لقد عارضتنا الريح منها بنفحة على كبدي من طيب أرواحها برد
فمازلت مغشيا علي وقد مضت أناة وما عندي جواب ولا رد

[21]
وإن قلت ردي بعض عقلي أعش به تولت وقالت ذاك منك بعيد

[22]
يقولون مجنون يهيم بذكرها وأقسم ما بي من جنون ولا سحر
إذا ما نظمت الشعر في غير ذكرها أبى وأبيكم أن يطاوعني شعري

[23]
يقولون جاهد يا جميل بغزوة وأي جهاد غيرهن أريد
لكل حديث عندهن بشاشة وكل قتيل عندهن شهيد

[24]
لقد عذبتني يا حب لبنى فقع إما بموت أو حياة
فإن الموت أروح من حياة تقوم على التباعد والشتات

[25]
يا ليتني ألقى المنية بغتة إن كان يوم لقائكم لم يقدر

[26]
وإني لأهوى الحشر إن قيل أنني وعفراء يوم الحشر ملتقيان

[27]
ولكنه باق على كل حادث وزائرنا في ظلمة القبر واللحد

[28]

أعوذ بك اللهم أن تشحط النوى ببثنة في أدنى حياتي ولا حشري

وجاور إذا ما مت بيني وبينها فياحبذا موتي إذا جاورت قبري

[29]

فيا ليتنا نحيا جميعا فإن نمت تجاور في الهلكى عظامي عظامها

[30]

وإني لأهوى الحشر إن قيل أنني وعفراء يوم الحشر ملتقيان

[31]

من كان من أخواتي باكيا أبدا فاليوم إني أراني اليوم مقبوضا

يسمعنيه فإني غير سامعه إذا علوت رقاب القوم معروضا

[32]

قد مات قبلي أخو هند وصاحبه مرقش واشتفى من عروة الكمد

وكلهم كان من عشق منيته وقد وجدت بها فوق الذي وجدوا

إني لأحسب أو قد كدت أعلمه أن سوف توردني الحوض الذي وردوا

[33]

ما إن صبا مثلي جميل فاعلمي حقا ولا المقتول عروة إذ صبا

[34]

خليلي فيما عشتما هل رأيتما قتيلا بكى من حب قاتله قبلي

[35]

ولو أن داع منك يدعو جنازتي وكنت على أيدي الرجال حييت

[36]

ولو شهدتني حين تحضر ميتتي جلا سكرات الموت عني كلامها

[37]

لقد هم قيس أن يزج بنفسه ويرمي بها من ذروة الجبل الصعب

فلا غرو أن الحب للمرء قاتل يقلبه ما شاء جنبا إلى جنب

[38]

أظلوم حان إلى القبور ذهابي وبليت قبل الموت في أثوابي

جرعتني غصص المنية بالهوى أفما بعيشك ترحمين شبابي

[39]

ما يعرف الحزن إلا كل من عشقا وليس من قال إني عاشق صدقا

للعاشقين نحول يعرفون به من طول ما حالفوا الأحزان والأرقا

[40]

ما أنكأ البين لقرح القلوب شيب رأسي قبل حين المشيب

أنحل جسمي وبرى أعظمي لذع حرارات فراق الحبيب...

أورث قلبي من جوى حبه داء عياء ماله من طبيب

Bibliography

Primary Sources

Al-Qur'an al-Karim.
The Holy Qur'an, trans. Yusuf Ali, Leicester: Islamic Foundation, 1975.
Al-'Abd, Tarafah (1979), *Diwan*, Beirut: Dar Beirut li al-tiba'ah wa al-nashr.
Abu Nuwas, al-Hasan b. Hani (2002), *Diwan*, ed. G. Schoeler, Damascus: Dar al-mada.
Abu Tammam, Habib b. Aws al-Ta'i, (1964) *Diwan Abi Tammam bi sharh al-Khatib al-Tabrizi*, ed. Muhammad 'Abduh 'Azzam, Cairo: Dar al-ma'arif.
Al-Abshihi, Shihab al-Din Muhammad b. Ahmad (1929), *al-Mustatraf fi kull fann mustadhraf*, Cairo: al-Matba'ah al-mahmudiyyah al-tijariyyah.
Al-Antaki, Daud (2003), *Tazyin al-aswaq fi akhbar al-'ushshaq*, Beirut: Dar al-bihar.
Al-A'sha, Maymun b. Qays (1966), *Diwan*, Beirut: Dar sadir.
'Atiyah, Jarir (1964), *Diwan*, Beirut: Dar sadir.
Al-Baghdadi, 'Abd al-Qadir b. 'Umar (1977), *Khizanat al-adab wa lubb lubab lisan al-'Arab*, ed. 'Abd al-Salam Harun, Vol. 6, Cairo: al-Hay'ah al-misriyyah al-'ammah li al-kitab.
Al-Bayhaqi, Abu Bakr Ahmad b. al-Husayn, *Kitab shu'ab al-iman*, http://www.ahlalhdeeth.com/vb/showthread.php?t=23108, 14 January 2009.
Al-Bukhari, Muhammad b. Isma'il (1987), *Sahih al-Bukhari*, ed. Mustafa dib al-Bagha, 3rd edn, Beirut: Dar Ibn Kathir.
Al-Bukhari, Muhammad b. Isma'il, *al-Jami' al-Sahih*, trans. M. Muhsin Khan, http://www.usc.edu/dept/MSA/fundamentals/hadithsunnah/bukharil. 1 February 2007.
Burd, Bashshar (1976), *Diwan*, ed. Muhammad al-Tahir b. 'Ashur, Tunis: al-Sharikah al-tunisiyyah li al-tawzi'.

Al-Dabbi, Al-Mufaddal (1983), *al-Mufaddaliyyat*, eds. Ahmad Shakir and 'Abd al-Salam Harun, 3rd edn, Cairo: Dar al-ma'arif.

Al-Dahhak, al-Husayn (1960), *Diwan*, ed. 'Abd al-Sattar Ahmad Farraj, Beirut: Dar al-Thaqafah.

Al-Ghazali, Abu Hamid Muhammad b. Ahmad (1997), *The Incoherence of the Philosophers*, trans. Michael E. Marmura, Provo, Utah: Brigham Young University Press.

Al-Ghazali, Abu Hamid Muhammad b. Ahmad (1980), *The Alchemy of Happiness*, trans. Claud Field, London: Octagon Press (for the Sufi Trust).

Al-Ghazali, Abu Hamid Muhammad b. Ahmad (1967–8), *Ihya 'ulum al-din*, Cairo: Mu'assasat al-Halabi.

Hamdun, Muhammad b. al-Hasan (2009), *al-Tadhkirah al-hamduniyyah*, 8 October.

Ibn 'Abd Rabbihi, Ahmad b. Muhammad al-Andalusi (1940), *al-'Iqd al-farid*, ed. Muhammad Sa'id al-'Aryan, Cairo: Matba'at al-istiqamah.

Ibn 'Arabi, Muhammad b. 'Ali (1999), *al-Futuhat al-makkiyyah*, ed. Ahmad Shams al-Din, Beirut: Dar al-kutub al-'ilmiyyah.

Ibn Daud, Abu Bakr Muhammad (1985), *Kitab al-zahrah*, ed. Ibrahim al-Samarra'i, 'Amman: Maktabat al-manar.

Ibn Hazm, 'Ali b. Ahmad al-Andalusi (1993), *Tawq al-hamamah fi al-ulfah wa al-ullaf*, ed. Ihsan 'Abbas, Beirut: al-Mu'asasah al-'arabiyyah li al-dirasat wa al-nashr.

Ibn Hazm 'Ali b. Ahmad al-Andalusi (1953), *The Ring of the Dove*, trans. Arthur J. Arberry, London: Luzac and Company, Ltd.

Ibn al-Jawzi, 'Abd al-Rahman b. 'Ali (1987), *Dhamm al-hawa*, ed. Ahmad 'Abd al-Salam 'Ata, Beirut: Dar al-kutub al-'ilmiyyah.

Ibn Manzur, Muhammad b. Mukarram (1984), *Mukhtasar tarikh Dimashq*, Damascus: Dar al-fikr.

Ibn Qayyim, al-Jawziyyah (1973), *Rawdat al-muhibbin wa nuzhat al-mushtaqin*, ed. Sabir Yusuf, Cairo: Maktabat al-jami'ah.

Ibn Qutaybah, 'Abdallah b. Muslim (1964), *'Uyun al-akhbar*, Cairo: al-Mu'asasah al-misriyyah al-'ammah li al-ta'lif wa al-tarjamah wa al-tiba'ah wa al-nashr.

Ibn Qutaybah, 'Abdallah b. Muslim (1958), *al-Shi'r wa al-shu'ara*, ed. Ahmad Muhammad Shakir, Cairo: Dar al-ma'arif.

Al-Isfahani, Abu al-Faraj 'Ali b. al-Husayn (1997), *al-Aghani*, Beirut: Dar ihya al-turath al-'arabi.

Al-Jahiz, Abu 'Uthman 'Amr b. Bahr (1987), *al-Rasail al-kalamiyyah*, Cairo: Maktabat al-hilal.

Al-Jahiz, Abu 'Uthman 'Amr b. Bahr (1980), *Kitab al-qiyan* [*The Epistle on Singing-Girls of Jahiz*], trans. A. Frederick L. Beeston, Warminster: Aris and Phillips.

Al-Jahiz, Abu 'Uthman 'Amr b. Bahr (1969), *al-Hayawan*, ed. 'Abd al-Salam Harun, Beirut, al-Mujamma' al-'ilmi al-Islami.

Al-Jahiz, Abu 'Uthman 'Amr b. Bahr (1965), *Rasail al-Jahiz*, ed. 'Abd al-Salam Harun, Cairo: Matba'at al-Khanji.

Al-Kindi, Imru' al-Qays b. Hajar (1958), *Diwan Imru' al-Qays*, Beirut: Dar sadir.

Kuthayyir 'Azzah, Kuthayyir b. 'Abd al-Rahman (2004), *Diwān Kuthayyir 'Azzah*, ed. Majid Tarad, Beirut: Dar al-kitab al-'arabi.

Majnun Layla; Abu Bakr al-Walibi (1994), *Diwan Majnun Layla*, ed. Jalal al-Din al-Halabi, Beirut: Dar al-najm.

Majnun Layla, Qays b. al-Mulawah (2003), *Diwan Majnun Layla*, ed. 'Adnan Zaki Darwish, 2nd edition, Beirut: Dar sadir.

Ma'mar, Jamil b. Abdallah (1980), *Diwan Jamil Buthaynah*, ed. Fawzi 'Atawi, Beirut: Dar sa'b.

Al-Marzuqi, Abu 'Ali Ahmad b. Muhammad (1951), *Sharh diwan al-hamasah li Abi Tammam*, ed. Ahmad Amin et al., Cairo: Lajnat al-ta'lif wa al-tarjamah wa al-nashr.

Al-Mutanabbi, Abu al-Tayyib Ahmad b. al-Husayn (1997), *Diwan, Sharh Abu al-Baqa al-'Ukburi*, ed. Kamal Talib, Beirut: Dar al-kutub al-'ilmiyyah.

Al-Naysaburi, Abu al-Qasim al-Hasan (1990), *'Uqala al-majanin*, ed. 'Abd al-Amir Muhanna, Beirut: Dar al-fikr al-Lubnani.

Al-Nuwayri, Shihab al-Din Ahmad b. 'Abd al-Wahhab (no date), *Nihayat al-arab fi funun al-adab*, Cairo: al-Mu'asasah al-misriyyah al-'ammah li al-ta'lif wa al-tarjamah wa al-tiba'ah wa al-nashr.

Al-Qayrawani, Ibn Rashiq (2000), *al-'Umdah fi sina'at al-shi'r wa naqduh*, ed. Al-Nabawi 'Abd al-Wahid Sha'lan, Cairo: Maktabat al-Kanji.

Qays Lubna, Qays b. Dharih (1998), *Diwan Qays Lubna (Qays b. Dharih)*, ed. 'Afif Nayif Ḥaṭum, Beirut: Dar sadir.

Al-Qurashi, Abu Zayd Muhammad b. Abi al-Khattab (1998), *Jamharat ash'ar al-'Arab*, Beirut: Dar sadir.

Al-Qushayri, Muslim b. al-Hajjaj (1987), *Sahih Muslim*, eds. Musa Shahin Lashin and Ahmad 'Umar Hashim, Beirut: Mu'asasah 'Izz al-Din li al-tiba'ah wa al-nashr.

Al-Qushayri, Muslim b. al-Hajjaj (1972), *Sahih Muslim*, trans. 'Abd al-Hamid Siddiqi, Lahore: SH Muhammad Ashraf.

Al-Qutami, 'Umayr b. Shaym (1960), *Diwan al-Qutami*, eds. Ahmad Matlub and Ibrahim al-Samirai, Beirut: Dar al-thaqafah.

Al-Safadi, Khalil b. Aybak (1990), *al-Ghayth al-musjam fi sharh lamiyyat al-'ajam*, Vol. 2, 2nd edn, Beirut: Dar al-kutub al-'ilmiyyah.

Al-Samarqandi, Abu al-Layth Nasr b. Muhammad (1966), *Qurrat al-'uyun*, trans. John Macdonald, 'Paradise', *Islamic Studies*, Vol. 5, No. 4, pp. 331–83, www.jstor.org/stable/20832856.

Al-Sarraj, Ja'far b. Ahmad (1992), *Masar'al-'ushshaq*, Beirut : Dar sadir.

Shaddad, 'Antarah (1992), *Diwan*, Beirut: Dar sadir.

Al-Suyuti, Jalal al-Din (1987), *The Book of Exposition*, trans. An English Bohemian, London: Darf Publishers Ltd.

Al-Tawhidi, Abu Hayyan (1951), *al-Hawamil wa al-shawamil*, eds. Ahmad Amin and al-Sayyid Ahmad Saqr, Cairo: Matba'at lajnat al-ta'lif wa al-nashr.

Al-Tawhidi, Abu Hayyan (1929), *al-Muqabasat*, ed. Hasan al-Sandubi, Cairo: al-Matba'ah al-rahmaniyyah.

Al-'Udhri, Jamil b. 'Abdallah; Majnun Layla; Qays b. Dharih (1992), *Diwan al-'udhriyyin: Jamil b. Ma'mar, Qays b. al-Mulawwah, Qays b. Dharih*, ed. Yusuf 'Id, Beirut: Dar al-jil.

'Umar, Abi Rabi'ah (2007), *Diwan*, ed. 'Abd al-Rahman al-Mistawi, Beirut, Dar al-ma'rifah.

'Urwah 'Afra, 'Urwah b. Hizam (1995), *Diwan 'Urwah b. Hizam*, ed. Antwan Muhsin al-Qawwal, Beirut: Dar al-jil.

Al-Washsha, Muhammad b. Ishaq (1884–5), *Kitab al-muwashsha*, Leiden: Brill.

Al-Walibi, Abu Bakr (1994), *Diwan Majnun Layla*, ed. Jalal al-Din al-Halibi, Beirut: Dar al-najm.

Zuhayr, Ka'b (1997), *Diwan*, ed. 'Ali Fa'ur, Beirut: Dar al-kutub al-'ilmiyyah.

Secondary Sources

Arabic

'Abd al-Karim, Khalil (1998), *al-'Arab wa al-marah hafriyah fi al-istir al-mukhayim*, Beirut: al-Intishar al-'Arabi; Cairo: al-Sina li al-nashr.

'Abdallah, Muhammad Hasan (1994), *al-Hubb fi al turath al-'arabi*, Cairo: Dar al-ma'arif.

Adunis (2002), *al-Thabit wa al-mutahawil*, Vol.1, London: Saqi.

Al-Alusi,'Adil Kamil (1999), *al-Hubb 'inda al-'Arab*, Beirut: al-Dar al-'arabiyyah li al-mawsuat.

Al-'Ani, Sami Makki (1983), *al-Islam wa al-shi'r*, Kuwait: al-Majlis al-watani li al-thaqafah wa al-funun wa al-adab.

Al-'Aqqad, 'Abbas Mahmud (1967), *Jamil Buthaynah*, Cairo: Dar al-ma'arif.
'Atwan, Husayn (1987), *Muqaddimah al-qasidah al-'arabiyyah fi al-'asr al-umawi*, Beirut: Dar al-jil.
'Ayyad, Bashir (2000), *Jamil Buthaynah imam al-muhibbīn wa al-majānīn: qirah mughayirah*, Cairo, Dar al-Ahmadi li al-nashr.
Al-'Azm, Sadiq Jalal (1968), *Fi al-hubb wa al-hubb al-'udhri*, Beirut: Manshurat Nizar Qabbani.
Badawi, Walid Mis'id (2004), 'al-Alfaz al-dallah 'ala al-husn wa al-qubh fi al-shi'r al-'udhri', Cairo University: Dar al-'ulum, unpublished masters dissertation.
Al-Bahbiti, Najib Muhammad (1961), *Tarikh al-shi'r al-'Arabi hatta akhir al-qarn al-thalith al-hijri*, Cairo: Mu'asasah al-khanji.
Bakkar, Yusuf Husayn (1980), *Ittijahat al-ghazal fi al-qarn al-thani al-hijri*, 2nd edn, Beirut: Dar al-Andalus.
Al-Batal, 'Ali (1984), *al-Ghazal al-'udhri wa idtirab al-waqi'*, 4/2, Cairo: Fusul, pp. 180–93.
Al-Batal, 'Ali (1983), *al-Surah fi al-shi'r al-'arabi hatta akhir al-qarn al-thani al-hijri*, Beirut: Dar al-Andalus.
Buluhi, Muhammad (2000), *al-Shi'r al-'udhri fi daw al-naqd al-hadith*, Damascus: Manshurat itihad al-kuttab al-'arab.
Burton, Richard (trans) (1962), *The Book of The Thousand and One Nights*, 6 Vols, New York: Heritage Press.
Al-Dahan, Sami (1981), *al-Ghazal mundhu nash'atihi hatta sadr al-dawlah al-'abbasiyyah*, 3rd edn, Cairo: Dar al-ma'arif.
Dayf, Shawqi (1999), *al-Hubb al-'udhri 'inda al-'Arab*, Cairo: al-Dar al-misriyyah al-lubnaniyyah.
Dayf, Shawqi (1978a), *Tarikh al-adab al-'arabi: al-'asr al-Islami*, 8th edn, Cairo: Dar al-ma'arif.
Dayf, Shawqi (1978b), *al-Fann wa mathahibuhu fi al-shi'r al-'arabi*, 10th edn, Cairo: Dar al-ma'arif.
Al-Dughli, Muhammad Sa'id (1985), *Ahadith ghazilah fi al-ghazalayn al-'udhri wa al-'umari wa imtidadatuhuma fi al-ghazal al-'arabi*, Damascus: Manshurat maktabat usamah.
Farrukh, 'Umar (1978), *Tarikh al-adab al-'arabi*, 3rd edn, Beirut: Dar al-'ilm li al-malayin.
Faysal, Shukri (1986), *Tatawwur al-ghazal bayna al-Jahiliyyah wa al-Islam*, Beirut: Dar al-'ilm li al-malayin.

Haddad, Qasim (1996), *Akhbar Majnun Layla*, London: Majmuʻat arabisk (Arabesque).
Haddarah, Muhammad Mustafa (1988), *al-Shiʻr al-ʻArabi fi al-qarn al-awwal al-hijri*, Beirut: Dar al-ʻulum al-ʻarabiyyah.
Hatum, ʻAfif (1997), *al-Ghazal fi al-ʻasr al-umawi*, Beirut: Dar al-sadr.
Hilal, Muhammad Ghunaymi (1960), *al-Hayah al-ʻatifiyyah bayna al-ʻudhriyyah wa al-sufiyyah: dirasat naqd wa muqaranah hawla mawduʻ Layla wa al-Majnun fi al-adabayn al-ʻarabi wa al-farisi*, Cairo: Anglo-Egyptian Press.
Al-Hufi, Ahmad (1973), *al-Ghazal fi al-ʻasr al-jahili*, Cairo: Dar nahdat Misr li al-tabʻ wa al-nashr.
Husayn, Taha (1976), *Hadith al-arbiʻa*, 12th edn, Cairo: Dar al-maʻarif.
ʻIsa, Ibrahim (1996), *al-Jins wa ʻulama al-Islam*, Cairo: Madbuli.
ʻIzz al-Din, Hasan al-Banna (1994), *al-Tayf wa al-khayal fi al-shiʻr al-ʻArabi al-qadim*, 3rd edn, Beirut: Dar al-manahil.
Jabri, Shafiq (2001), *Dirasat al-aghani*, 2nd edn, Damascus: Dar al-bashaʼir.
Jadidi, Al-Tahir Labib (1988), *Susyulujiya al-ghazal al-ʻarabi: al-shiʻr al-ʻudhri namudhajan*, trans. Mustafa al-Misnawi, Beirut: Dar al-taliʻah.
Al-Jawari, Ahmad ʻAbd al-Sattar (2006), *al-Hubb al-ʻudhri nashʼatuhu wa tatawwuruhu*, Beirut: al-muʼasasah al-ʻarabiyyah li al-dirasat wa al-nashr.
Al-Jihad, Hilal (2007), *Jamaliyyat al-shiʻr al-ʼarabi. Dirash fi falsafat al-jamal fi al-waʼi al-shiʼri al-jahili*, Beriut: markaz dirasat al-wihdah al-arabiyyah.
Khulayf, Yusuf (1997), *al-Hubb al-mithali ʻinda al-ʻArab*, Cairo: Dar Quba.
Mubarak, Zaki (1945), *al-ʻUshshaq al-thalathah*, Cairo: Matbaʻat al-maʻarif wa maktabatuha.
Al-Mukhtar, Hamid (1983), *Jamil Buthaynah wa al-hubb al-ʻudhri*, Baghdad: Maktabat al-shuruq.
Najm, Khristu (1982), *Jamil Buthaynah wa al-hubb al-ʻudhri*, Beirut: Dar al-raʼid al-ʻarabi.
Al-Nass, Ihsan (1976), *al-Ghazal fi ʻasr Bani umayyah*, Damascus: Dar al-fikr.
Al-Qitt, ʻAbd al-Qadir (1987), *Fi al-shiʻr al-Islami wa al-umawi*, Beirut: Dar al-nahdah al-ʻarabiyyah.
Qulaymah, Bayyar (2004), *Jamil Buthaynah raʼid al-ghazal al-ʻafif*, Beirut: Dar al-fikr al-lubnani.
Al-Ramadi, Jamal al-Din (1976), *Jamil b. Maʻma shaʻir al-hubb wa ʻashiq Buthaynah*, Cairo: al-Hayʼah al-misriyyah al-ʻammah li al-kitab.
Sabrah, Ahmad Hasan (2001), *al-Ghazal al-ʻudhri fi al-ʻasr al-umawi*, Alexandria: al-Sadiqan li al-nashr waʼl-iʻlan.

Sadiq, 'Abbas (2002), *al-Ghazal al-'udhri*, Amman: Dar 'alam al-thaqafah.
Salah, 'Id (1993), *al-Ghazal al-'udhri haqiqat al-zahirah wa khasa'is al-fann*, Cairo: Maktabat al-adab.
Salamah, Raja (2003), *al-'Ishq wa al-kitabah: qira'ah fi al-mawruth*, Cologne: Manshurat al-jamal.
Salim, Muhammad 'Adnan and Sulayman, Muhammad Wahbi (1997), *Mu'jam kalimat al-Quran al-'azim*, Beirut: Dar al-fikr al-mu'asir.
Sarkis, Ihsan (1981), *al-Zahirah al-adabiyyah fi sadr al-Islam wa al-dawlah al-umawiyyah*, Beirut: Dar al-tali'ah.
Al-Shak'ah, Mustafa (1979), *Rihlat al-shi'r min al-Umawiyyah ila al-'Abbasiyyah*, Beirut: 'Alam al-kutub.
Shawqi, Ahmad (1989), *Majnun Layla*, Cairo: Maktabat Misr.
Al-Shibi, Kamil Mustafa (1997), *al-Ghazal al-'udhri wa makanatuhu al-fikriyyah wa al-diniyyah fi al-'asr al-umawi*, Beirut: Dar al-manahil.
Sulayman, Musa (1954), *al-Hubb al-'udhri*, 2nd edn, Beirut: Dar al-thaqafah.
Tajwar, Fatimah (1999), *al-Marah fi al-shi'r al-Umawi*, Damascus: Manshurat itihad al-kuttab al-'Arab.
Al-Tarabulsi, Muhammad al-Hadi (2006), *al-Buna wa al-ru'a*, Safaqas: Dar Muhammad 'Ali li al-nashar.
Tawili, Ahmad (2001), *Kutub al-ḥubb 'inda al-'Arab*, Beirut: Riyad al-rayyis li al-kutub wa'l-nashr.
'Urawi, Muhammad Iqbal (2009), 'Mustawayat hudur al-Jasad fi al-khitab al-qur'ani', *'Alam al-fikr*, 37:4, pp. 11–31.
Vadet, Jean-Claude (1979), *al-Ghazal 'inda al-'Arab*, trans. Ibrahim al-Kilani, Damascus: Manshurat wizarat al-thaqafah wa al-irshad.
Al-Yusuf, Yusuf (1978), *al-Ghazal al-'udhri: dirasah fi al-hubb al-maqmu'*, Damascus: Manshurat ittihad al-kuttab al-'arab.
Al-Zahi, Farid (1999), *al-Jasad wa al-surah wa al-muqaddas fi al-Islam*, Casablanca: Afriqya al-sharq.

English language

Abu-Lughod, Lila (1986), *Veiled Sentiments: Honor and Poetry in a Bedouin Society*, Berkeley and Los Angeles: University of California Press.
Ali, Kecia (2016), *Sexual Ethics and Islam. Feminist Reflections on Qur'an, Hadith, and Jurisprudence*, 2nd edn, London: Oneworld Publications.
Allen, Roger, Kilpatrick, Hilary and Moor, Eduard de (1995), *Love and Sexuality in Modern Arabic Literature*, London: Saqi Books.

Arberry, Arthur John (1957), *The Seven Odes: The First Chapter of Arabic Literature*, London, George Allen and Unwin Ltd.

Ashtiany, Julia, Johnstone, Thomas M., Latham, J. Derek., Serjeant, Robert. B. and Smith, G. Rex (eds) (1990), *Abbasid Belles-Lettres*, Cambridge: Cambridge University Press.

Baba, Rahman (2005), *The Poetry of Rahman Baba: Poet of the Pukhtuns*, trans. Robert Sampson and Momin Khan, Peshawar: University Book Agency.

Bataille, Georges (1986), *Eroticism, Death and Sensuality*, trans. Nary Dalwood, San Francisco: City Lights Books.

Bausani, Alessandro (1991), '*Ghazal*' in *Encyclopaedia of Islam*, Vol. 2, No. 2, Leiden: Brill.

Beeston, Alfred F. L. (ed.) (1983), *Arabic Literature to the End of the Umayyad Period*, Cambridge: Cambridge University Press.

Behrens-Abouseif, Doris (1999), *Beauty in Arabic Culture*, Princeton, NJ: Markus Wiener.

Bell, Joseph N. (1979), *Love Theory in Later Hanbalite Islam*, New York: State University of New York Press.

Biesterfeldt, Hans H. and Gutas, Dimitri (1984), 'The Malady of Love', in *Journal of the American Oriental Society*, Vol. 104, No. 1, pp. 21–55.

Bloch, R. Howard (1991), *Medieval Misogyny and the Invention of Western Romantic Love*, Chicago: University of Chicago Press.

Boitani, Piero and Torti, Anna (1999), *The Body and the Soul in Medieval Literature*, Cambridge: D. S. Brewer.

Bouhdiba, Abdelwahhab (1985), *Sexuality in Islam*, trans. Alan Sheridan, London: Routledge and Kegan Paul.

Bürgel, Johann C. (1989), 'The Lady Gazelle and Her Murderous Glances', in *Journal of Arabic Literature*, Vol. 20, No. 1, pp. 1–11.

Bürgel, Johann C. (1979), 'Love, Lust, and Longing: Eroticism in Early Islam as Reflected in Literary Sources', in *Society and the Sexes in Medieval Islam*, ed. A. L. Sayyid-Marsot, California: Undena Publications.

Capellanus, Andreas (1941), *The Art of Courtly Love*, trans. John J. Parry, New York: Columbia University Press.

Dols, Michael (1992), *Majnun: the Madman in Medieval Islamic Society*, Oxford: Clarendon Press; New York: Oxford University Press.

Fisher, Sheila and Halley, Janet E. (eds) (1989), *Seeking the Woman in Late Medieval and Renaissance Writings: Essays in Feminist Contextual Criticism*, Knoxville: The University of Tennessee Press.

Foucault, Michel (1990), *The History of Sexuality*, trans. Robert Hurley, London: Penguin Books.
Freud, Sigmund (no date), *Beyond The Pleasure Principle*, London, The International Psycho-analytical Press.
Freud, Sigmund (1989), 'Creative Writers and Day Dreaming', in *20th Century Literary Criticism*, ed. David Lodge, London and New York: Longman, pp. 73–9.
Gibb, Hamilton A. R (1963), *Arabic Literature: An Introduction*, 2nd rev. edn, Oxford: Clarendon Press.
Giffen, Lois (1972), *Theory of Profane Love among the Arabs: The Development of the Genre*, New York: New York University Press; London: University of London Press.
Goldziher, Ignáz (1966), *Short History of Classical Arabic Literature*, Hildesheim: G. Olms.
Gould, Thomas (1963), *Platonic Love*, London: Routledge and Kegan Paul.
Grabar, Oleg and Robinson, Cynthia (eds) (2001), *Islamic Art and Literature*, Princeton, NJ: Markus Wiener Publishers.
Grunebaum, Gustave E. von (ed.) (1973), *Arabic Poetry Theory and Development*, Wiesbaden: Otto Harrassowitz
Hamori, Andras (1990), 'Love Poetry (*Ghazal*)', in Julia Ashtiany, Thomas M. Johnstone, J. Derek Latham, Robert B. Serjeant and G. Rex Smith (eds), *Abbasid Belles-Lettres*, Cambridge: Cambridge University Press.
Hamori, Andras (1974), *On the Art of Medieval Arabic Literature*, Princeton, NJ: Princeton University Press.
Hillenbrand, Robert (1982), 'La dolce vita in early Islamic Syria: the evidence of later Umayyad palaces', in *Art History*, Vol.5, No.1, pp. 1–35.
Houwen, Luuk A. J. R. (ed.) (1997), *Animals and the Symbolic in Mediaeval Art and Literature*, Groningen: Egbert Forsten.
Jacobi, Renate (2003), *Die Udhra: Liebe und Tod in der Umayyadenzeit*, workshop held at the Wissenschaftskolleg, Berlin, 1–2 July, www.wiko-berlin.de/index.php
Jacobi, Renate (2000), '"Udhri', in Peri J. Bearman, Thierry Bianquis et al. (eds), *Encyclopedia of Islam*, Vol. 10, Leiden: Brill.
Jacobi, Renate (1998), '"Udhri poetry' in *Encyclopedia of Arabic Literature*, London and New York: Routledge, pp. 790–4.
Jacobi, Renate (1996), 'Al-Khayalan – A Variation of the Khayal Motif', in *Journal of Arabic Literature*, Vol. 27, pp. 1–12.
Jacobi, Renate (1992), 'Theme and Variations in Umayyad Ghazal Poetry', in *Journal of Arabic Literature*, Vol. 23, No. 2, pp. 109–19.

Jacobi, Renate (1985), 'Time and Reality in Nasib and Ghazal', in *Journal of Arabic Literature*, Vol. 16, pp. 1–17.
James, Sharon L (2003), *Learned Girls and Male Persuasion: Gender and Reading in Roman Love Elegy*, Berkeley, CA; London: University of California Press.
Jayyusi, Salma Khadra (1983), 'Umayyad Poetry', in A. F. L. Beeston (ed.), *Arabic Literature to the End of the Umayyad Period*, Cambridge: Cambridge University Press.
Jones, Alan (1992), *Early Arabic Poetry, Vol. 2: Select Odes*, Oxford: Ithaca Press, Reading for the Board of the Faculty of Oriental Studies, Oxford University.
Katz, Marion (2002), *Body of Text: The Emergence of the Sunni Law of Ritual Purity*, Albany: State University of New York Press.
Khairallah, Asad (1980), *Love, Madness, and Poetry: An Interpretation of the Majnun Legend*, Beirut: Orient-Institut der Deutschen Morgenländischen Gesellschaft.
Khan, Ruqayya Y. (1997), 'Sexuality and Secrecy in the Medieval Arabic Romance of Majnun Layla' (unpublished PhD, Department of Asian and Middle Eastern Studies, The University of Pennsylvania).
Khan, Ruqayya Yasmine (2019), *Bedouin and 'Abbasid Cultural Identities: The Arabic Majnun Layla Story (Culture and Civilisation in the Middle East)*, New York: Routledge.
Khuri, Fuad I. (2001), *The Body in Islamic Culture*, London: Saqi Books.
Kilpatrick, Hilary (2003), *Making the Great Book of Songs. Compilation and the Author's Craft in Abu al-Faraj al-Isbahani's Kitāb al-aghānī*, London: Routledge.
Kinany, Ahmad K. (1951), *The Development of Ghazal in Arabic Literature (Pre-Islamic and Early Islamic Periods)*, Damascus: Syrian University Press.
Kugle, Scott A. (2006), *Sexuality, Diversity and Ethics in the Agenda of Progressive Muslims*, http://www.geocities.com/vidyak1/scottkugledoc.pdf, 5 March.
Law, Jane Marie (ed.) (1995), *Religious Reflections on the Human Body*, Bloomington and Indianapolis: Indiana University Press.
Lecker, Michael (2005), *People, Tribes, and Society in Arabia around the Time of Muhammad*, Aldershot: Ashgate.
Lentz, Thomas W. and Lowry, Glenn D. (1989), *Timur and the Princely Vision: Persian Art and Culture in the Fifteenth Century*, Los Angeles: LA County Museum of Art.
Lewis, Clive S. (1973), *The Allegory of Love. A Study In Medieval Tradition*, Oxford: Oxford University Press, pp. 2–3.

Lodge, David (ed.) (1989), *20th Century Literary Criticism*, London and New York: Longman.

Lomperisem, Linda and Stanbury, Sarah (eds) (1994), *Feminist Approaches to the Body in Medieval Literature*, Philadelphia: University of Pennsylvania Press.

Lyall, Charles J. (1918), *The Mufaḍḍaliyat: Vols 1–2. An Anthology of Ancient Arabian Odes Compiled by al-Mufaḍḍal, son of Muhammad; according to the recension and with the commentary of Abu Muhammad al-Qasim b. Muhammad al-Anbari*, Oxford: Clarendon Press.

Maghen, Ze'ev (2005), *Virtues of the Flesh – Passion and Purity in Early Islamic Jurisprudence*, Leiden: Brill.

Malti-Douglas, Fedwa (1991), *Woman's Body, Woman's Word: Gender and Discourse in Arabo-Islamic Writing*, Princeton, NJ: Princeton University Press.

Manzalaoui, Mahmoud (1986), 'Swooning Lovers: a Theme in Arab and European Romance', in *Comparative Criticism*, Vol. 8, pp. 71–90.

Manzalaoui, Mahmoud (1979), 'Tragic Ends of Lovers: Medieval Islam and the Latin West', in *Comparative Criticism*, Vol. 1, pp. 37–52.

Massad, Joseph A. (2007), *Desiring Arabs*, Chicago: The University of Chicago Press.

Meisami, Julie S. and Starkey, Paul (eds) (1998), *Encyclopedia of Arabic Literature*, Vol. 2, London: Routledge.

Menocal, Maria R. (1994), *Shards of Love: Exile and the Origins of the Lyric*, Durham, NC and London: Duke University Press.

Miquel, André (1998), *Majnun Layla wa Tristan*, trans. Ghassan al-Sayyid, Damascus: Dar al-awa'il.

Paxson James J. and Gravlee, Cynthia A. (eds) (1998), *Desiring Discourse. The Literature of Love, Ovid through Chaucer*, Selinsgrove: Susquehanna University Press.

Pellat, Charles (1969), *The Life and Works of Jahiz*, trans. David M. Hawke, London: Routledge and Kegan Paul.

Pinder-Wilson, Ralph H. (1958), *Persian Painting of the Fifteenth Century*, London: The Faber Gallery of Oriental Art.

Poplawski, Paul (ed.) (2001), *Writing the Body in D. H. Lawrence: Essays on Language, Representation, and Sexuality*, London: Greenwood Press.

Raven, Wim (1980), 'Ibn Dawud al-Isbahani and Greek Wisdom', in *Union Européenne des Arabisants et Islamisants: 10th Congress, Edinburgh, 9–16 September: Proceedings*, ed. Robert Hillenbrand, pp. 66–9.

Robinson, Cynthia (2001), 'The Love, His Lady, Her Lady, and a Thirteenth-Century Celestina: A Recipe for Love Sickness from al-Andalus', in Oleg Grabar and Cynthia Robinson (eds), *Islamic Art and Literature*, Princeton, NJ: Markus Wiener Publishers.

S., Kamal (2006), *Islam and Sacred Sexuality*, www.gaia.web.org.waia-wicca. 16 April.

Sawa, George D (1985), 'The Status and Roles of the Secular Musicians in the Kitāb al-Aghānī (Book of Songs) of Abu al-Faraj al-Iṣbahānī', *Asian Music*, Vol. 17, No. 1, pp. 69–82.

Al-Sayyid-Marsot, Afaf Lutfi (ed.) (1977), *Society and the Sexes in Medieval Islam*, Malibu, CA: Undena Publications.

Sells, Michael A. (1994), 'Guises of the *Ghul* Dissembling Simile and Semantic Overflow in the Classical Arabic *Nasib*', in ed. Suzanne P. Stetkevych, *Reorientations: Arabic and Persian Poetry*, Bloomington: Indiana University Press.

Seybold, John (1994), 'The Earliest Demon Lover: The *Tayf al-Khayl* in *al-Mufaddaliyat*', in S. Stetkevych, *Reorientations: Arabic and Persian Poetry*, ed. Suzzane Stetkevych, Indiana: Indiana University Press.

Seyed-Gohrab, Asghar A. (2010), 'Leyli o Majnun', in *Encyclopædia Iranica*, http://www.iranica.com/articles/leyli-o-majnun-narrative-poem, 21 April.

Shakespeare, William (1975), *Othello*, Oxford: Clarendon Press.

Shoaf, R. Allen (1992), *Chaucer's Troilus and Criseyde: Essays in Criticism*, New York: Medieval and Renaissance Texts and Studies.

Smith, W. Robertson (1885), *Kinship and Marriage in Early Arabia*, Cambridge: Cambridge University Press.

Spentzou, Efrossini and Fowler, Don (eds) (2002), *Cultivating the Muse: Struggles for Power and Inspiration in Classical Literature*, Oxford: Oxford University Press.

Stchoukine, Ivan (1954), *Les peintures des manuscrits timurides*, Paris: Paul Geuthner.

Stetkevych, Jaroslav (1993), *The Zephyrs of Najd: the Poetics of Nostalgia in the Classical Arabic Nasib*, Chicago and London: University of Chicago Press.

Stetkevych, Suzanne P. (ed.) (1994), *Reorientations: Arabic and Persian Poetry*, Bloomington: Indiana University Press.

Stetkevych, Suzanne P. (1993), *The Mute Immortals Speak: Pre-Islamic Poetry and Poetics of Ritual*, Ithaca: Cornell University Press.

Stewart, Devin (2008), *Emory Resources on the Middle East*, www.mesas.emory.edu/gmesc/pdf/10_Love_Theory_Unit_All.pdf, 3 June.

Tinkle, Theresa (1996), *Medieval Venuses and Cupids: Sexuality, Hermeneutics, and English Poetry*, Stanford: Stanford University Press.

Tuetey, Charles G. (1977), *Imrulkais of Kinda, Poet (The Poems-the Life-the Background)*, London: Diploma Press.

Van Gelder, Geert (2000), *Of Dishes and Discourse: Classical Arabic Literary Representations of Food*, Richmond: Curzon Press.

Walther, Wiebke (2006), *Women In Islam*, trans. C. S. V. Salt, Princeton, NJ: Markus Wiener Publishers.

Wright, Elizabeth (1984), *Psychoanalytic Criticism: Theory in Practice*, London and New York: Methuen.

Wright, J. W. and Rowson, Everett K. (eds) (1997), *Homoeroticism in Classical Arabic Literature*, New York: Columbia University Press.

Zeitlin, Froma I. (1996), *Playing the Other: Gender and Society in Classical Greek Literature*, Chicago: University of Chicago Press.

Zolondek, Leon (1960), 'An Approach to the Problem of the Sources of the *Kitab al-Aghani*', in *Journal of Near Eastern Studies*, Vol. 19, No. 3, pp. 217–34.

Zwettler, Michael (1978), *The Oral Tradition of Classical Arabic Poetry*, Columbus: Ohio State University Press.

Index

Abbasid period, 7, 10–11, 15–16, 36–8, 45–6, 216
'Abd al-Karim, Khalil, *Al-'Arab wa al-marah hafriyyah fi al-istir al-mukhayim (The Arab Concept of Women)*, 104–6
Al-'Abd, Tarafah, *mu'allaqah*, 92
'Abdallah, Muhammad Hasan, 51
al-hubb fi al-turath al-'Arabi, 21–2
'Ablah, 90, 181
absence of the object of desire, 51, 141–51, 169–75
Abu Nuwas, al-Hasan b. Hani, 45, 146
Abu Tammam, Habib b. Aws al-Ta'i, 145
Abu'l-Qasim al-Hasan al-Naysaburi, *'Uqala' al-majanin' (The Wise Fool)*, 222–3n
Abu-Lughod, Lila, 167, 184n
adab, 57–8, 128–9, 205
Adam and Eve, 79–80n
adultery, 48, 64–5, 82n
adventurous love, 12, 34–5
'Afra', 96–7, 101, 147, 199–200, 202–3, 211, 212
Al-Ahnaf, 'Abbas b., 3, 36, 42, 213, 215, 216, 220–1n
Al-'Ajjaj b. Ru'bah, 161n
akhbar (historical anecdotes), 38, 40, 46
Ali, Kecia, 64
Al-Amidi, *al-Muwazanah bayna al-ta'yyan*, 41
'Amr b. Hijr, 87–8
Andalusians, 214–15, 225n
Al-Antaki, Daud
Tazyin al-aswaq, 7, 214
'Antarah, 180–1
Al-'Aqqad, 'Abbas Mahmud, 19, 110, 171
Aristotle, *Poetics*, 41
Al-'Askari, al-Hasan, *al-Sina'atayn (The Two Industries)*, 42
Al-Asma'i, 158n, 205
'Atiyah, Jarir, 133, 143
Avesta, 45
'Ayshah b. Talhah, 220n

Al-'Azm, Sadiq Jalal, 172
Fi al-hubb wa al-hubb al-'udhri, 17
'Azzah
absence of the object of desire, 170
compared to the sun, 92
desire for possession of, 168–9
ethereal nature of beauty, 117
face of, 96
form of, 101
heroic gesture, 182
Kuthayyir's devotion to, 53n
phantom presence of, 142
residence of, 146, 149

Bakkar, Yusuf Husayn, 18
Banu 'Amir tribe, 2, 12
Basrah, 45
Bataille, Georges, 178, 197, 219n
Erotism: Death and Sensuality, 21
Al-Batal, 'Ali, 4, 9–10, 93, 106–7
Bayad wa Riyad, 214–15, 225n
beauty
ethereal nature of, 110–18
female, 86–91
Bedouin tribes
Abu-Lughod, 184n
Arabic language, 105–6
children, 167
and courtly love, 70
Husayn, Taha, 16
and Islam, 20, 208
Jamil and chaste love, 14, 17–18, 171–2
madness, 205
marriage, 185n
and Platonic love, 77
rise of 'udhri poetry, 8–11
speech, 135
women and publicity, 72
Bellamy, James A., 61, 80–1n
beloved
body of the, 85–126

face of the, 96–9
form of the, 100–2
glow of the, 91–3, 96
one ideal, 164, 165–7
presence in nature of the, 151–5
presence and absence of the, 127–63
residence of the, 146–51
scent of the, 100
Berbers, 214–15
Biesterfeldt, Hans H., 194
birds, 69, 115–16, 152
  crows, 196, 219n
  doves, 95, 140, 152, 162–3n, 196
Bloch, R. Howard, 167–8
blood, 74–6, 193–7, 219n
Bonaparte, Marie, 168
bondage metaphor, 176–7
Bouhdiba, Abdelwahhab, 30–1n, 60, 140
  Sexuality in Islam, 20–1, 62–3
Bouncompagno da Signa, 157n
Burd, Bashshar, 45, 136, 140
Bürgel, Johann C., 6, 37, 50, 96, 133–4
  'Love, Lust, and Longing', 18
Buthaynah
  absence of the object of desire, 171–2
  authenticity of, 14
  beautiful, 48
  chastity, 67–8, 70
  complained about, 175–7, 179–80
  corpulent female body, 104
  ethereal nature of beauty, 111–12, 114–15, 117–18
  face of, 96–8
  faithfulness, 35
  fire, 197
  form of, 100
  gazelles, 94
  glances, 131
  glow of, 93
  inuendoes, 18
  malady and wasting away, 201–2
  marriage, 75
  phantom presence of, 144
  physicality, 47, 49–50
  poet's imagination, 110
  presence in nature, 153
  speech, 135–40
  ugliness, 48

camels
  corpulent female body, 104–6
  fainting, 136
  gazelles and, 153
  glances, 130
  and lovers, 22
  malady and wasting away, 198–200

residence of the beloved, 148
scent of the beloved, 100
celibacy, 61–2, 78–9n, 80–1n, 183n
chastity (*'iffah*)
  Bedouins, 16, 33–7
  Bedouins and Islam, 17–18, 64–73
  definitions, 78–9n
  ghazals, 37
  and physicality, 46–52
  and sensuality, 56–84
  speech, 139
  and *'udhri* love, 15
children, 71, 78, 116, 152, 166–7, 184n, 228
complaining, 175–80
corpulent female body, 104–8
'courtly love', 3, 38, 42–3, 70, 75, 83n, 225n
crying, 7, 90, 175–6, 195–8

Al-Dahhak, al-Husayn b., 45, 145
Dayf, Shawqi, 8, 45, 46
death, 208–15
  chastity (*'iffah*) and, 71
  desire leads to, 36, 189, 194
  destiny, 116–17
  eroticism and, 21, 197
  glances, 130, 132
  Khan, 22
  malady and wasting away, 199–200, 202–3
  marriage and, 74
  martyr of love, 223n
  one ideal beloved, 165–6
  poets and, 160n, 224n
  speech, 137
  tortured love and, 43
  'udhri poetry, 2–6
  wish, 26n
  see also fatal love
desert
  Abu-Lughod, 184n
  Bedouin tribes and Islam, 17–18
  gazelles, 95
  Husayn, Taha, 16
  and madness, 153–5, 157n, 172–3, 206–8
  Majnun and, 182, 188n, 204
  'udhri love, 77
  'udhri poetry, 2–3, 5, 8–10
desire
  absence of the object of, 169–75
  adab, 128
  beauty and, 48
  chastity (*'iffah*) and, 16, 18, 51–2, 56, 70–2, 226
  complaining, 175–9
  crying, 198
  fainting, 137
  glances, 131–2, 158n
  heroic gesture, 182

desire (cont.)
    Islam and, 58, 64–6
    literary creativity and, 17, 184n
    love as malady in, 190, 192, 201
    madness, 36
    marriage, 73
    one ideal beloved, 35
    phantom presence of the beloved, 144–6
    physicality, 46–7, 53n
    poets and, 67–9, 185n, 227–8
    for possession, 167–9
    Qur'an, 21
    residence of the beloved, 147, 150–1
    secrecy, 20
    sexuality, 61
    speech, 138–9
    'udhri love, 8
    see also longing
Al-Din 'Attar, Farid, 85
divorce, 10, 60, 166, 184n
Dols, Michael, 11, 27n, 154, 206, 207–8
    Majnun: The Madman in the Medieval Islamic World, 19
Don Juan, 172
du'a', 176, 194
Al-Dughli, Muhammad Sa'id, 95

Egyptian literature, 190
eyes
    anecdotes, 48
    beauty and, 230
    'Chinese' eyes, 103
    complaining, 175–6
    corpulent female body, 104
    crying, 195–8
    fainting, 203
    female beauty, 87–95
    glances, 128–34
    Ibn al-Jawzi, 157n
    malady and wasting away, 191
    one ideal beloved, 165
    poets and, 109–12
    Qur'an, 63, 65
    residence of the beloved, 147
    see also glances

fainting, 136–7, 202–5
    lover's body, 231
    Majnun, plate 1, 103
    Sufis, 45, 221n
    tragedy, 209
faithfulness
    chastity ('iffah), 56–7
    doves, 162n
    Jamil, 35–6
    'udhri love, 4, 6, 8

fatal love, 3, 4, 6, 165, 176, 178; *see also* death; martyr of love
Faysal, Shukri, 8–9, 82n
female singers (*al-qiyan*), 42, 45, 181
fire, 22, 77–8, 144, 172, 196–8, 216
French romances, 174
Freud, Sigmund, 168–9, 184n
    'Creative Writers and Day Dreaming', 21
fuqaha (scholars of religious sciences), 37, 57–8, 62, 71

gazelles, 93–6, 121n
    Layla, 151–5
    Majnun, 222n
    murderous glance of, 133–4
    phantom presence of the beloved, 145
    and slave girls, 161n
    'Umar, 120–1n
gestures, 24, 127–8, 131, 134, 147, 156, 157n
Al-Ghazali, Abu Hamid Muhammad b. Ahmad, 81n, 85, 155
ghazals
    beloved's body, 91–2
    definition, 25n
    face of the beloved, 98
    glances, 132
    malady and wasting away, 202, 216
    poets and, 170
    roots, 33
    Sufis, 44–5
    vs. 'udhri ghazal, 33–7
    Umayyad period, 16, 32–3, 90–1, 181
Gibb, Hamilton A. R., *Arabic Literature: An Introduction*, 15
Giffen, Lois Anita, 192, 210, 218n, 223n
    Theory of Profane Love Among the Arabs: The Development of the Genre, 22
glances, 128–34, 231
    chastity ('iffah) and, 66
    evil, 61
    fainting, 203
    Jamil, 27n, 47
    murderous, 133–4
    sensuality in Paradise, 63
    stolen, 83n
Gould, Thomas, 77
Greeks, 77, 190, 193, 215
Grunebaum, Gustave E. von, 77
Gutas, Dimitri, 194

Haddad, Qasim, *Akhbar Majnun Layla*, 11
Al-Hafi, Bishr, 81n
Hamori, Andras, 13, 112, 177, 180, 181
    Abbasid Belles-Lettres, 15–16
Al-Harith b. Khalid, 37
Hatum, 'Afif, 14, 30n

al-Ghazal fi al-'asr al-umawi [The *Ghazal* in the Umayyad Period], 17–18
hawa (desire) *see* desire
Heine, Heinrich, *Der Asra*, 11
heroic gesture, 6, 180–2, 183
Hijaz desert, 9–10, 15–16, 32, 34
Hilal, Muhammad Ghunaymi, 33, 34, 45, 70
   Al-hayah al-'atifiyyah bayn al-'udhriyyah wa al-sufiyyah, 12
Hillenbrand, Robert, 123n
homosexuality, 45
houris, 5, 21, 63, 66
Husayn, Taha, 8, 14, 33, 203–4
   Hadith al-arbi'a, 12, 16
husbands
   'Ayshah b. Talhah, 220n
   death, 212
   desire for possession, 167
   fainting, 204
   gestures, 157n
   marriage, 74–6, 78, 83n
   physicality, 49
   portrayal of Layla in Persian book painting, 103
   Qur'an, 60, 65–6
   speech, 135
   'udhri poets, 4
   ugly, 172

Ibn 'Abbas, 212
Ibn al-Jawzi, 'Abd al-Rahman b. 'Ali, 129–30, 205
   Dhamm al-hawa, 210
Ibn al-Jazzar, 190
Ibn al-Muqaffa, *Kalilah wa dimnah*, 41
Ibn al-Nafis, 85
Ibn 'Arabi, Muhammad b. 'Ali, 136, 137, 155, 174
Ibn Daud, Abu Bakr Muhammad, 215, 218n
   Kitab al-zahrah, 7, 42, 97, 128–9, 192, 198, 201, 210
Ibn Hazm, 'Ali b. Ahmad al-Andalusi, *Tawq al-Hamamah (The Ring of the Dove)*, 214
Ibn Hazm, 'Ali b. Ahmad al-Andalusi, 53n, 178–9, 180
   Tawq al-Hamamah (The Ring of the Dove), 72, 83n, 128–9, 138–9, 223n
Ibn Qayyim al-Jawziyyah, 51, 112, 128, 205
   Rawdat al-muhibbin, 7, 71–2, 156–7n
Ibn Qutaybah, 'Abdallah b. Muslim
   al-Shi'r wa al-shu'ara, 7, 37, 41, 47–8, 53n
   Jamil and Kuthayyir, 14
   Majnun, 27n, 137–8, 204, 205–6
   'udhri ghazal, 38
   'udhri poetry, 109
   'Uyun al-akhbar, 135–6, 136–7
Ibn Sina, 71, 217n

Al-Qanun, 190–1
Treatise on Love, 194
ideal woman, 3, 5–6, 110, 165
'iffah (chastity) *see* chastity
Indian aceticism, 46
inuendoes, 18
'Isam, 87–8
Al-Isfahani, Abu al-Faraj 'Ali b. al-Husayn
   husbands, 75–6
   libertinism, 55n
   Majnun's gaze, 129
   women and adventurous love, 34–5
   Kitab al-Aghani ('The Book of Songs'), 35; anticipation, 170; desire for possession, 168–9; fainting, 202–3; fire, 198; Kuthayyir, 25n; Majnun's authenticity, 12; Majnun's madness, 177, 206; malady and wasting away, 199; moral and ethical issues, 45–6; physicality, 46–7; poetic fragments, 7; storytellers (*ruwah*), 14; *'udhri ghazal*, 38–9
'ishq, 22, 71, 189, 190–4, 205, 217n
Islam
   'devout hero', 181
   ethics, 34
   Majnun, 207–8
   monotheism, 36, 58–9
   Muslim ascetic, 179
   promiscuity forbidden by, 17–18
   and rise of 'Udhri poetry, 8–9
   sexuality and, 20–1, 60–4
   shari'ah doctrine, 65
   tragedy, 223n
'Issa, Ibrahim, *al-Jins wa 'ulama al-Islam*, 62

Jacob (prophet), 203
Jacobi, Renate
   beloved's presence in nature, 151
   blamer (*'athil*), 6
   death, 214
   Encyclopedia of Arabic Literature, 15
   fatal love, 5–6
   ghazals, 32–3
   khayal, 141–2, 145
   'udhri love, 66–7, 77
Jadidi, al-Tahir Labib, 8, 36
   Susyulujiya al-ghazal al-'Arabi: al-shi'r al-'udhri namudhajan, 18
Al-Jahiz, Abu 'Uthman 'Amr b. Bahr
   al-majdulah, 107–8
   Al-maqamat, 41
   Bedouin tribes, 16
   female singers (*al-qiyan*), 45
   glances, 128
   Kitab al-Nisa, 108
   Kitab al-qiyan, 42
   Majnun's authenticity, 12

Al-Jahiz, Abu 'Uthman 'Amr b. Bahr (*cont.*)
  malady and wasting away, 191–2
  Risalat al-Qiyan, 72
  speech, 135
Jamil
  absence of the object of desire, 171–2
  anecdotes, 14
  beauty, 48
  beloved's presence in nature, 153
  chastity ('*iffah*), 67–8, 70
  complaining, 175–7, 179–80
  corpulent female body, 104
  crying, 195
  Diwan, 35, 116–17
  ethereal nature of beauty, 111–12, 114–15, 117–18
  eyes, 110
  face of the beloved, 97–8
  faithfulness, 35–6
  fire, 197
  form of the beloved, 100–2
  gazelles, 94
  glances, 131
  glow of the beloved, 93
  inuendoes, 18
  Layli and Majnun, 11
  literary creativity, 19
  madness, 206–7
  malady and wasting away, 201, 202
  marriage, 75
  martyr of love, 9, 210–11, 213
  phantom presence of the beloved, 141, 143–4
  physicality, 47, 50
  pre-Islamic poets, 33
  residence of the beloved, 148
  scent of the beloved, 100
  speech, 134–40
  '*udhri* poets, 2–3, 27n, 30n
  wealth, 10
Al-Jawari, Ahmad 'Abd al-Sattar, 12–13, 77
  al-Hubb al-'udhri nash'atuhu wa tatawwurhu [*'Udhri* Love: Its Origin and Progression], 16–17
Jayyusi, Salma Khadra, 4, 7, 10, 11, 186–7n
Joseph (prophet), 65, 70, 190
Al-Junayd, 155
Al-Jurjani, 'Ali, *al-Wasatah bayna al-Mutanabbi wa khusumuh (Meditation between al-Mutanabbi and his opponents)*, 41

Khairallah, As'ad E.
  authenticity, 13
  desire for possession, 169
  fainting, 221n
  Jamil, 175

Love, Madness and Poetry: An Interpretation of the Majnun Legend, 19
  madness, 207–8, 222n
  Majnun, 27n, 154
  poetry and psychology, 182
  Sufis, 186n
Khan, Ruqayya Yasmine
  deferral of union, 173–4, 182
  eyes, 131–2
  fire, 198
  gazelles, 95, 222n
  madness, 206
  Majnun, 162n
  Majnun and Islam, 207–8
  marriage, 75
  Najd, 150–1
  poets as lovers, 170–1
  Sexuality and Secrecy in the Medieval Arabic Romance of Majnun Layla, 20, 25n
  speech, 136, 138
  women and publicity, 72
Al-Khara'iti, Abu Bakr, *I'tilal al-qulub (The Malady of Hearts)*, 192
khayal, 141–6, 161n
Khuri, Fuad I., *The Body in Islamic Culture*, 79–80n
Kilpatrick, Hilary, 39
Kinany, Ahmad K., 6, 7, 8, 77, 109, 116, 179
Kratchkovsky, I. Y., 12
Krueger, Roberta L., 174
Kugle, Scott A., 'Sexuality, Diversity and Ethics in the Agenda of Progressive Muslims', 63
Kuthayyir 'Azzah, Kuthayyir b. 'Abd al-Rahman
  absence of the object of desire, 170
  anecdotes, 14, 53n
  complaining, 178
  crying, 195
  ethereal nature of beauty, 115–17
  face of the beloved, 96, 99
  form of the beloved, 100–2
  gazelle, 94–5
  phantom presence of the beloved, 142
  poets as lovers, 168–9
  residence of the beloved, 146, 147, 149
  scent of the beloved, 134
  speech, 131, 140
  sun and moon, 92
  '*udhri* poets, 3, 10, 25n

Layla
  authenticity, 12
  complaining about, 177–8
  crying, 196
  death, plate 3
  desire for possession of, 167–8, 173–4

ethereal nature of beauty, 112–14
face of, 96, 99
fainting, plate 1, 203–4
gazelles, 94, 96
glances, 129–32
heroic gesture, 181–2
Khamsa (Qunitet), plate 3, plate 5
longing, 68–70
madness, 206, 208
malady and wasting away, 201–2
marriage, 74–5, 83n
Najd, 149–50
in Persian book painting, 102–4
phantom presence of, 144–5
physicality, 48–9
poetry, 171
presence in nature, 151–5
residence of, 148
secrecy, 19–20
Shiraz minature painting, 123n
speech, 137–8
Sufis, 11
sun and moon, 92–3
Lewis, Clive S., 75, 83n
libertinism, 45–6, 227
Lisan al-'Arab, 79n, 189
Loewe, Carl, *Der Asra*, 11
longing,
   desire for possession, 167–8, 228
   ethereal nature of beauty, 116–17
   ghazals, 43
   glances, 128
   houris, 66
   madness, 208
   malady and wasting away, 189
   phantom presence of the beloved, 143–8
   poets and, 90
   beloved's presence in nature, 152
   Qays and Lubna, 76
   Salamah, Raja, 22
   'udhri love, 26n
   'udhri poetry, 67–9
   see also desire
lover's body, 189–225
Lubna
   death, 211
   divorce, 10
   ethereal nature of beauty, 111
   fire, 197
   form of, 101
   glances, 133
   husbands, 75–6
   longing, 69–70
   malady and wasting away, 201
   marriage, 78, 166–7
   phantom presence of, 142

Al-Madini, Zuhayr, 192
madness, 205–8
   desire leads to, 36
   fatal love, 177
   glances, 129–30
   Ibn 'Arabi, 155
   Khairallah, 222–3n, 222n
   Majnun, 19
   malady and wasting away, 192–4
   poetry and psychology, 182
   'udhri love, 5, 172–3, 189
   and wisdom, 221n
Maghen, Ze'ev, 57–8, 66, 79n, 85
al-Mahdi, Caliph, 45
Maimonides, Moses, *The Travels of Sir John Mandeville*, 81n
al-majdulah, 107–8
Majnun
   Abbasid period, 10–11
   anecdotes, 28n, 41
   authenticity of, 12, 27n
   beloved's presence in nature, 151–5
   compared with Tristan, 19
   crying, 195–8
   death, plate 3, 212–14
   desire for possession, 167–8, 171
   ethereal nature of beauty, 112–14, 162n
   fainting, plate 1, 203–4
   fatal love, 177–8
   form of the beloved, 100–1
   gazelles, 94–6
   glances, 129–32, 134
   glow of the beloved, 91–3
   heroic gesture, 181–2
   Islam, 9
   Khamsa (Qunitet), plate 2, plate 3, plate 4
   love and death, 6
   madness, 19, 36, 205–8, 222n
   malady and wasting away, 200–2
   marriage, 73–5, 83n
   phantom presence of the beloved, 141, 144–5
   physicality, 48–9
   portrayal of Layla in Persian book painting, 102–4
   and Qays, 188n
   residence of the beloved, 147–51
   scent of the beloved, 100
   secrecy, 20
   sensuality, 68–70
   Shiraz minature painting, 123n
   speech, 137–40
   Sufis, 44–5, 173–4, 186n
   'udhri poets, 2–3
   wine, 98–9
malady and wasting away, 198–202
   in classical Arabic literature, 190–4

malady and wasting away (cont.)
   death, 212
   Majnun, 178–9
   martyr of love, 213
   medical case, 215–16
   thinness, 220–1n
   tragedy, 209
Al-Malik b. Marqwan, Caliph 'Abd, 110, 117
Manzalaouni, Mahmoud, 137, 204–5, 205, 210, 221n
   'Swooning Lovers: a Theme in Arab and European Romance', 20
   'Tragic Ends of Lovers: Medieval Islam and the Latin West', 20
marriage, 73–6
   Islam, 56–7, 64–5, 78, 228, 232
   Jamil and Buthaynah, 35
   Jayyusi, 183n
   Khan, 20
   Layla, 83n, 182
   nikah (marriage), 60–2
   Qays and Lubna, 166
   Qur'an, 80n
   sexuality, 60–2
   Sufis, 81n
   'udhri love, 172–3, 187n
   'udhri poets, 4, 183
   zanadiqah (approved sibling marriage) movement, 45
martyr of love
   death, 208–15
   Giffen, 22
   Islam, 9
   Jamil, 30n
   Kitab al-wadih al-mubin fi dhikr man istushhida min al-muhbin, 43
   Majnun, 11, 36
   speech, 134–5
   Tawq al-Hamamah (The Ring of the Dove), 223n
   'udhri love, 3
   'udhri poets, 1, 6–7, 33
   see also death; fatal love
al-Marzubani, Muhammad, *Kitab al-riyad*, 192
Massad, Joseph A., *Desiring Arabs*, 21
Massignon, Louis, *Encyclopedia of Islam*, 77
medical literature, 190–4, 200–1, 215–16, 217n
Miquel, André, 19, 151
moral and ethical issues, 23, 40, 45–6, 227
Mother Goddess, 106–7, 118, 229
Mughultay, *Kitab al-wadih al-mubin fi dhikr man istushhida min al-muhbin*, 43, 209–10
Al-Muraqqish al-Akbar, 33, 160n
Al-Muraqqish al-Asghar, 98
Al-Mutanabbi, Abu al-Tayyib Ahmad b. al-Husayn, 132–3
mythology, 14, 91, 93, 95–6, 215, 229

Najd, 149–51, 162n, 204
Najm, Khristu, 49
nasib, 32–3, 89–90, 146
Al-Nass, Ihsan, *al-Ghazal fi 'asr bani Umayyah* [The *Ghazal* in the Era of the Umayyad Dynasty], 16
Nawfal, 74, 83n
Nizami
   Khamsa (Qunitet), plate 1, plate 2, plate 3, plate 4, plate 5, 44, 102–4, 123n
   Layli and Majnun, 11, 174–5
Al-Numayri, Abu Hayyah, 137
Al-Nuwayri, Shihab al-Din Ahmad b. 'Abd al-Wahhab, 162n
Nihayat al-arab, 7

One Thousand and One Nights, 137, 205, 221n
oral tradition, 12–13
Ovid, 218n

painting and sculpture, women described as, 123n
Paradise
   chastity, 80n
   hur al'ayn, 113
   longing, 69
   Maimonides, 81n
   sensuality in, 20–1, 30–1n, 62–3, 86
Parry, John Jay, *The Art of Courtly Love*, 218n
pearls, 59, 63, 87, 135, 136
Persian book painting, portrayal of Layla in, 102–4
Persian poetry, 41, 44–5, 174–5
phantom presence of the beloved, 127, 141–6, 156, 160n, 174, 200, 231
physicality, 16–17, 68, 226–7
   in the *'udhri* tradition, 46–52
Platonic love, 76–8
poets as lovers, 169–75, 184–5n, 224n
presence of the beloved, 51, 85, 127–41, 230–1
'profligacy movement' (*mujun*), 45–6

qasidah, 90, 104, 141, 146–7, 218n
Al-Qayrawani, Ibn Rashiq, *al-'Umdah fi sina'at al-shi'r wa naqdih (The Pillar in the Creation and Criticism of Poetry)*, 42
Qays, A'sha, *ghazals*, 125n
Al-Qays, Imru'
   face of the beloved, 97
   form of the beloved, 102
   gazelles, 94
   glances, 133
   glow of the beloved, 91–2
   Mu'allaqah, 89
   women as symbols of desire, 35
Qays Lubna, Qays b. Dharih
   beloved's presence in nature, 153–4

complaining and embracing, 176–7
desire for possession, 167
divorce, 184n
eyes, 94
form of the beloved, 101
glances, 133
husbands, 75–6
longing, 69–70
and Majnun, 188n
malady and wasting away, 179, 201
marriage, 78, 166
martyr of love, 211
phantom presence of the beloved, 142
residence of the beloved, 148–9
suicide, 214
sun and moon, 111
'udhri love poets, 3, 33, 37
water, 197, 219n
wealth, 10
Qudamah b. Ja'far, *Naqd al-shi'r (Criticism of Poetry)*, 41
Al-Qitt, 'Abd al-Qadir, 12, 28n
Qur'an
  Bedouin tribes, 9
  body in, 57–64, 79–80n, 85–6
  chastity (*'iffah*), 64–6
  crows, 219n
  fainting, 203
  glances, 128
  houris, 5
  love as malady, 190
  sexuality, 20–1
  Sura 36, 202
  water, 98–9
Quraysh tribe, 38
Al-Quss, 37
Al-Qutami, 'Umayr b. Shaym, 137

Raven, Wim, 215
Al-Razi, 217n
reciters (*al-rawah*), 12, 13, 14
Robinson, Cynthia, 225n
Al-Rummah, Dhu, 3, 10, 164

Al-Safadi, Khalil b. Aybak, *Sharh lamiyyat al-'Ajam*, 132–3
Sahih al-Bukhari, 65–6
Salamah, Raja, 37, 219n
  al-'Ishq wa'l-kitabah: qira'h fi al-mawruth, 22
Al-Sarraj, Ja'far b. Ahmad, 202
  Masari' al-'ushshaq (Death of the Passionate Lovers), 7, 43, 202, 208–9
secrecy, 19, 20, 25n, 150–1
Sells, Michael A., 95
sensuality
  absence of the object of desire, 170–1, 228
  and chastity, 56–84
  classical Arabic literature, 22
  corpulent female body, 104
  ethereal nature of beauty, 112, 230
  in Paradise, 20–1, 30–1n, 62–3, 86
  physicality, 46–52
  sensual urban (*sarih*), 33–7
  '*udhri* poetry, 16–18, 50–2
sexuality, 56–84
  female beauty, 86
  Paradise, 80n
  positive perspectives on, 60–4
  studies, 16–17, 20–1, 25n
Seybold, John, 143–4
Al-Shak'ah, Mustafa, *Rihlat alshi'r min al-umawiyyah ila al 'Abbasiyyah* [Poetry from the Umayyad Era to the Abbasid Era], 17–18
Shakespeare, William, 205
  Othello, 106
Al-Sharif al-Murtada, *tayf al-khayal*, 144–5
Shawqi, Ahmad, *Majnun Layla*, 11, 83n
Al-Shibli, Kamil Mustafa, 155
Shurayk b. 'Abdullah, 194
soul (*nafs*)
  beloved's presence in nature, 153
  body and, 85
  crying, 196
  glances, 129
  Ibn Hazm, 53n
  immortality of, 117
  Islam, 8
  madness, 205
  malady and wasting away, 190–3
  Najd, 150
  Sufis, 103
speech, 134–41, 156
  Buthaynah, 159n, 176
  ethereal nature of beauty, 111–12
  glances, 130–4, 231
  Jamil, 180
  Majnun, 206
  marriage, 75
  presence of the beloved, 127
  Qur'an, 59
  residence of the beloved, 147
Stanbury, Sarah, 155, 158n
Stendhal, *De l'amour*, 11
Stetkevych, Suzanne P., 14, 146, 150
storytellers (*ruwah*), 14, 51–2, 227
Sufis
  body, 85–6
  celibacy, 81n
  fainting, 221n
  Majnun, 155, 174, 186n
  Majnun and Layla, 11
  portrayal of Layla in Persian book painting, 103

Sufis (*cont.*)
  'udhri ghazal, 44–5
Sufyan b. Ziyad, 165
Sulaym, Umm, 79n
Sulayman, Musa, 77–8
  al-Hubb al-'udhri [*'Udhri* Love], 16–17
sun and moon, 91–3, 106, 111, 119–20n, 229
sunnah, 62–3, 64–6, 78
Al-Suyuti, Jalal al-Din, *al-Idah fi 'ilm al-nikah*, 63–4

Tajwar, Fatimah, *al-Marah fi al-shi'r al-Umawi*, 68
Al-Tawhidi, Abu Hayyan
  al-hawamil wa'l-shawamil, 145
  Al-Muqabasat, 192
tayf, 141–6
tayf al-khayal, 141–6
tragedy, 6, 19–20, 209
Troilus and Criseyde, 204–5
Turkish poets, 11

'Ubaydallah b. 'Abdullah b. 'Utbah, 37
'Udhrah tribe, 2, 25n, 112, 165, 199
Al-'Udhri, Abu Mishar, 214
'udhri poetry
  authenticity of, 12–14
  as a literary tradition, 10–11
  overview, 2–7
  rise of, 8–10
  scholarship on, 15–22
'Umar, Abi Rabi'ah
  anecdotes, 50
  Buthaynah, 48
  gazelles, 120–1n
  ghazals, 15, 34–5, 90
  speech, 139
  women, 35, 37, 183–4n
Umayyad period, 4, 9–10, 16, 32–3, 36–7, 181
Umm-Iyas, 87–8
'Urawi, Muhammad Iqbal, 58–9

Urdu literature, 11
Al-'Urji, 34
'Urwah b. Hizam
  chastity (*'iffah*) and Islam, 69
  death, 118, 211–13
  fainting, 202–3
  form of the beloved, 101
  glances, 132
  malady and wasting away, 179, 198–201
  phantom presence of the beloved, 142
  residence of the beloved, 147
'udhri poets, 3–4

Al-Walibi, Abu Bakr, 41
Walid b. Yazid, Caliph, 37, 45
Walther, Wiebke, 46
Al-Waqi'ah, Sura, 26n
Al-Washsha, Muhammad b. Ishaq, 140, 201, 215–16
  al-Muwashsha, 43, 67, 70–1
Western literature, 19–20
wine
  Burd, 45
  face of the beloved, 97–100
  fatal love, 178
  gazelle, 95
  metaphors, 87–9
  as sacred, 229
  speech, 136
wisal, 130
wolf, 41, 96
Wollheim, Richard, 184n

Al-Yaman, Waddah, 157n
Yeats, W. B., 185n
Al-Yusuf, Yusuf, 9

Zolondek, Leon, 39
Zoroaster, 45
Zuhayr, Ka'b b., 101–2

EU representative:
Easy Access System Europe
Mustamäe tee 50, 10621 Tallinn, Estonia
Gpsr.requests@easproject.com